You, _Tania_ ,

have what it takes to courageously and successfully *"Identify and Untie the Knots That Tie Up Your Life."*

Remember —
You may have been delayed,
But you're RARELY denied!

A life of better health, balance, harmony, potential, significance, and prosperity awaits you.

Best Wishes for Your "Untie the Knots" Journey.

Sincerely,

Ty Howard

Ty Howard

2-29-2008

UNTIE
the KNOTS™
THAT TIE UP
YOUR LIFE

**A Practical Guide to Freeing Yourself From Toxic
Habits • Choices • People • Relationships**

Ty Howard

**KNOTS
FREE
Publishing**
Baltimore, Maryland

This book is dedicated with love and affection

to my mother,

Theresa Howard,

and her never quit, hardworking, guiding, and caring spirit.

In the words of Abraham Lincoln,

"All that I am and will ever be, I owe to my mother!"

This book is my way of standing proudly, along with the rest of your children and grandchildren, to applaud you.

Thank YOU,
Mom

A Firm, Tight Hug from Your Son, Ty

Acknowledgments

Writing this book has been significantly transformative yet sometimes difficult due to the determination, commitment, and passion I put into my efforts. It has been an undertaking that I could not have completed without the help and support of many important and in some instances "key people" in my life.

I must acknowledge and first thank Berlinda, my life partner, who has brought so much joy and substance into my life. I'm grateful for her patience and understanding when my life's work forces me to focus and takes me away. I'm also grateful for her valuable input into my teaching and particularly into this book. Without her sense of adventure and unwavering spiritual core, my life would be much more chaotic. Her keen ability to help me see the other side of things is always welcomed and greatly appreciated.

Thanks also to my daughter, Nakiarra, for believing in and encouraging Daddy to keep writing. Each day I wrote, I only had to look into her beautiful and hopeful eyes for inspiration to continue.

Thank you to Natasha Mobley for being an exceptional office assistant with lots of understanding and multi-tasking while I was writing this book. We both encountered days where my book project and the other 900 jobs we had to complete became a tug-of-war. Still, she hung in there with me by rising to the occasion to make sure nothing slipped through the cracks. That was definitely teamwork at its best!

Thank you to Laura and Robert Bland and Virginia and James "Pop-Pop" Howard. Although my grandfathers are now deceased, I could not have asked for a better set of grandparents. I've learned from them how and why to accept God into my life.

They taught me many principles that are the core values and positive beliefs that guide me today. My grandmother's taught me how to share sincere warmth, kindness, care and love. My grandfather's taught me how to share the wisdom of a teacher, be accountable to my family, and firm, yet fair, with my love, discipline and praise.

Thank you to Madertino, Zachary, Lakisha, Big Charles, Little Charles, Ahmad, Big Lorne, Little Lorne, Catherine "Benjie," Coleman and Florence Chandler, and Skittles for being my immediate family members who contribute to my lasting legacy and inspire me to continue living and fulfilling my dreams.

Special thanks go to Chris Justice, my editor. He helped to make my best even better when it came to writing this book. He worked with each word, each sentence, each paragraph, and each chapter as if the book was his. His energy, feedback, and suggestions kept me passionately writing and rewriting from the first typed word to the completed manuscript. I am definitely looking forward to teaming up with him once again for my next book project in the near future.

Special thanks to Sylvia Baffour, renowned Life Coach, and Alicia "Rena" Lewis for their time, service, and support. They may not have known it at the time, but they were my BIGGEST supporters and confidants throughout this project. Even though I kept telling Rena "NO!" you can't see and read the next chapter in the book before I complete the manuscript, she would always call me back the next day to share feedback, which was always greatly appreciated because it enabled and empowered me to return to the chapter to refine what I wrote a day or two before. I called Sylvia at the last minute to give my completed manuscript another set of eyes to check for readability and flow, and she generously gave her time, not just for one day, but an entire week. You two women are my "Sheros" when it comes to the work and completion of this book project!

Special thanks to Laura Burns, my caricature artist, for creating and providing her art for my book. Her work is truly awesome.

Special thanks to Keith Harrell for encouraging me to give birth to the Untie the Knots Process. I do not know if Keith remembers this, but I called him on the phone seven years ago to explain my passionate process of *Untying the Knots That Tie Up Your Life*. His response was both challenging and life-changing. He said, "Ty, you have to give birth to this process." Six years later, we stand at a point where this book is proof that I took his advice and gave birth to the process.

Special thanks to Willie Jolley for being there whenever I needed him! We both know there are people in our business and in this world who won't give people the time of day. However, when it comes to Willie, he is my ambassador and role model for service. He truly and selflessly gives so much of himself to others—that's why the Universe rewards his genuine servitude tenfold.

Special thanks to Harvey Alston, my #1 mentor, for being a reliable mentor and coach. His honest yet firm guidance has made my journey in the professional speaking business and in life in general much easier.

Thanks for the work, support, and faith of a handful of good people who believed in me, pushed me, and still supported me: Bobby Lowman, Dr. Diana Elliott, Tamika Harris-Dean, Craig Valentine, Mark Tabron, Dee Jolley, Natalie Greene, Dr. Jamie Washington, Dr. Alicia Harvey-Smith, James Amps III, Art Jackson, Torin Ellis, Craig Thompson, John Carrington, Elizabeth Stemley, Sheryl Nelson, Dr. Raymond Winbush, Dr. Joann Christopher-Hicks, James "Jim" Mullen, Tracy McGee, Lloyd Nimrod, Zee Green, Sabrina Chamblee, Alisa Underwood, Ralph Underwood, Iris Sauber, Stephanie Poplar, Debbie Dozier, Edwin Quinn, Portia Burke, Frank and Lillian Coleman, Paris Law, Quinton Gipson, Darrell Williams, Derrick Hayes, Larry Young, Minh Pham, Dr. Wolfe Rinke, Dr. Jack Cole, Dr. Dennis Kimbro, Patrick Combs, Dr. Dilip Abayasekara, Darlene Campbell,

Angela Draughn, Blanca Rosa Romero, Pegine Echevarria, Leon Shepherd, Renee Madden, Todd Hazzleton, Bill Ecker, Carolyn Gamble, Sebastian Bruce, Ronald Culberson, Mark Brown, Dan Poynter, Doni Glover, Ben Garber, Georgia Muhammad, Winston Sherman, Bessie Johnson, Karen Bontrager, Darryl Hunter, Michele Hunt, Fran and Joe Princehouse, Annelie Weber, Michael Aronin, Elizabeth Cockey, Winston Barber, John Alston, Norm Hull, and Steve Siebold.

Last but certainly not least, special thanks to those who have taught and inspired me along my life's journey; this includes my teachers, students, and many Unsung Heroes. Some have been all three to me. Although your name may not be individually listed in these Acknowledgements, you haven't been forgotten. Thank you too for your contribution and loyalty and sharing your successes with me. You are the reasons why my life has been so filled with love, purpose, laughter, significance, and prosperity. You are appreciated.

Table of Contents

Part 4: NEVER QUIT! NEVER STOP! DON'T EVER GIVE UP!

Part 5: ONCE IS NEVER ENOUGH—LET'S DO IT AGAIN!

Foreword

Attitude is 100% of everything you do!

After more than two decades of speaking to people about the power of attitude, I know a positive attitude is your most priceless possession and one of your most valuable assets. To a great extent, your attitude determines the overall quality of your life.

In the aftermath of events like September 11, major corporate scandals, economic downturns, the constant threat of terrorism, and Hurricane Katrina, I am convinced more than ever that people need to learn how to control and manage the quality of their lives through a positive mental attitude. It's not a secret that life seems to reward us most when we approach the world with a positive attitude. But somehow this knowledge and daily practice escapes us when we mix into our lives toxic habits, choices, people, and relationships. These are toxic obstacles that delay and derail us from living our dreams.

My friend, Ty Howard, a.k.a. Mr. Untie the Knots, has written a timely and necessary book for people who seek solid techniques designed to help free them from some of life's most challenging obstacles. His book, ***Untie the Knots That Tie Up Your Life: A Practical Guide to Freeing Yourself from Toxic Habits, Choices, People, and Relationships***, is not only a powerful text for continuous guidance, but a reference tool you will find yourself referring back to time and time again. Ty says, "When toxic knots go unattended in your life for long periods of time, they begin to choke and prevent you from living life to the fullest—from fulfilling and living *your* dream!" This is a book that you should not take lightly. It will become a must-have reference guide for your personal library.

In this significant book, Ty weaves together his own life experiences with an easy-to-follow process that can help free you from toxic bondage. In each section, he discusses an "untie the knots" concept, illustrates it with anecdotes, and teaches specific strategies for integrating it into your life—all with an easygoing, friendly, and inspiring style.

You are beginning a journey that has the potential to greatly improve your habits, choices, interactions with people, relationships, and overall quality of life. Isn't that super-fantastic?

The book that you now hold in your hands was written for you, regardless of your current position or level in life. The passion and thorough guidance in this book could bring you the freedom to live, freedom to achieve, freedom to love, freedom to progress, freedom to believe, freedom to forgive, freedom to overcome, freedom to break away, freedom to confidently empower and encourage others, and freedom to utilize a positive mental attitude every day.

Yes, this book has great potential; however, you will need to apply the process and principles in **Untie the Knots That Tie Up Your Life**. Just reading this book will not change or take your life to new heights. As you apply the "untie the knots" concepts, you will begin to renew and free your mind, body, and spirit from toxic bondage. You will put yourself on course for better living, achievement, growth, and prosperity.

Just as attitude is a choice, freedom is also a choice. Each and every day we have a choice about how imprisoned or liberated we will feel in the world around us. Ty Howard has done you a wonderful service by writing this road map on how to choose, create, and live an out-of-bondage life: a life with fewer knots, a life with more manageable obstacles, and a significant life with greater potential. Read the stories, apply the principles, and enjoy the journey!

Keith Harrell, CSP, CPAE
Dr. Attitude
Author of *Attitude Is Everything*
October 2006

Introduction

I love the practice and feeling of freeing myself from toxic habits, choices, people, and relationships, and I trust the idea of living a free and prosperous life also appeals to you. I have written this book with the enthusiasm of sharing with you what I have learned about this empowering concept.

First, are you curious about how this book started?

In 1995, I began my passionate journey speaking to people about how to live and work successfully. It has been a humbling and privileged experience to see firsthand the countless men and women whose lives have been positively impacted by their decisions to discipline themselves to strive for a life with fewer knots and significant potential. There is nothing better than improving the quality of your life and living your dreams!

Over the years, I have attended countless seminars, read hundreds of books, listened to hours of tapes, and interviewed scores of successful people about the subject of self-development. I've quickly learned that all the great speakers spoke from their life experiences. They told their stories openly, confidently, humorously, and intuitively. The one feature that stood out most, more than anything else, was the great orators all developed a philosophy behind their message. Many other speakers just spewed motivational fluff and feel-good messages; however, the great speakers purposefully and skillfully shared their philosophy about their subject. They taught people a solid process that could improve some aspect of their lives, if it was applied continuously.

I recall sitting up late at night into the wee hours of the morning pondering two questions: 1) What would be my greatest life's message? and 2) What would be the philosophy behind my message based on my life's experiences? I'm proud to now say my many life experiences have propelled me to where I am today. My time in foster care at an early age shaped my perspectives on the fact that there will be situations in life I can and cannot control. Being raised by a single mother in one of the toughest low-income neighborhoods in Baltimore, Maryland taught me that even when your circumstances may not be the most favorable, you can still plan and prepare for a better future. Becoming a teenaged father taught me that even though my father was an absentee parent, I could break the toxic cycle by becoming a responsible and accountable father to my child. Serving 10 years as an enlisted sailor in the U.S. Navy taught me that discipline, focus, and goal accomplishment were necessary to move positively forward in life. Working on a supervisory and managerial level in Corporate America prepared and groomed me for becoming the founder, and full-time Chairman and CEO of a very successful diverse business based in Baltimore County, Maryland. Let's face it...we all have our own life's journey. We will never be able to rewrite the beginning of our lives; however, if we still have breath and ability in our mind, body, and spirit, we can definitely influence and direct where our life ends.

Many of us have suffered from one or several challenging knots in our lives at one time or another. Sometimes, it feels like they'll never come undone, and they'll get tighter and tighter. Sometimes, it feels like they'll drive you crazy! And if you do not learn how to identify and boldly *Untie the Knots That Tie Up Your Life*, these knots can pose a serious threat to your whole life: your health, relationships, career, goals, and finances. Don't despair. There are answers, solutions, strategies, and real-life examples that can assist you in setting yourself free to manifest the life you desire.

In creating the philosophy and process for this guide, I realized why most people are tied-up, bound-down, and stuck in an inescapable position. Learning how to effectively deal with or work through toxic habits, choices, people, and relationships is not taught in school alongside history, math, and science. Consequently, people don't know what to do or say when a toxic obstacle or behavior delays or derails them from their dream. They often are DELAYED (stuck between two points in life that will not allow them to move closer to their dream) or DERAILED (completely off track and in a place in life that has no scenery or relation to their dream). Both positions are unhelpful and highly unproductive.

What is the "Untie the Knots" Process?

The Untie the Knots Process is a philosophy and process that teaches and empowers people to successfully identify, defeat, and free themselves from toxic habits, choices, people, and re-lationships. This then allows them to create and live a healthier, happier, significant, and prosperous life.

My goal was to develop real-life and practical tools (strategies, ideas, principles, and techniques) that people may use imme-diately to handle the daily challenges they face. I didn't want to waste time on theories and case studies. Platitudes don't help much when people are openly or silently screaming for help because of toxic knots that are threatening their health, family, relationships, career, finances, growth, development, peace-of-mind, productivity, spirituality, and happiness.

Untie the Knots That Tie Up Your Life deals with fundamental emotions, ideas, choices, behaviors, and positions. It is an em-powering read and easy to apply. Allow it to change and improve you. There's no need to live life in self-imposed toxic knots and bondage that keep you from enjoying a full, active, rewarding, and happy life!

The material in this book is not simply motivational or inspi-rational. You will learn that regardless of your age, wealth, po-sition, career, gender, education, or marital status, a life with fewer knots can make an incredible difference. This book is also a guide for attaining new levels of accomplishment in all areas of your life, not just in personal achievement, but also with rela-tionships in your home, work, school, church, or community.

Does your life feel overwhelming, unbalanced, stagnant, painful, or disappointing?

Have you become the image of success that everyone talks about and marvels over, yet silently, deep inside, you feel empty or filled with regrets?

Have you done everything you know possible to bury and release bad memories, fears, and poor choices from your past? Yet somehow, they just keep returning to haunt your new relationships?

Have you wanted to take a new, positive, and fulfilling direction in life but don't know how and where to start?

Do your current habits and behaviors have people avoiding you, employers terminating you, and opportunities passing you by?

Do you have a chronic pattern of constantly starting and never finishing projects and tasks due to procrastination, excuse making, and frequent distractions?

If you answered "YES" to any of the above questions, *Untie the Knots That Tie Up Your Life* was written for you.

In the chapters that follow, I will give you the tools you need to successfully identify and *Untie the Knots That Tie Up Your Life*. I will provide you with a process that includes 10 "Infusers" that, when practiced daily, will turn your toxic obstacles into positive, empowered freedoms and then into rewarding action. An "Infuser" is a fundamental principle that when put into constant action creates momentum and energy for positive motivation, change, and growth. Each Infuser focuses on fundamental principles of self-development and personal growth. The theme that runs throughout the "untie the knots" process, like threads holding together a quilt, is that in learning to identify and *Untie the Knots That Tie Up Your Life*, you can create a life of better health, balance, significance, harmony, potential, and prosperity. Here's a brief description of each of the Infusers that will help you free yourself from toxic habits, choices, people, and relationships.

Infuser #1: Reinstate a Positive Attitude

If you are serious about breaking free from these knots, you must adopt a positive mental attitude. You must be committed to developing and working constantly with a positive attitude, regardless of your past experiences or current situations or circumstances. Attitude is a choice. And the choice that you make from this point forward will be the difference between whether you stay tied-up or you set yourself free. I will explain to you empowering strategies about how to maintain a positive and controlled attitude daily, even during extremely challenging situations.

Infuser #2: Refocus

How will you change the direction of your life if you're not aware of what direction you're currently in? You will mark where you currently are, update yourself on where you truly want to be, then set new written goals so you can chart and execute your revised personal life plan.

Infuser #3: Choose

Decide true freedom and life is what you want and then go where you can produce those results. I will offer you the benefits and rewards of what can happen when you commit to "deciding to do you" 100% of the time, regardless of what the world may throw your way.

Infuser #4: Identify

To successfully break away from anything that has delayed or derailed you in the past, you must summon the bold confidence to now identify it as a toxic habit, choice, person, or relationship. You will learn how to honestly identify, accept, write down, and forgive yourself for all your knots of delay. You will also learn how to identify your innate gifts and talents so you can connect to and begin driving your life's passion and purpose toward your destiny.

Infuser #5: Simplify

Remove clutter, confusion, stress, and distractions from your life daily, and watch new, desirable opportunities appear. I will offer you keys to organize and simplify your life so you can observe, think, prioritize, refine, and perform at your peak daily.

Infuser #6: Believe

It takes your strong will and unshakable faith to make the impossible possible. I will explain to you the power behind a healthy belief system and how to effectively remove toxic habits, choices, people, and relationships from your life. All of which can block your path to success.

Infuser #7: Move

Don't just stand there filled with knowledge: Do it! Quit procrastinating and making excuses. My ultimate goal is to inspire, teach, and empower you to create an updated personal life plan, boldly face your fears, and move forward daily in executing your new personal life plan.

Infuser #8: Bring Your "A" Game

The winners in life don't just show up; they bring their BEST preparation, plan, and effort to the world every day! You will also learn the characteristics of the living freely process, the three ways people respond to it, and seven strategies for embracing your new way of living.

Infuser #9: Persist

How strongly do you want what you now see? No more excuses...no more procrastination...no more wasted and unproductive days! Stay the course! I will offer five proven strategies to prevent self-sabotage and outside-sabotage from tying you up again and provide you with a quick check system to monitor and maintain your personal radar for potential daily hazards.

Infuser #10: Leave a Mark of Significance

It's one experience in living to have simply come and gone. It's another experience in living to have purposely decided to create and live a life of significance: a life that will enable you to leave behind a lasting legacy that will contribute to your family's heritage and also allow the many others who come after you to learn and grow from your efforts. You will learn the benefit of linking your passion and life's purpose to someone other than you. If you connect what you're doing and striving for to the improvement of your family, community, and the world around you, you will increase the probability that you will leave a lasting mark of significance...a lasting legacy...for friends, family, community, and the world. Those you love and care for will benefit from your significance for many years to come. All because you decided to create and live a life of significance versus an insignificant life of chaos and procrastination.

As imperfect human beings, we will never be 100% knot free; however, we can still create and live a significant life that we feel good about and enjoy. This will require continuous work, commitment, and determination. But you're definitely worth it! You too deserve a life of better health, balance, harmony, potential, reward, prosperity, and happiness. I've organized the book into bite-size strategies and chapters. I purposely designed this guide to be a reference guide throughout the rest of your life. Its main goal is to hopefully influence and alter the way you currently think. When a person begins to think and act with a more positive attitude, then he or she can begin to improve and move their life in the direction of consistently fulfilling their goals, dreams, and aspirations. One can only do this when toxic habits, choices, people, and relationships don't tie up them up.

Remember, this is an investment in you. The light is green: The time is now. You're more than worthy. You may have been delayed, but you're rarely denied. Never quit! Never stop! Don't EVER give up! And, once will never be enough. Let's learn this process, apply it, and do it again-and-again!

You're on the verge of identifying and untying your knots. I wish you a knot breaking, *green and growing* journey. Let's get started...now, GO!

P.R.E.P.A.R.E. for Untie the Knots Success

SEVEN SUGGESTIONS FOR MAXIMIZING THE POTENTIAL OF THIS BOOK

1) **Plan:** Develop an unshakeable, tireless desire to master the principles of breaking away from toxic habits, choices, people, and relationships. Come prepared to read and enjoy this book. You will need writing pads, pens, highlighters, stress release products, a personal organizer, and a journal.

2) **Read:** Read each chapter twice before going onto the next one. Underline or highlight each important idea, tip, principle, or strategy. This book is divided into six units that contain three chapters each for a total of 18 chapters. A conclusion is included after each chapter, and a summary is included at the end of each unit. The book also offers periodical "Timeouts". Timeouts offer you an opportunity to pause and reflect on where you've been, where you currently are, and where you're headed. The first three chapters are primer chapters and are meant to condition and set your mind, attitude, and willpower in the right mode for planning, reading, engaging, practicing, accepting, realizing, and executing the power this life-changing guide offers. Chapters 4 through 18 introduce and guide you step-by-step through the Untie the Knots Process. These are the chapters that will help and empower you to successfully identify and break free from your toxic habits, choices, people, and relationships.

3) **Engage:** Stop frequently to think about what you're reading. Underline or highlight each important idea, tip, principle, or strategy for quick recall. Read over this material several times until you are thoroughly familiar with these

concepts. Adapt these ideas to your own situation and then take action. Write your learning experiences along the way in your personal organizer and personal journal.

4) **Practice:** Review this book twice each month. Stop frequently to ask yourself how you can apply each suggestion. Apply each new idea, strategy, or principle you encounter that is most meaningful to your knots. Practice applying them daily. Use this guide to help solve your daily problems. Practice doesn't make perfect, but practice helps you improve.

5) **Accept:** Accept any behaviors or mistakes that you discover while reading this book as a learning experience. Do not become discouraged and quit. Look at all the identified toxic behaviors and mistakes as opportunities for growth, fun, and empowerment. Stay the course, stay focused, stay committed, and you will *"untie your knots."*

6) **Realize:** Know that it will take hard, committed work and long hours to *"untie the knots"* that have tied up your life. Your knots did not enter your life overnight; do not expect them to disappear overnight. When you successfully identify and *"untie a knot,"* realize it by writing that success in your personal journal and celebrating it in a meaningful way.

7) **Execute:** If you wish to get the most out of this book, there is one non-negotiable requirement, one essential step that is more important than any other strategy, principle, or technique. That requirement is execution. Aristotle once remarked, *"What we have to learn to do, we learn by doing."* If you're not willing to take continuous action while reading and journeying through this book, your time and investment will be a waste of time. However, if you do commit yourself to taking the continuous, necessary steps of action by executing the principles, strategies, and personal plan that you will create as a re-

sult of reading this book, you will develop a life of better health, balance, significance, harmony, potential, and prosperity. A life that will leave a mark—a life that will leave your family and the world a lasting legacy. You purchased this book because you're looking for change, and you are looking to take constant action. Yes? All right, let's go!

UNTIE the KNOTS™
THAT TIE UP
YOUR LIFE

"One starts an action simply because one must do something."

— *T.S. Eliot*

Chapter 1

A POSITIVE ATTITUDE...

"We cannot change our past. We cannot change the fact that people act in a certain way. We cannot change the inevitable. The only thing we can do is play on the one string we have, and that is our attitude."

— *Charles Swindoll*

The Power of a Positive Attitude

As my dear friend and trusted advisor, Keith Harrell, a.k.a. Dr. Attitude, believes and explains passionately to every audience, "Attitude is everything! Attitude is a choice!" He skillfully moves through his dynamic and insightful motivational presentation about attitude to communicate this important message: "I've suggested to you today little adjustments that can change your thinking in a big way. By changing your thinking, you can change your beliefs. By changing your beliefs, you can change your actions and your life."

Keith is 100% correct!

Having a positive attitude can help you cope much more easily with life's daily affairs. A positive attitude brings optimism into your life and makes it easier to avoid the ill-effects of worrying and negative thinking.

If you adopt a positive attitude as a way of life, it will bring constructive changes into your life, and over time, will make you happier, healthier, and more successful.

It's true. With a positive attitude you'll begin to see the bright side of life, you'll become more action-oriented, and you'll expect the best to happen—and it will!

A positive attitude is certainly a state of mind that is well worth developing and strengthening!

Here are some benefits of a positive attitude:
- Achieve short- and long-term goals
- Attain success faster and more easily
- Increase self-esteem
- Increase happiness
- Gain more energy
- Improve self-love and self-respect
- Improve inner power and strength
- Inspire and motivate yourself and others
- Gain confidence to tackle challenges
- Decrease stress
- Persevere through obstacles
- Gain more respect

There is great power in developing and maintaining a positive attitude. A positive attitude says, "YES! You Can Achieve Success!"

A Positive Attitude Is Important for Continuous Success

The great motivational speaker Zig Ziglar says, *"A positive attitude will not help you to do everything; however, it can help you to do everything better than a negative attitude will."*

If you're seriously expecting and wanting to succeed in life, then you will be required to bring forth your positive attitude constantly.

Positive attitudes drive successful people in the following ways:
- Facilitate positive thinking
- Unlock constructive thinking
- Foster creativity
- Increase expectations of success

- Heighten optimism
- Ignite motivation to accomplish goals
- Provoke inspiration
- Empower a "never surrender" attitude
- Awaken abilities to positively critique oneself
- Raise self-confidence
- Display self-esteem
- Steer hunger to seek solutions
- Direct focus and opportunities

Being driven by a positive attitude affects not only you and the way you look at the world, but also your family, work, community, friends, and colleagues. If your positive attitude is strong, it can become contagious. If you're a person already choosing and using a positive attitude daily, you know exactly what I mean.

Quickly Evaluate Your Current Attitude

Most people who fail in life do so because of their ATTITUDE. If you bring a negative attitude to the world each day, the game is over for you before it begins. Nothing in life is more powerful than BRINGING A POSITIVE ATTITUDE to all situations you encounter throughout your day. The attitude you project to others depends primarily on the way you look at your life and the world. To measure your current attitude toward life, complete this quick exercise.

Circle the extent to which you agree or disagree with each statement.

	Strongly Agree	Agree		Disagree	Strongly Disagree
1. There is nothing demeaning about assisting or serving others.	5	4	3	2	1
2. I can be cheerful and positive to everyone regardless of age or appearance.	5	4	3	2	1
3. On bad days, when nothing goes right, I can still find ways to be positive.	5	4	3	2	1
4. I feel my current attitude allows me to continuously succeed.	5	4	3	2	1
5. I am enthusiastic about life.	5	4	3	2	1
6. Encountering difficult "people" occasionally throughout the day will not cause me to be negative.	5	4	3	2	1
7. My ability to maintain a positive attitude daily is easy.	5	4	3	2	1
8. If someone requests my help or feedback on a project when I am working and focusing on something else, it wouldn't bother me at all to stop what I'm doing and assist them.	5	4	3	2	1
9. I receive great pleasure when others compliment or recognize me in front of others for something I've done.	5	4	3	2	1
10. Doing well in all aspects of my life is very important to me.	5	4	3	2	1

Now add up your circled numbers: **TOTAL SCORE** _____

If you scored above 40, you have an excellent attitude towards life. If you scored between 25 and 40, you seem to have some reservations that require some necessary inner work before you make positive thinking a way of life. A rating below 25 indicates that you have been exhibiting a negative attitude and have most likely created conflict and difficulties along the way. It's never too late to change the way you think and to begin developing a positive attitude. You too can begin leading a happy and successful life.

The Effects of a Negative Attitude

Do you see difficulty in an opportunity? If you answered, "Yes," then you are negative at the moment.

When you exhibit a negative attitude and expect failure and difficulties, that's what you get.

It was James Allen who said, *"All that you accomplish or fail to accomplish is the direct result of your thoughts."*

I can recall a short rhyme on attitude my fifth grade homeroom teacher, Ms. Hayward, would share with our class at the beginning of each school day:

> *"If you think you cannot,*
> *you can't.*
> *If you think you will lose,*
> *you have lost.*
> *If you think you can,*
> *you can.*
> *If you think you can win,*
> *you have won."*
>
> — Author Unknown

Ms. Hayward would then frequently explain to our class there are no useful benefits to having and maintaining a negative attitude. She said negative attitudes only bring people these problems:

- ☹ Poor health
- ☹ Strained muscles in your face due to frowning
- ☹ Blockage to learning
- ☹ A stinking way of thinking
- ☹ Low energy
- ☹ Limited success
- ☹ Difficulties, troubles, and problems
- ☹ Sleepless nights

☹ Low motivation
☹ A weak and aimless belief system
☹ Pessimism
☹ Poor self-esteem
☹ Poor friends
☹ Fewer chances to have a positive outcome in life
☹ Blockage to one's vision
☹ Stunted growth and development
☹ Low grades
☹ Struggles and unhappiness in life

The five minutes Ms. Hayward used each day to encourage us to choose a positive attitude pushed me to excel and achieve each day.

Quickly Break Out of a Bad Mood

Often, we find ourselves in a bad mood due to an isolated situation that causes us to have an immediate negative attitude about life or the current situation. If you ever find yourself in a bad mood, apply one or more of the following seven steps to quickly bring yourself and your thinking back into a positive state:

1. **Switch your thinking to a more positive place.**

   Remember, your attitude is a choice. When a situation or person gets you frustrated or in a bad mood, switch your thinking to a more positive place.

   If you're in a bad mood because of something your friend did, do not harp on it. Switch your thinking to the rewarding and exceptional day you had at work that day.

   You can switch your thinking to a more positive place by thinking of something positive like a recent accomplishment, your family, a positive affirmation, or a peaceful and calming place.

2. **Change your environment.**

   There comes a time when your bad mood has become so tangled in a web of negative thinking that the best solution to pursue is to change your environment.

Cordially excuse yourself from the presence of the person or group that you're with so you may step away into another environment to gather yourself and regain your positive attitude.

3. **Listen to uplifting music or a motivational tape or cd.**
   There are many people who listen to and benefit from positive music or motivational tapes. Studies have shown that music and motivational tapes can help a person to change a negative attitude into a more positive and productive one.
   Try listening to-
   - a) *Goals : Setting and Achieving Them on Schedule* by Zig Ziglar (Audio CD)
   - b) *Everyday Grace: Having Hope, Finding Forgiveness, and Making Miracles* by Marianne Williamson (Audio CD)

4. **Read something positive, affirming, or peaceful.**
   Reading quotes, affirmations, and positive books and articles can bring peace and the return of your positive attitude. It's very common today to see posters or printed quotations and affirmations inside an employee workspace.
   Try reading-
   - a) *Attitude is Everything (Revised Edition): 10 Life-Changing Steps to Turning Attitude into Action* by Keith Harrell (Paperback)
   - b) *A Setback Is a Setup for a Comeback* by Willie Jolley (Paperback)

5. **Telephone someone in your Positive Support Circle.**
   Positive Support Circles are necessary and beneficial. When bad moods or challenging times occur, call a trusted, non-judgmental person in your Positive Support Circle. I call my circle my "Fab Five Team." Your circle members should know you well enough that they can hear you out and offer sound suggestions and strategies to bring you back into a positive state.

6. Exercise.

Exercising is one of the most effective ways to eliminate a bad mood. When you're exercising, your mind shifts toward what you're doing, and you're focusing on the positive results you're striving for while working out. Exercising is healthy, relaxing, challenging, fun, and rewarding.

7. Smile. Smile. Smile.

It sounds too simple to be true; however, smiling works! When a bad mood strikes you unexpectedly, just smile, smile, smile. And from ear to ear. No one has to know why you're smiling so hard.

When you smile purposefully, not only will people wonder why you're smiling, but it's also healthy for your body and peace of mind. So, go ahead right now---and SMILE!

I'm sure you figured out by now that all bad moods are negative attitudes. Some are short-term, and some are long-term. Still, you have a choice to determine how long your bad moods will stay. Don't give that choice to anyone or anything else!

Six Bad Attitudes to Avoid Displaying

There are many negative attitudes tying people up today; however, the following six bad attitudes I believe tip the scale:

1) The — I Don't Want to Be Bothered Attitude

This is a negative attitude where the person using it reacts to anyone who comes into his or her space with negative body, facial, or non-verbal gestures.

<u>Suggestion for improvement</u>: Learn how to teach and encourage yourself to look and be attentive with a welcoming smile and positive body language when others come into your space. You might find yourself in situations where the world smiles back and welcomes you.

2) The — I'm Angry at the World Attitude

This is a negative attitude where the person using it provides a negative response to anyone or any situation because he or she feels that someone or something has done them wrong.

<u>Suggestion for improvement</u>: Learn how to teach and encourage yourself to look for the good and the positive in any situation. You might find that there are more good and positive things in the world that you've been missing.

3) The — I Don't Like People Attitude

This is a negative attitude where the person using it chooses to not like a particular group of people because of hearsay, family beliefs, experience, or simply choice.

<u>Suggestion for improvement</u>: Learn how to teach and encourage yourself to get to know a person or group first before passing a "one-size fits all" judgment. You might discover that not everyone is bad, ugly, or negative.

4) The — I Know It ALL Already Attitude

This is a negative attitude where the person using it replies to every opportunity for growth and learning as if it's a waste of his or her time. Why? Because they know it ALL already!

<u>Suggestion for improvement</u>: Learn how to teach and encourage yourself to be open to the fact that you can learn something new each day and from anyone. You might learn that even a six-year-old can teach you something useful.

5) The — I Say Whatever Comes Out of My Mouth Attitude

This is a negative attitude where the person using it chooses to say whatever comes out of his or her mouth, normally without even thinking about it.

<u>Suggestion for improvement</u>: Learn how to teach and encourage yourself to think for at least five seconds before you respond to anyone or any situation. You might

find yourself being welcomed and embraced more than being avoided or pushed away.

6) The — I Don't Need Anyone's Help Attitude

This is a negative attitude where the person using it chooses to turn away or responds negatively to people or organizations trying to help him or her with self-development, human services, or life.

Suggestion for improvement: Learn how to teach and encourage yourself to seek and welcome help from others. You might find yourself accomplishing ten times as many goals in life because we win in life with people.

If your negative attitudes, words, gestures, barriers, and beliefs become your preferred weapon or tool of choice, do not fault anyone else when you find yourself on the outside looking in.

Six Positive Attitudes to Display

There are many positive attitudes freeing people today; here are six positive attitudes that I believe have most successful people soaring high:

1) The — Attitude of Gratitude

This is a positive attitude in which a person is appreciative, grateful, and thankful for *all* that others have done for them.

2) The — Attitude of Respect

This is a positive attitude in which a person respects the personal space, property, ideas, work, relationships, and beliefs of others, including their own.

3) The — Attitude of Optimism

This is a positive attitude in which a person using it chooses to look for the positive in all situations presented to them.

4) The — Attitude of Service

This is a positive attitude in which a person seeks out opportunities to give their time through service to help make the life of someone else better and more manageable.

5) The — Attitude of a Life-Long Student

This is a positive attitude in which a person using it chooses to learn from everyone and everything so they can continuously learn and grow each day.

6) The — Attitude of Humility

This is a positive attitude in which a person chooses to move his or her pride and ego out of the way to display a genuine sense of humility to the world. Being humble doesn't mean shrinking around others, it just means recognizing the value in others and the right for them and their opinions to co-exist with yours.

When you're in constant control of a positive and productive attitude, you will lead yourself to higher levels of achievement and fulfillment. You can start by learning and displaying the above "Six Positive Attitudes to Display."

Trade Your Negative Attitude for a Positive Attitude

If you have a negative attitude, you can always trade it in for a positive attitude!

My first question to you is, when you're around someone with a negative attitude, are you drawn to them or repelled away?

If you are repelled by their attitude, why adopt that as your attitude of choice and expect things to come your way?

My second question to you is, why wouldn't you trade a negative attitide in?

We all can benefit from better health, balance, harmony, potential, significance, and prosperity in our lives.

All learned habits and behaviors can be broken and replaced with new and more positive habits and behaviors.

All you have to do is make today the day you choose to commit yourself to develop, focus on, and use a positive attitude from this point forward throughout life. Once you do that, contact someone in your Positive Support Circle, share your new goal with him or her, and ask that person to help you with this new commitment.

Try it for 30 days! When you arrive at Day 30, that evening, go out and celebrate. On Day 31, extend your Positive Attitude Goal to 60 days. Each time you accomplish this goal, reset your goal by extending it an additional 30 days. Remember to celebrate each and every successful accomplishment you reach while attaining this goal. You'll soon discover your trade in was well worth the effort.

Five Strategies for Maintaining a Positive Attitude

1. Words to Use

Our words have power: the power to uplift, build, and encourage.

Here are words to use in your positive attitude vocabulary. The words on the left have negative connotations for most people, so replace them with the words on the right, which have more positive connotations.

Negative	Positive
I want	I choose or desire
I'm thinking about	I will
I've never done it before.	It's an opportunity to learn something new.
It's too complicated.	Let's look at it from a different angle.
I don't have the resources.	Necessity is the mother of invention.
There's not enough time.	Let's re-evaluate some priorities.
There's no way it will work.	I will try to make it work.
I don't have the expertise.	I'll find people who can help me.
It's good enough.	There's always room for improvement.
It's too late for me to change.	Let's take a chance.
I'm not going to get any better at this.	I'll give it one more try.
I'm never going to learn how to manage my attitude.	I'm going to try to learn how to manage and commit to a positive attitude.

Remember: Practice makes improvements, and improvements are always possible.

If you tend to have a negative outlook, don't expect to become an optimist overnight. But eventually, your self-talk will automatically contain less self-criticism and more self-acceptance and empowerment.

2. Change Your Mental Attitude with "I Am Statements"

Many people create and use "I am statements" to empower and guide them through their day.

At the end of each night, create two to ten "I am statements" to read aloud slowly, three times confidently, while looking at yourself in a mirror.

What is important here is a soft focus with your eyes, and SLOW, mild-mannered talking. If you feel you are rushing even a tiny bit, you should slow down and begin again. Maintaining a slow, relaxed pace is crucial.

Here are a few examples of "I am statements":
- I am Powerful.
- I am Successful.
- I am Wealthy.
- I am a Very Successful Business Person.
- I am an Encouraging Parent.
- I am the Top Sales Person on My Team.
- I am Loving.
- I am Beautiful.
- I am a Winner.
- I am Committed to Positive Thinking Today.

To make your "I am statements" work for you, make them:
- Unique
- Personal
- Positive
- Empowering
- Inspiring
- Valuable

These "I am statements" become your personal guiding affirmations. Over time, they will encourage you, inspire you, and drive you to maintain a positive attitude even during challenging times.

3. Positive Sparks That Can Bring You a Positive Attitude

If you keep yourself connected to feeling joyful and doing positive things, you will find yourself more often than not in a positive state of mind.

Below is a quick list of Positive Sparks That Can Bring You a Positive Attitude

Constantly smiling	Playing with a pet
An Inspirational Quote	Success / Goal Accomplishment
Spending time with family	Giving
Mentoring	Writing a personal letter to thank someone for helping you
Inspirational Music	Volunteering
Pictures of children	Dancing

These are just a few positive activities that can keep you connected to, enjoying, and maintaining your positive attitude.

I personally challenge you to add five more strategies to the above list.

4. Your Positive Support Circle

If you do not have a Positive Support Circle, I strongly encourage you today to seek and develop one.

Create a list of five people within your circle that without question or hesitation you consider to be "Positive Ambassadors". These are people who care about you and are non-judgmental. At the same time, these are people who will listen to you, yet will give their honest feedback or suggestions when you're right or wrong.

Outside of personally choosing to maintain and control a positive attitude, your Positive Support Circle should be one of your most powerful resources when it comes to assisting you in maintaining a positive attitude.

Warning: Do not take this strategy lightly. When you contact and gain agreement from your Positive Support Circle team members, respect them and their time by following-up with them and keeping them informed of your overall growth, progress, and development.

5. Consistently Drive and Apply Your Positive Attitude Daily

Enthusiasm! Enthusiasm! Enthusiasm!

A positive attitude is the vital fuel that moves you along in your journey, and it requires that you drive it and drive it daily!

For every event or situation that comes along, you are completely free to choose the attitude with which you respond. And the attitude you choose will determine how much positive value you gain from whatever is happening.

With many aspects of your life, there are restrictions and limitations imposed upon you from outside forces. Yet with your own attitude, you have total, unlimited control.

And your attitude can make a big difference, with people, with events, and with what you learn about the moments that make up each day.

Choose not to allow your attitude to merely follow you along. Drive it enthusiastically and positively so it brings you inner peace, success, improved relationships, better health, and new levels of freedom.

We were all put on this Earth with everything we needed at birth to believe, achieve, succeed, and live our dreams. So, we all have a purpose to fill, a cause to serve, and a job to do. And it starts with attitude!

Poem: *A Positive Attitude*

Each day is a new day,
A day for you to choose,
Hmmm... Which attitude will I use?
Attitude...
It's what you think,
It's how you feel,
It's how you act,
That makes it real.
Attitude...
It's your body language,
It's the expressions on your face,
It's your rhythm and tone of voice...
All which communicate to others,
If things can be a hazard or safe.
Attitude...
It can attract people to you,
It can shun people away.
It can have you surrounded by positive friends and
family,
Or by your lonesome, turning, old and gray.
Attitude...
It can take you places,
It can leave you behind.
It can bring you happiness,
Yet, have you losing peace of mind.
Make this day,
A day where you control your inner voice.
By choosing a positive attitude,
An attitude of your choice.

~ Ty Howard

Chapter Conclusion

In this chapter, I explained to you the power of a positive attitude and why it is important for continuous success. I provided you with an assessment tool that allowed you to quickly evaluate the state of your current attitude. I explained to you the effects of a negative attitude and how to break out of a bad mood. I shared with you six bad attitudes to avoid displaying, six positive attitudes to display continuously, and methods about how to trade a negative attitude for a positive attitude. And I gave you five practical and easy-to-apply strategies that can help you maintain a positive and healthy attitude each and every day.

When you continuously choose a positive attitude as a standard and positive habit—you will take your life to a whole new level.

Embrace the profound words of Keith Harrell, *"Attitude is everything! Attitude is a choice. By changing your thinking, you can change your beliefs. By changing your beliefs, you can change your actions and your life."*

Chapter 2

...PLUS CONTINUOUS— DETERMINATION, FOCUS, AND ACTION...

"We may experience many defeats but we must not be defeated."

— *Maya Angelou*

Do you know the top three reasons why people stop getting what they want in life?

They are a
1) Lack of Determination.
2) Lack of Focus.
3) Lack of Action.

People who are continuously determined, focused, and action-oriented, prosper. They plan, move, and execute for continuous success.

Think about it: the greatest accomplishments ever achieved have resulted from the transmission of positive thoughts into will power, focus, and action.

Here are a few examples that I recall:

a) Madam C.J. Walker, who was one of America's first black female millionaires;
b) Roger Bannister, was the first person to run a four-minute mile in 1954;
c) Bill Russell, who led his team to 11 NBA championships in 13 seasons between 1957 and 1969;
d) Dr. Martin Luther King Jr., who made his most famous "I Have A Dream Speech" in 1963;

e) Libby Riddles, who was the first woman to win the Iditarod Trail Sled Dog Race in 1985;

f) Dr. Ben Carson, pediatric neurosurgeon, who successfully separated Siamese twins in 1987;

g) Tiger Woods, who at age 21 became the youngest person to win the Masters Golf Tournament in 1997;

h) Ms. Bea Gaddy, known as Baltimore's Mother Teresa, who started feeding Baltimore's homeless, unemployed, and hungry people each Thanksgiving in 1981, and by 2000, before she passed away in 2001, grew her legendary holiday feast of a few dozen neighbors to a sprawling all-day affair, with as many as 20,000 people, on the grounds of a nearby middle school; and

i) Theresa Howard, my mother, who successfully raised four children on her own with what she had and what she knew. Her children finished school and stayed off drugs and away from the prison system.

What did the above great accomplishments have in common? They defied the odds and critics.

There are many, many great accomplishments that we may draw from throughout the world. The ones I mention above are the ones that have influenced and inspired me throughout my life. They are significant to me because, whether those people knew it or not, their proud accomplishments inspire and fuel my drive each day as I continuously commit to being "determined".

Do you have your own list of people whose great accomplishments fuel and inspire you?

It does not matter if the people on your list are older than you, younger than you, alive, or deceased. It's powerful to have people and a power higher than you to draw from when you begin to lose determination, focus, and the desire to take action.

Continuous determination, focus, and action are vital if you intend to successfully apply and practice the Untie the Knots Process.

Continuous Determination, Focus, and Action are VERY Powerful!

If you don't believe me, seriously think about this next quote for at least a couple minutes:

> *"I got my start by giving myself a start."*
> — Madam C.J. Walker

Madam C.J. Walker did not mention any magic formula or magic pill. Just driven Determination, Focus, and Action were Madam Walker's meal tickets.

And if you want to seriously break free of your knots to achieve better health, happiness, balance, relationships, prosperity, and significance, it's time to prepare yourself to turn on your innate switch to Continuous Determination, Focus, and Action.

Let's take a look at what these three concepts are about on a more individualized scale.

DETERMINATION

> *"The person who can drive themself further once their effort gets painful is the person who will win."*
> — Roger Bannister

What is Determination?

Dictionary.com defines "determination" as "a fixed purpose or intention."

Merriam-Webster Dictionary defines "determination" as a "firm or fixed intention to achieve a desired end."

Determination is one of the most powerful feelings we can command. It can push us beyond our predetermined expectations.

Determination helps us build character. It helps us honor and fulfill our commitments. Determination fuels the core of our being when fears, doubt, pain, and challenges set in. Determination makes us move, commit, focus, and act on our ideas, goals, dreams, and aspirations.

Here are a few examples of determination in action:

> *I am still in the process of learning to "stretch," but I start by identifying what I can already do - what I am comfortable doing and feel good at. Then I say to myself (sometimes in writing), "I can do more." I can do better; what is it BEYOND what I already can do that I want to be able to do? Then I write down goals or ideas and make efforts to "stretch" myself.*

(From Kathy, an adult with hearing and mobility impairments)

> *I set my personal, academic, and career goals by knowing where my limits are and working around them. If someone says I can't do something, and I haven't tried it before, that just makes me more determined to prove them wrong. If I fail, at least I tried. However, tomorrow, knowing me, it will be a new day, a new me, and a new way that I will try again. That's what counts.*

(From Maria, a college student who grew up in foster care)

> *I became a teenage mother of twin boys at age 17. All who knew me told me my life was practically over. I completely ignored them and was determined to graduate, go onto college, and succeed. I enrolled in college part-time after I graduated high school. I took two classes each semester and stuck with them by using my twin boys and beliefs for success as the ultimate goal of inspiration. Due to life challenges here and there, I walked across the graduation stage to receive my undergraduate degree 12 years later. Six years after that, I*

walked across another graduation stage to receive my master's degree. Now my twin boys have a standard within our small family to strive to uphold.

(From Tamika, a teenage mother of twin boys)

My parents helped me maintain high expectations for myself. They taught me never to say, "I can't," at anything I try. Today, I travel the world encouraging audience participants to "Rise Above" their limitations through the use of determination.

(From Michael Aronin, professional comedian and inspirational speaker with cerebral palsy)

The Power of Determination

"I am not discouraged, because every wrong attempt discarded is another step forward."
— Thomas Edison

When a positive attitude and well-built character join hands with the power of determination, nobody in this world can stop such a powerful being. No one! Who wants to step in front of a self-assured and determined seven-ton elephant moving purposely toward victory?

Determination is the tool we use to push ourselves to learn everything that life and the world has to teach us. It is the tool we use to defeat discouragement and turn our failures into opportunities. Determination is the tool we use to turn our setbacks into victories and to give us the will to win even when pain sets in. It is the tool we use to survive when survival is our only option. Determination is the tool we use to reach our goals to live our dreams. It is the tool we use to believe in ourselves when it appears no one else will. Determination is the tool we use to recover from health issues. It is the tool we use to rebuild after crisis and tragedy, and it aids us in learning to master the skill of patience. Determination is the tool we use to feed, clothe, shelter, and care for our family. It's the ultimate tool we use to nourish our faith and starve our doubts to death.

This asset called Determination is POWERFUL!!!

Are you determined?

I hope at this point you are.

Because it will require you to use pit bull-like determination to successfully identify and break free of your knots of delay.

The Effects of Low or No Determination

"Defeat never comes to any man until he gives in to it."
— Josephus Daniels

When a person reaches a point where he or she is discouraged, unmotivated, uninspired, or undetermined, his or her life appears to be in a downward spiral. Life becomes a constant struggle and challenge. An individual in this weakened state will usually exhibit some or all of the following behaviors:

❖ Feels life is overwhelming
❖ Disconnects from goals and dreams
❖ Experiences low motivation
❖ Holds negative attitudes about life
❖ Becomes indifferent to success and accomplishment
❖ Accepts being average, routine, or mediocre
❖ Distracted into doing non-productive activities
❖ Sleeps excessively above all else
❖ Articulates negative statements
❖ Chooses to stay home rather than explore
❖ Refuses to try something more than once
❖ Owns no self-confidence or self-esteem
❖ Prefers anti-social behaviors
❖ Conjures many excuses
❖ Prevents learning

- ❖ Loses interest in hobbies or talents
- ❖ Procrastinates
- ❖ Feels hopeless

For most people in these states, they must pick themselves back up and turn their strong determination switch back on. For others, it may require the help of a licensed professional.

Consult your medical professional if this lack of determination has been paired with feelings of depression, loneliness, crying, or thoughts of hurting yourself. Clinical Depression is a serious illness that results from chemical imbalances in the brain. Often times it is treatable. It's your life, so be careful with it, and visit a doctor if you're the least bit concerned about such depression. A visit to a medical professional's office could be a valuable decision.

Remember: We win in life with people! Licensed professionals can be an additional option in assisting us along our journey toward freeing ourselves from toxic habits, choices, people, and relationships.

Why Most People Lose Their Determination

"Unless you're willing to try, fail miserably, then try again, success won't happen."

— Phillip Adams

Have you ever stopped to wonder why most people lose their determination in life?

Here are a few reasons:

They failed at something.
- This individual may have had a constant string of success but failed at something big which caused the individual to quit on all goals and dreams.

Their ego was bruised.
- This individual may have experienced a situation where a weakness they had was revealed to the world, and instead of working to strengthen this weakness, they decided to give up on striving for their goal altogether.

They experienced a health challenge or surgery.
- This person was very driven until he or she was diagnosed with a challenging health issue. Once this event happened, the individual quickly adopted a "What's the use of trying or doing anything else at this point" attitude.

They lost belief in their goals.
- This person allowed the many distractions and challenges of life to disconnect them from their goals. As time passes, their goals become irrelevant and unreachable.

They take on too much.
- These individuals have a problem saying no to others. Because of this self-sabotaging behavior, they end up taking on so much they spread themselves thin and burn out.

An unexpected change in life occurs.
- This person experiences an abrupt relationship break-up, loss of a job, loss of a loved one, or the birth of a child, and this change knocks the wind out of their sail.

They decided to put their efforts into pushing other people.
- These individuals spend so much time encouraging and pushing others to succeed they have no energy and focus left to pursue their own goals and dreams.

They haven't experienced success or accomplishment in sometime.
- This is the person who hasn't experienced any type of real success over an extended period of time (two years or more). These individuals are at a point in their lives where they feel completely discouraged and hopeless.

They live by and surrender to other people's standards and opinions of them.
- These individuals allow others to tell them that certain goals aren't for them and that they do not have the education or resources to live and achieve their dreams. So, they believe what the other person told them and quit trying.

They possess low self-confidence, low self-esteem, and a low self-image.
- These people never see anything good or appealing about themselves and posses a low regard for themselves. Their low level of self-confidence, self-esteem, and self-image prevents them from connecting with and working effectively with others.

They lack driven and determined people in their circle of friends.
- This is the person who hangs out with a bunch of buzzards (toxic and negative friends), and birds of a feather flock together. These buzzards do not have drive. They would rather spend their time doing non-productive or negative activities than pursuing goals and dreams.

They haven't connected their life to an identified purpose.
- These individuals feel, "What's the use?" because they haven't taken the time to connect with and identify the "Why?" or "purpose" or "cause" they're working toward fulfilling. So, they choose to simply exist by floating wherever life pushes them.

They no longer believe they have what it takes.
- These people had "it" —Determination, Focus, and Action— at one time in life; however, now that they have reached a certain age, they feel they no longer have what "it" takes to drive their desires and dreams through the finish line.

They are constantly overwhelmed by fear.
- This person is afraid of a specific challenge that exists before them or even a potential new level of success.

The fear is so frightening they decide to get comfortable where they are in life and never try to move forward with their goals or dreams.

Do you know at least one person who fits any of the examples above?

Life can become quite scary when you lack determination. Life becomes mundane, boring, and routine. It becomes a constant, meaningless struggle that is not much fun. Why? Because deep down inside you know that you're not exerting the highest level of determination possible—that you're not putting out your best!

If this person happens to be you, don't worry...there are strategies to help you turn your determination switch back on.

You will need lots of focused, driven determination fueled by plenty of steps of necessary action to break free from your knots and begin accomplishing your goals.

Seven Proven Ways to Turn Your Innate Determination Switch Back On

"Those who want to succeed will find a way; those who don't will find an excuse."

— Leo Aquila

We experience moments and periods in our life where our innate determination switch gets turned off. Should this happen to you, do the following:

1) **Do something:** The fact is sometimes we just have to get started, even if we're not motivated. Staring at the walls and doing the same activities that keep you in the negative place you are stuck in will keep you unmotivated and undetermined. Many times, the quickest way to get motivated and determined again is to do something productive. Start by gathering a writing pad and pen.

Write down on the writing pad a list of three tasks you would like to accomplish starting tomorrow. Also, write into your plan for tomorrow how you will work on each item individually and will take action until the last task is completed. This is the beginning of helping you to turn your determination switch back on.

2) **Do something different:** Maybe your lack of determination is the result of pure boredom. If you're doing the same activities over and over again, day after day, your brain shuts down and tunes out. We all need growth and stimulation. Try to discover a goal you can work on that will stretch your mind, challenge your knowledge, or force you to work on something different.

Doing something different may mean doing something new *outside* your work life. Motivation and determination for your work can return when you feel inspired by the success you experience in other areas of your life. Volunteer, take a class, or learn a new skill. Even reading books on topics you haven't previously explored can bring new insights for determination.

3) **Get moving:** Getting your body moving early the next morning so you can start accomplishing your three new goals will begin to make the blood flow to your brain. Your physical excitement will get the mental energy flowing. Freshen up, prepare your clothes, get dressed, eat a healthy breakfast, and begin your day. As your day progresses, monitor the progress you've made toward accomplishing each of your goals. As you complete each goal, check it off on your list. Repeat this process until you've accomplished all three goals. Another way to get your body moving is by going to the gym to exercise, walking around your neighborhood, or going out to play and be active with your kids. When your body is in motion, blood flows to your brain, which increases your ability to think and encounter new ideas.

4) **Carry a notebook:** Inspiration often comes when you least expect it. Capture those great ideas when they emerge so when you're not as motivated, you'll have something to fall back on. Always have a small notebook, some index cards, or something else to write on and something to write with. Sitting in the

movie theater, driving in the car (wait until you've stopped to write, though), taking a walk, and writing during those last few minutes before you fall asleep are often the times when the best ideas emerge. If you have a pen and paper handy, you can preserve those great ideas and then get right back to what you were doing without anxiety. And those ideas and that notebook will be ready for you when you're facing another tough day of work.

5) **Create a deadline:** Often, the best motivation that drives determination is having a deadline to meet. A deadline forces you to commit yourself to arrive and have a goal or task completed on time. If you set a goal to have your bedroom closet cleaned and organized, setting a timer for 20 minutes can be a great motivator. Often, once you get through that first 20 minutes, you'll be motivated to continue. If you have a goal that is important to complete, but not urgent, make it urgent by setting a deadline and writing it in your calendar.

6) **Enlist a friend:** You can reinforce your deadline by enlisting a friend, colleague, or coach to help you. When you tell someone else that you're planning to do something by a specific date and time, it creates an expectation. We don't like to embarrass ourselves or let other people down, so we're much more likely to get it done so we don't have to admit to someone else that we didn't do it. Ask your friend, mentor, colleague, or coach to keep you accountable by following up to make sure you've done what you said you were going to do when you said you were going to do it.

7) **Celebrate ALL accomplishments:** No matter how small or large your accomplishments are from this point forward, record and celebrate each and every one of them. When you take the time to stop and celebrate your accomplishments, you give yourself an opportunity to reward your efforts. Rewards also give you the opportunity to stay connected to your beliefs, goals, dreams, and aspirations. And the more you find yourself celebrating, the more you're going to be determined to push yourself towards your ultimate goal of breaking free of your knots and living and celebrating your dream.

Let's face it, at one point or another, we all have found ourselves un-motivated, uninspired, discouraged, lost, de-energized, and undetermined. We all have stumbled. We all have fallen. We all have failed. That's why it's your responsibility to get back up, and try again, no matter how small a task, goal, activity, or errand. If you can complete it, you are already on your way. Make today the day you get up; turn your determination switch back on, and don't look back.

How to Stay Committed to Driving Your Determination

"The achievement of your goal is assured the moment you commit yourself to it."

— Mack Douglas

To stay committed to driving your determination, pursue a project or goal only if you're sure you have the will, time, and energy to start it and work it through to accomplishment. When difficulties, obstacles, and complications cross your path, counteract those distractions by discovering what motivates you, and use the strategies for turning your determination switch back on to develop and maintain an active, determined lifestyle. If by chance you should stumble or fall in the area of determination, just pick yourself back up, dust yourself off, take notes, and learn from the experience. Then plug yourself back into your determination outlet, turn your switch back on, and start anew!

FOCUS

"If you try to do too much, you will not achieve anything."

— Confucius

What is Focus?

Dictionary.com defines "focus" as "to concentrate: to focus one's thoughts."

The American Heritage Dictionary defines "focus" as "a central point of focus, to converge on or toward; be focused."

People often ask me what I think are the most important keys to achieving success. There are many, but the one key that I see as being the most essential—yet often ignored—is focus.

Any meaningful goal worth pursuing requires directed and committed efforts from beginning to end. Doing some of the tasks that are necessary will not be enough. Many people do not accomplish their goals or live their dreams because they don't stay focused all the way through to successful accomplishment.

In today's fast-paced and busy world, you will find hundreds of distractions that compete for your time, energy, and focus. Common distractions include children, family, friends, neighbors, phone calls, mail, household chores, hobbies, video games, television, Internet, electronic gadgets, cars, recreation, sports, visitors, community groups, work, school, and many more.

Distractions can seriously erode your focus and ability to work effectively. Many distractions are unavoidable. Yet, you can still take certain steps to minimize your distractions so you can regain your mind's full focus and attention.

Remember: Continuous achievement comes to those who remain steadfast and to those who stay focused and positively committed to their goals no matter what. Why? These people know the true power of focus.

The Power of Focus

> *"Get out of the block, run your race, stay relaxed.*
> *If you run your race, you'll win. Channel your*
> *energy. Focus."*
>
> — Carl Lewis

We all have the choice to run our own race—to channel our energy and to stay focused. The level of success you will achieve in life will be based on how well you develop and maintain your constructive habits. Your ability to focus and channel your efforts in the same direction will be one of the most rewarding habits you can develop for the constant empowerment of your life. The developed habit of focus is what makes the pursuit of freedom and goal accomplishment so inspiring to those who use it to create their best life or a better life for others.

> *Orville and Wilbur Wright, the Wright Brothers, used focused energy on December 17, 1903 when they successfully flew the first controlled power-driven airplane.*

> *George Washington Carver, American agricultural chemist, used focused energy to revolutionize the Southern agricultural economy in the early 1900s by showing that 300 products could be derived from the peanut.*

> *Gertrude Ederle used focused energy when she swam the English Channel in a record-breaking 14 hours, 31 minutes in 1926.*

> *Dr. Slava Fyodorov of Russia, in a case of eye trauma in the 1970s, used focused energy to bring about the practical application of refractive surgery (laser eye surgery) through radial keratotomy.*

These people also knew and used the power of focus. In doing so, their actions proved that they chose not to leave the accomplishment of their goals in someone else's hands. They chose to focus their energy and efforts on a successful, rewarding end.

The fact of the matter is successful people have successful habits. Unsuccessful people don't. The ability to commit yourself to stay focused until you accomplish your most meaningful goals is powerful.

Think about your life right here, right now. Can your level of focus use more development, more strengthening, and more determination? Make the powerful choice right now to regain and begin developing and channeling your focused energy and efforts for a more productive tomorrow and rewarding future.

The Effects of Low or No Focus

"I'm not here to just make a living, I'm here to make a difference."

— Helice Bridges

There are many effects of low or no focus. Here are five of the most common effects of low or no focus:

1) Distracted constantly and easily

These individuals find themselves unable to stay focused because they think they will miss out on something, or they have taken on too much work to accomplish in a short period of time.

Solution: *Don't think it, ink it.* When you write down your goals, they appear not only on paper, but they become real to you. This gives you a proven guide to what's most meaningful for your time. If it's not on your list of goals, most likely it's a distraction.

2) Produces unproductive days

These people find themselves constantly on the go and doing almost anything just to keep busy. Yet, by the end of the day, they have not accomplished any meaningful goals that will bring them closer to fulfilling their life's purpose or living their dream.

Solution: *Don't think it, ink it.* This time, at the end of each day, write down on a 3x5 index card two to five goals that are most meaningful to you creating or living your life's purpose. The very next morning, read the index card aloud to yourself, then put it in your wallet or in your purse. Throughout the day, work to accomplish each goal, and draw a line through the goals that you accomplish. If you do not accomplish one for that day, carry it over to the next day.

3) Struggles through life

These individuals find themselves constantly struggling through life because they have no clue about where they're headed or why they're headed that way. These people don't know what they want out of life.

<u>Solution</u>: *Stop! Sit. Think. Write.* Focus on only a few goals at a time. Sit down with a pen and writing pad, and think about these goals for five minutes without writing anything on the page. After five minutes have passed, write down three meaningful goals you would like to accomplish in your life within the next two years. Under each "Thing I Would Like to Accomplish," write two ways you may successfully accomplish this goal. Now organize these goals by ordering them according to those you can accomplish soonest. After you've completed this step, begin working on Goal Number One until you've accomplished it. Continue working through your list until you accomplish all five.

4) Indulges in procrastination and excuse-making

These individuals find themselves starting but never finishing tasks, projects, or goals. When asked, "Why not?" they always have has a good reason for not producing desired results.

<u>Solution</u>:*To achieve and stay focused on your objectives, create an action plan.* Your written plan of action should spell out what steps you will take to successfully complete the tasks or projects you've created for that day-what household chores to do and when, for example. It should also include steps to take if another task required more time to complete. For example, if you went to the community college campus to register for the upcoming semester and it took you two additional hours to complete this task, you may need to carryover a few of your "action plan" items for that day to the next day. Your plan of action should also include a list of support people to call when you encounter a problem or a challenge that you're having difficulty handling yourself. Using a detailed written plan of action will help you become more independent and successful in accomplishing tasks, projects, and

goals. And, it can also help you to break free of the toxic knots of procrastination and excuse making once and for all.

5) Sabotages their belief system by convincing themselves that life has nothing for them

These people find themselves at a point in their life where they feel their goals and dreams have passed them by. "It's just not meant to be for me" is a common thought.

<u>Solution</u>: *Speak your goal into existence.* An affirmation is a positive statement of your intended outcome. I now have achieved _____ (fill in the blank). The more sensory-rich you can make your affirmations, the more effective they will be. This technique will help you feel the presence of your objectives and build belief.

F.O.C.U.S. Acrostic

I created an acrostic for the word FOCUS many years ago. I share it with audiences whenever I speak about the power of focus.

I enthusiastically communicate to the audience that successful people, when it comes to focus, all have—

<u>F</u>aith
- A belief in a determined Higher Power or source that keeps them believing that their goals, aspirations, and dreams are attainable.

<u>O</u>rganization
- Successful, focused people do not operate in a bunch of clutter and confusion. They tend to organize their work areas, thinking areas, and life from the inside out.

<u>C</u>ommitment
- They are so driven towards the successful accomplishment of a goal or objective that it's non-negotiable when it comes to whether or not they will achieve their goal. All distractions are minimized to their lowest form.

Unshakeable Spirit

- Successful, focused people have a spirit that will not be shaken or derailed should unexpected challenges come their way. They will promptly deal with challenges, then pick up their goal, right where they left off.

Service

- All successful, focused people know they will acquire ten times more when they give their time, money, material things, and service to other people who need it more. This statement is definitely true: "What you give is what you get."

Are you F.O.C.U.S.ed?

How to Stay Committed to Driving Your Focus

"The person attempting to travel two roads at once will get nowhere. The superior person is committed to focus."

— Mencius (Mengzi Meng-tse)

Success in identifying and "untying your knots" of delay is entirely and completely reliant upon you and the decisions you make.

You had your reasons for deciding to purchase this book. You should always keep your reasons in the forefront of your mind. You must always rely upon yourself and your dedication to succeed.

Your friends and family might be annoyed they cannot gain your attention upon their own whim; however, when you achieve new levels of success because you remained focused, everyone will see and understand your previous commitment and dedication to your goals.

Success is within your reach, if only you can stay focused on your goals. You must decide to reach for your goals, and then, you must have the discipline necessary to reach them.

ACTION

"Life happens at levels of event, not words."

— Alfred Adler

What is Action?

Dictionary.com defines "action" as "a way or manner of moving."

The American Heritage Dictionary defines "action" as "a habitual or vigorous activity; energy."

Stop for a moment and consider your dreams, hopes, and ambitions. They are yours for a reason. They are yours because you are in the best position to drive, follow, and fulfill them. They are yours because they will compel you to create and live a significant life filled with meaning, purpose, and happiness.

Still, none of this will happen if you do not take the necessary steps of action.

The Power of Action

"All human actions have one or more of these seven causes: chance, nature, compulsions, habit, reason, passion, desire."

— Aristotle

If you want to improve the results in your life, you must accept the fact that you can no longer do the same old things the same old way. It's been said time-and-time again, *"If you do what you've always done, you'll always get what you've always got."*

Making a commitment to change or improve your life is a big step. It will require continuous, necessary steps of action!

Action brings forth movement and momentum. It brings forth the need to assess and adjust. Action brings forth new ideas, fears, and inspiration. It brings forth motivation and increases hope and belief. Action brings forth new energy, opportunity, and support teams. It brings forth the need for research and finding resources. Action brings forth failure and outcomes with the chance to learn a new way. In the end, continuous action brings forth success and great accomplishment.

There's little to no power in standing still. However, there is great power in taking continuous, necessary steps of action!

Jackie Robinson burst onto the scene in 1947, breaking professional baseball's color barrier and bringing the Negro Leagues' electrifying style of play to the majors. He quickly became baseball's top drawing card and a symbol of hope to millions of Americans.

In 1948, Mother Teresa devoted herself to working among the poorest of the poor in the slums of Calcutta. Although she had no funds, she depended on Divine Providence and started an open-air school for slum children. Soon, she was joined by voluntary helpers, and financial support was also forthcoming. This made it possible for her to extend the scope of her work.

From 1960 to 1981, Muhammad Ali floated, stung, punched, prophesized, and transformed the sport of boxing and became the world's most adored athlete.

Dr. Maya Angelou is hailed as one of the great voices of contemporary literature and as a remarkable Renaissance woman. In January 1993, she became only the second poet in U.S. history to have the honor of writing and reciting an original work at a Presidential Inauguration.

Continuous, necessary steps of action have great power when they are used to pursue a goal or effort with great meaning.

Where are your current steps of action leading you?

Why Most People Stop Taking Action

"Every profession is great that is greatly pursued."

— Oliver Wendell Holmes

If you gave people today who are not taking action on their goals, dreams, and ambitions an opportunity to explain to you "Why?" I'm sure you would hear a million excuses.

Nonetheless, here are my top four reasons why most people today stop taking action.

1) They listen to what someone else has told them.
   More times than not, there are more people listening to the logic and reasoning of people who really don't know what they're talking about.
   Solution: *It is wise to ask for advice from other people; however, do your own homework and research.* Discover the names and resources yourself so you can move your life confidently forward. Do not accept every answer as fact because there is a lot of incorrect information out there. You will be surprised when you learn how wrong those eager to give advice are.

2) They experienced failure one too many times, so they quit.
   These people do work towards a goal wholeheartedly; however, they experienced failure in their mind's eye one too many times. As a result of repeated failures, they have made the decision to quit and give up their goals.
   Solution: *Learn to accept failure as a part of the process on your way to success.* Realize that most (97%) people fail on their way to success. If one or more doors get slammed in your face, don't quit. Go to the next door, then the next door, then the next door. If that doesn't work, go back to the first door, and keep knocking with positive steps of action, until you knock it open or knock it down! Persistence wears down resistance. Remember: a "No" is a "Yes" waiting to happen.

3) They have no identified goals or sense of direction.

   These people do not see the benefit of writing down their goals or feel they are too busy to write down their goals. This poor habit puts them in a position in life where they land wherever life pushes them.

   Solution: *This is a critical step. Don't think it, ink it.* Again, when you write your goals down, they not only appear on paper, but they become written upon your consciousness.

4) The people they hang around have little to no ambition.

   These people choose to hang out with people who do not have any goals or ambitions for themselves. So, every time a person within the group wants to make a big change in his or her life to improve life or move it forward, one of the crabs within the basket reaches up to pull them back down into a no-action-taking state.

   Solution: *Find some new friends—QUICKLY!* If you are the smartest among your ten closest friends, find some new friends that are at least one or two levels higher than you. Surrounding yourself with people who are driven and successful will be very empowering.

How to Stay Committed to Taking Necessary Steps of Action

"The most effective way to do it is to do it."

— Toni Cade Bambara

Once you find yourself taking the necessary steps of action for continuous success, the most challenging part will be staying committed.

Learn, remember, and apply the following formula—

The Continuous—Determination, Focus, and Action Formula

Success = Idea + Determination + Focus + Action

Idea – Determination – Focus – Action = wishful thinking, struggling, floundering, self-sabotage, tied up in knots, wasted time, and lost recourses.

Chapter Conclusion

*"Unless commitment is made, there are only
promises and hope; but no plans."*

— Peter Drucker

Like all successful habits, developing the habits of continuous determination, focus, and action will take effort and daily discipline. If you're feeling a little bit overwhelmed right now, don't worry. That's quite normal. Together, we're going to take it one step at a time. Schedule sufficient time to learn and practice the strategies shared in this chapter. Commit to getting started today. Take the first step. Creating a successful future takes determination, focus, and action. That's the reason why most people don't do it. However, by deciding to read this book you have already taken the first step to rise above the crowd. Continue forward confidently. Accept the challenge. Prepare yourself. And expect some major breakthroughs.

Chapter 3

...CAN BREAK YOU AWAY TO FREEDOM

"There are always risks in freedom. The only risk in bondage is breaking free."

— *Gita Bellin*

FREEDOM is a mental state—a condition of the spirit; it is the condition of minimal constraint. Naturally, in a society or community, there must be some constraints: the burglar cannot have the freedom to steal, the thug cannot have the freedom to mug, and the businessman cannot have the freedom to excessively pollute or not pay taxes. But if we get right the balance between personal freedom, social order, and governed integrity, the vast majority of citizens can live happily by acknowledging and utilizing the principles and resources of freedom.

F.R.E.E.D.O.M.

F
Fueled

R
Resources,

E
Education, and

E
Empowerment

D
Driven daily to

O
Open opportunities for positive

M
Movement

or

F
Focused,

R
Resilient

E
Energy,

E
Enthusiasm, and

D
Determination

O
Orchestrating opportunities for positive

M
Movement

When we focus and fuel available principles and resources, we create a positive movement within us to live freely. We all are free to change our thoughts, improve our knowledge, and understand ourselves so we can change our attitudes and beliefs—the inner part of each of us. These positive habits and principles are the fuel that drives freedom.

The Effects of Living Tied Up

"Two wrongs don't make a right, but they make a good excuse."

— Thomas Szasz

You may be wondering why it is important for you to *"identify and untie the knots that tie up your life."* If you do not take time to identify and untie your knots, you've made the decision to live your life with the following toxic conditions:

Continuous worrying

> Solution: Take each of these worrisome thoughts and write down an alternative thought that is a more believable challenge to the worry. Then write down two positive ways you can take action to remove each worrisome thought. If you find it impossible to remove a worrisome thought, seek professional help.

Endless struggle

> Solution: Stop. Think about why you're in endless struggles. Write down a complete list of your current struggles. Then write down beside each struggle two positive ways you can take action toward alleviating each struggle from your life, one-by-one. If you find it difficult to remove a particular struggle, seek help from a family member, friend, or professional.

Continual health problems

> Solution: If you haven't already visited the hospital or clinic for a complete exam, call to make an appointment and see a doctor today. If you do not have health insur-

ance, call your community clinic or hospital and speak to someone who helps people with no health insurance to receive check ups. If you have already been seen, examined, and diagnosed by a doctor, it doesn't hurt to get a second opinion from another doctor. Also, try changing your eating habits and daily exercise.

Endless financial frustrations

<u>Solution</u>: Stop. Write down your current list of financial debts or frustrations. Rank them according to their degree of severity so you can resolve the one that's going to take the longest to fix. Set a written goal with an estimated "Resolve by date," and take action on removing each financial frustration, one-by-one, until you eliminate your ultimate financial challenge.

Thoughtless loss of personal vision

<u>Solution</u>: It's true what the Bible states, "Without a vision the people will perish." Sit down this evening and write a positive vision for your life. A positive vision of your life after you have successfully identified and untied the knots that entangle your life. Make your personal vision statement positive, unique, enthusiastic, lofty, believable, and achievable. A good personal vision is one that requires you to reach outside your comfort zone for extraordinary accomplishments.

Reckless, unhealthy relationships

<u>Solution</u>: Stop. Look at your current circle of friends. Write their names down on a list. Beside each name, write one of the following statements: "Good for Where I'm Headed" or "Not Good for Where I'm Headed." If you have to think more than twice about whether someone is good for where you're headed, most likely, they're not. For all the "Not Good for Where I'm Headed" people, begin to distance yourself from them. You can still say "Hello" to them; however, it's best to remove toxic people and relationships from your personal circle now, if you're serious about living freely.

Poor understanding of opportunities

<u>Solution</u>: Stop. Write down a list of three goals that you could honestly achieve within the next 30 days. It doesn't matter if these goals are small or medium-sized. You just have to be able to achieve them within the next 30 days. Write down the list of resources and people who can assist you in achieving these three goals. Now take action. Don't stop until you achieve all three. The truth of the matter is that opportunity is everywhere. It takes some people to begin experiencing purposeful success again for them to begin seeing all the opportunities that are around them each day.

Unfulfilling advancement in life

<u>Solution</u>: Stop. Look at where you are in life right now. Write down where you would like to be in two years. Now, write a plan of action and execute your plan of action. Do not allow toxic distractions or any outside people to stop you.

Constant decline in quality of living

<u>Solution</u>: Stop. If your life has been going down hill, it's time for you to acknowledge it. Write down specifically how your life has been going down hill. This will give you an opportunity to see what has been happening and what your attitude and habits have been. Now, write down a list of 10 ways you can improve the quality of your living, beginning today. Then start doing and executing your strategies. Most of us know what type of life we want and know how to obtain it; however, we fail to execute the steps and strategies. This puts your life in a state of decline: The only way to coast is to go down hill. So, execute your onward and upward quality of life plan today.

Misguided sense of direction

<u>Solution</u>: Stop. Write your new plan of direction for your life right now. Post this plan in your bedroom, kitchen, office, etc. This will remind you where you're headed. This will also help you identify and remove toxic distractions.

Unmotivated belief system

Solution: Stop. If your belief system is currently shot and polluted, I want you to write down 25 things. First, write down, on a separate sheet of paper, 10 negative thoughts about your life that are not empowering you. Second, write down, on a separate sheet of paper, 15 positive thoughts about you and your life that could inspire and empower you. Ball-up and throw away your list of negative thoughts. Keep your list of positive thoughts in your pocket, wallet, or pocketbook daily. Read this list seven times each day. The more positive, inspirational thoughts about you that go into your mind daily, the more positive expectations and results come from you.

Uncontrollable family problems

Solution: Stop. Think about the current state and quality of the relationships within your family. Write down the toxic behaviors and problems that currently exist within your family. Write down how you can help your family fix each problem. Now, set a day, date, and time for you and the other members within your family to sit down and discuss the importance of how and why you should all work together to *"untie the knots."* A family that prays together stays together. A family that acknowledges its faults and failures together stays together. A family that works out problems together stays together. A family that has fun together stays together. A family that succeeds together stays together. And, a family that learns and grows together stays together.

Unsatisfying job fulfillment

Solution: Stop. Think about your current job. Is it really what you envisioned yourself doing for work five or more years ago? If not, you have two choices: 1) Change the condition or 2) Change your position. Change the condition simply means to go to your supervisor or manager and discuss ways that could make your job more fun and pleasing. Change your position means you can look for other positions different from the one you're currently at in your current organization. However, you may need to find a new job with another company so you can reconnect yourself with positive job fulfillment and peace of mind.

Ineffective decision-making
>   <u>Solution</u>: Stop. Making decisions can be intimidating and time-consuming. And while there is no easy way to just make them, here are a few tips that can help you make better decisions: A) Mark out the parameters of the decision clearly: What choices do you have? Are there more than two? B) Jot down a list of pros and cons for each decision. Prioritize which considerations are very important to you and which are less important to you. C) Think honestly about any fears, motives, or biases guiding your thinking. Recognize them for what they are. D) Recognize that you might learn things in hindsight that would have changed your decision had you known about them earlier. This thought is normal and should not be allowed to stall your decision-making. E) Make the decision.

Ongoing self-sabotaging behavior
>   <u>Solution</u>: Stop. The process of changing a bad habit into a good one can be challenging. Write down a list of self-sabotaging behaviors that currently have you "tied up in knots," and apply these "Five ITS to Self-Rewarding Habits" to each one. 1) *Acknowledge it*. Write down specifically what this self-sabotaging behavior is and how it's affecting you on a daily basis. 2) *Control it*. Write down two ways that you can immediately gain control of this toxic behavior. 3) *Remove it*. Write down three ways that you can remove this toxic behavior from your life, completely, within the next 30 days. 4) *Replace it*. Write down two potential positive habits that can replace this old bad habit. 5) *Maintain it*. Write down five strategies about how you plan and will stay committed to utilizing the two new positive habits that replaced your self-sabotaging habits.

You may have noticed that most of the above <u>Solutions</u> in this section required you to write things down in one way or another. As you continue your journey by reading on, you will discover that this is not my primary solution for everything; however, in the early phases of the Untie the Knots Process, it is required for you to write out what's happening in your life so you can see the details as clearly as possible. You will find yourself using the information you create from the above writing assignments again-and-again throughout your Untie the Knots "journey;" be sure to keep this information where you can find it quickly.

Being tied up creates hopelessness, excuses, and chaotic habits that waste time and prevent us from living a productive and rewarding life; it also undermines our sense of self-worth, leaving us feeling unsuccessful and helpless. Watch out for it. When you feel and catch yourself drifting towards one or more of the above toxic conditions, turn yourself around by applying one of the suggested solutions. Then apply another. Then another.

If you practice this new habit on a daily basis, you will be on the right path to living freely, to *"untying your knots"* for your FREEDOM.

What It's Like to Live Freely

"The energy of the mind is the essence of life."

— Aristotle

If you take the time to *"identify and untie your knots,"* you've made the decision to live life with the following healthy conditions:

- ✓ Continuous peace of mind
- ✓ Endless accomplishment
- ✓ Improved health conditions
- ✓ Unlimited financial independence
- ✓ Keen personal vision
- ✓ Rewarding relationships

✓ Resilient understanding of opportunities
✓ Meaningful advancement in life
✓ Constant increase in quality of living
✓ Dedicated sense of direction
✓ Ambitious belief system
✓ Orderly family development
✓ Increased career fulfillment
✓ Effective decision making ability
✓ Self-empowering behaviors

One of the greatest planning tools is your imagination. Take a few minutes to mentally picture living your life freely with the above healthy conditions; imagine empowering your life continuously with positive habits, choices, people, and relationships. Imagine what your life will be like two years from now, five years from now, and ten years from now as you begin to incorporate into your life the tips and principles you will learn and apply from reading this guide. Once you visualize what you need to do, you'll be amazed at how smooth and free your life can become.

If true freedom is what you want, then you're going to have to plan your work, visualize your success, and work your plan.

Why Most People Are Not Living Freely

"I am the master of my fate; I am the captain of my soul."

— William Earnest Henley

The million dollar question is this: If we are so free, why are there more people living *"tied up in knots"* than there are living in a state of true freedom and personal accomplishment?

Most people, even though they could be truly free, are not living freely for three clear and concise reasons:
1) They believe one person can't make a difference.
2) They fear standing up and challenging an unfavorable situation or habit.

3) They accept a "this is all I'm going to be" attitude.

Marian Wright Edelman said it best when she said, *"We must not, in trying to think about how we can make a big difference, ignore the small daily differences we can make which, over time, add up to big differences that we often cannot foresee."*

If you are serious about freeing yourself by "identifying and untying your knots," you are required to update and renew your belief system.

First, take out your writing pad and pen.

Second, write at the top of a blank page the following title: "My Belief Restoration Story."

Third, skip three lines, and then write a four-paragraph answer to your story, which should begin like this:
- *Paragraph 1*: The last person I helped to resolve a problem was __(person's name)__. I specifically helped __ (same person's name)__ in the following way. Specifically, explain the problem or challenge this person was facing.
- *Paragraph 2*: My efforts resulted in __(same person's name)__ doing or accomplishing what?
- *Paragraph 3*: Helping __(same person's name)__ made me feel what?
- *Paragraph 4*: Write down three ways you feel that you can continue making a difference in the lives of the people you love and your community.

Fourth, once you're done writing your "My Belief Restoration Story," put it inside an envelope and do not seal it. You will carry this story with you for the next 30 days to read in the morning, at lunch, and before you go to bed.

If you are serious about "untying your knots for freedom," you will find yourself eager to complete this assignment to update and renew your belief system.

It was Mahatma Gandhi who said, *"You can chain me, you can torture me, you can even destroy this body, but you will never imprison my mind."*

If you are serious about freeing yourself by "identifying and untying your knots," you are required to boldly face your fear of standing up and changing an unfavorable situation or habit.

Neither this book nor all the self-help or clinical professionals in the world can help you if you choose to stay tied up in an unfavorable situation or habit. You need to decide in your mind right now whether you're going to commit to making changes for the better. That you're going to start boldly standing up within yourself as we journey through this book, and say, "No MORE! I will no longer allow toxic situations and habits to tie me down—or hold me back!"

Turn to another blank page in your writing pad and write down your quick list of current unfavorable situations and habits that have you tied up. Just write them down for now. I will share with you in "Chapter 9: Step 3: Acknowledging and Pushing Through Your Fears" and "Chapter 12: Step 6: Defeating Toxic Habits, Choices, People, and Relationships" proven strategies and specific "How Tos" on how to break free of your unfavorable situations and habits.

You have to boldly face your fears because you know it's the right thing to do. Because you're sick and tired of being tired. Because you know change and growth has to happen. Because you know you deserve much better than what a current situation, person, or habit is giving you. Because you know success and freedom is for you too!

Together, let us boldly say it again, right now, "No MORE! I will no longer allow toxic situations and habits to tie me down—or hold me back!"

William Boetcker's powerful statement on personal acceptance drives the nail into the wall, *"You can succeed if nobody else believes it, but you will never succeed if you don't believe in yourself."*

If you are serious about freeing yourself by "identifying and untying your knots," you are required to personally accept and ignite the fact within your heart and mind that you will accomplish more in life from this point forward. You will do more. You will be more. You will live more. You will see more. You will learn more. You will travel more. You will step out of your comfort zone more. And you will continuously network and succeed more.

Take out your writing pad and pen again. Find a blank page and draw a line down the middle of that page from top to bottom. At the top of the page, on the left side of the line, write the words "Low Points of My Life," and at the top of the page, on the right side of the line, write the words "High Points of My Life."

First, write your list of "Low Points of My Life." Second, write your list of "High Points of My Life."

Once you have your list of "lower" or "higher" points, you have the means to compare points of your life to one another. How does your life today compare with your life five years ago? Are you richer? Happier? Healthier? Smarter? Freer? Growing?

Next, decide how you want to push things to improve your quality of life. You can accept your current position as adequate opting to simply maintain it and stay tied up. Or you can strive to achieve something greater, and create a life of better balance, health, financial independence, significance, and prosperity. A life that is free and continuously growing.

Remember: Personal acceptance starts in the mind, is fueled by your heart, and is distinguished by your actions.

Chapter Conclusion

The freedom that I'm going to guide, coach, and mentor you toward, as a result of your reading and applying what you learn in this book, will not come easy. Nor will it happen overnight. Prepare yourself now to work on your habits, choices, people skills, and relationships from where you are right now until your time on this Earth is done.

The only place where freedom comes before work is in the dictionary.

That is why when you free yourself and break away from each and every knot, I want you to stop to celebrate each specific knot you've untied. The Untie the Knots Process is a challenging and demanding one; however, it's one that encourages ongoing self-rewards and celebration.

You have what it takes to create and live a free life. Within you is the potential for extraordinary accomplishment. Do not voluntarily tie yourself up or allow someone else to tie you up. A life in bondage is a life that denies us the chance to fully express our gifts, talents, and strengths. If you are tied up right now, don't worry; this guide will assist you in gaining freedom. If you're not tied up right now, that's GREAT; this guide will assist you in maintaining your freedom and in making your life even better.

The key is this: true freedom will only come and stay with you when you have faith. Faith in yourself, faith in the Untie the Knots Process, and faith in your determined Higher Power.

Unit Summary

When you're willing to lose something toxic to gain something worthwhile, you're ready to take a risk. Taking risks requires stepping out of your comfort zone while standing on faith. Your willingness to take the risk may well determine how rewarding and fulfilling your life turns out.

The first three chapters of **Untie the Knots That Tie Up Your Life** were written to act as primers for your journey. I want to make sure that your mind, attitude, heart, spirit, and faith are properly conditioned and pointed in the right direction.

Let's recap the three chapters that make up Unit 1:

Chapter 1: A Positive Attitude

Chapter 2: Plus Continuous—Determination, Focus, and Action

Chapter 3: Can Break You Away To Your Freedom

We've encountered the following **Infusers** *(Freedom Break Away Tools)* that were referred to in the introduction of this book:

Infuser #1: Reinstate a Positive Attitude
If you're serious about breaking free from the knots that tie up your life, you are required to adopt a positive mental attitude. You will have to be committed to developing and working constantly with a positive attitude, regardless of past experiences or current situations or circumstances. Attitude is a choice. And the choice you make from this point forward may mean staying tied up (STUCK) or setting yourself free.

Infuser #3: Choose
Decide true freedom and life is what you want and then go where you can produce those results.

Infuser #4: Identify

To successfully break away from anything that has delayed or derailed you in the past, you must summon the bold confidence to now identify it as a toxic habit, choice, person, or relationship.

Infuser #6: Believe

It takes your strong will and unshakable faith to make the impossible possible.

Infuser #7: Move

Don't just stand there filled with knowledge: Do it! Quit procrastinating and making excuses.

We've covered a lot in this unit (Chapters 1-3). Make sure you read it more than once because the material will uplift your mind and soul. Adopt the ideas and strategies to your own situation and then take action. Again, I emphasize the importance of following through with necessary steps of action. These are essential tools to help you make positive attitude, determination, focus, action, and freedom permanent habits in your life. In a few weeks you, your family, friends, and co-workers will notice a big change in your character. You will feel healthier, happier, prosperous, excited, and inspired to accomplish one goal after another.

The next unit (Chapters 4, 5, and 6) will introduce you to and begin your official journey into the Untie the Knots Process. These three chapters will help you identify your current toxic knots, begin to untie your current toxic knots, and make the decisions to begin "doing you" positively and daily. It will require honesty, realism, and commitment on your part. So, be ready to get real, stay real, and deal with the real you in the present.

You cannot rewrite the beginning script of your life; however, you can influence and direct your present and future. Meet me at the beginning of Unit 2, Part 1: THE TIME IS NOW, so we can start your journey!

Time OUT!

Just to recap some of the major concepts you've read about thus far, find and write in your journal the answers to the following questions:

- What's the Untie the Knots Process?
  Refer to the Introduction of the book to find the answer.

- What's an Infuser?
  Refer to the Introduction of the book to find the answer.

- What are four benefits of having a positive attitude?
  Refer to "The Power of a Positive Attitude" section in Chapter 1 for the answer.

- What are three strategies for maintaining a positive attitude?
  Refer to the "Five Strategies for Maintaining a Positive Attitude" section in Chapter 1 for the answer.

- What are the three reasons why people stop getting what they want in life?
  Refer to the first page of Chapter 2 for the answer.

- What is Ty's definition of the word "freedom"?
  Refer to the first page of Chapter 2 for the answer.

"We are made wise not by the recollection of our past, but by the responsibility for our future."

— George Bernard Shaw

PART 1

THE TIME IS NOW

"You can't turn back the clock. But you can wind it up again."

— *Bonnie Prudden*

In Part 1...

You will learn the nine steps of the Untie the Knots Process and how each step brings you closer to creating a life of better health, balance, significance, harmony, potential, and prosperity. I will also show you the importance of boldly standing up within yourself as you begin your Untie the Knots journey. I will teach you how you can treat the lessons you gain from the Untie the Knots Process with the same joy that you treat your hobbies and pastimes. You will learn that no matter your age, your position or station in life, your gender, educational level, or marital status, a life with fewer knots can make an incredible difference. This part offers green and growing information to keep you upbeat and moving forward.

Chapter 4

BOLDLY STANDING UP WITHIN
TO CHANGE AND GROW

"Think success, visualize success, and you will set in motion the power force of the realizable wish."

— Norman Vincent Peale

Do you know someone who is tied up in procrastination, poor choices, excuse making, addiction, self-pity, laziness, the past, denial, clutter, fear, distraction, materialism, worry, debt, confusion, toxic relationships, conformity, continual pain, anger, mediocrity, an unfulfilling job, or stress?

Someone who is so tied up they're sick and tired of being tied up?

You know what's even worse: to be someone who is tied up and not even know it.

How do I know? I was once one of those people.

When I was two-years old, my older brother Zachary and I were ripped out of my mother's home, in the middle of the night, by the Baltimore City Child Protective Services and placed into foster care at the Saint Vincent's Center, a part of the Catholic Charities of the Archdiocese of Baltimore. For the next five years, this was our home. As the years passed, my brother and I were allowed weekend stays at my biological mother's home to transition back into her life. The cold nights and uncertain moments at Saint Vincent's made me afraid and often angry. Afraid because this wasn't my mother's home and angry because I wasn't at home with my mother.

My brother often talked to me about us some day going back to live with Mommy. To me, someday wasn't soon enough. There was a nurse at Saint Vincent's who took me to her office to talk to me and assure me by encouraging me to draw pictures of my brother, older sister, and myself living and having fun together. My brother's talks and the nurse's assurance techniques worked; however, my inner anger and frustrations built back up and shattered all hope for the picture of "some day soon."

At the age of seven, "someday soon" did arrive. My brother and I were returned to our biological mother's home to live with her permanently. At the time, my mother lived in South Baltimore in a poor community known as Cherry Hill. My brother and I were definitely happy to be back home with Mommy; however, we weren't aware of our new challenges.

My mother quickly enrolled us into the nearby elementary school, Arundel Elementary School, where we continued our education. Mommy taught and preached to us at an early age, "Learn as much as you can! Do your BEST when it comes to school and education!" She would often take her pointer finger knuckle and tap me on my head while she said, "Once you put it up here in your head, no one can ever take that away, boy! Education! Education! Education!" I bought into Mommy's education sermon, hook-line-and-sinker.

However, a funny thing happened when my brother and I showed up in our separate classrooms at the elementary school. The other students quickly noticed that even though we were black students, like them, we didn't speak like them, walk like them, or act like them. We didn't speak like the other students in our class because while at Saint Vincent's we were taught a more rigid and structured way of speaking. We didn't walk or act like the students in our class because we had spent time in another environment that was more disciplined and less chaotic. So, my brother and I found ourselves being picked on, teased, and often in fights.

In the beginning, being in a community of people that looked like me but being rejected by my own kind caused me to once again grow angry and upset. This time, my anger and frustrations pushed me to act out. When this happened in school, it placed me quickly in the principal's office. I recall days when I literally yelled at Ms. Jule, our elementary school principal, shouting out that "I wouldn't be this way if I hadn't spent time in foster care... if my father was in my life...if I had friends in school who didn't think I was weird because I didn't talk or walk like them!"

When my anger and frustration happened in the community, it often resulted in me being brought home to my mother by an angry adult or even the police. And once again, I returned to yelling, "I wouldn't be this way if I hadn't spent time in foster care...if my father was in my life...if I had friends in the community who didn't think I was weird because I didn't talk or walk like them!"

This deeply rooted rage became my weapon and excuse of choice for every troublesome situation I found myself in.

Unknown to me at the time, these were becoming my knots. Knots of delay, decay, and destruction.

I carried this self-sabotaging rage and these knots with me into my high school years. Life became a big challenge: trying to be good while avoiding trouble was difficult. It seemed like every time I took one victorious step forward, I was knocked two steps backward. I still tried my best to remain committed to Mommy's standards for education. It was crazy for me to even try to walk through my mother's doors with low or failing grades, so I buckled down and tried to maintain good grades.

I started my high school experience at Baltimore Polytechnic Institute in Baltimore, Maryland. Poly was a college preparatory school and one of the top two public schools in Baltimore City at the time. I had made my mother, family, friends, and myself very proud when I was accepted into Poly.

When I arrived at Poly, I quickly noticed something: I was no longer one of the smartest students in the school like I was in middle school. Now, over 95% of the students in the school were smart and bright. I felt intimidated. How else could I stand out?

Give a teenager enough idle time to think, and an answer will appear. It may not be the best or brightest answer; however, an answer will emerge.

I decided at the beginning of my tenth grade year at Poly that I would become the school bully and work to run the school. I worked hard. By the middle of my tenth grade year, I formed the Ten Horsemen, which was far more than ten teenagers; it was actually almost 45% of the entire tenth grade class. I could make other students tease other students, take stuff from other students, and even fight other students.

At the end of my tenth grade school year, my mother and I found ourselves sitting in Principal Dohler's office. I was expelled from Poly due to my behavior and poor academic performance. I was not working hard enough to continue the traditions and standards of the school. Mr. Dohler told my mother, "Ms. Howard, your son Ty isn't a failing or lazy student at all. He actually performs very well academically when he wants to. He treats his talents and abilities like a light switch. He turns them on when he wants to, and he turns them off when he wants to. During the past two years, Ty has become somewhat of a puppeteer here at Poly. He has managed to dangle several other students from a string and has enticed them to do whatever he wants them to do. When the situation or conflict dissolves, your son is never there when those other students are brought back to my office. However, when I start suspending and calling parents, Ty's name comes up at the top of every list of those responsible for the incident."

My mother was very angry and disappointed to hear Principal Dohler's description of what her son had been up to in school while she was out working two to three jobs to make ends meet.

But before she could get a single word of frustration out of her mouth, I quickly went back to my creed: "I wouldn't be this way if I hadn't spent time in foster care...if my father was in my life... if I had friends in school who didn't think I was weird because I didn't talk or walk like them!"

These were now my knots. My knots of delay, decay, and destruction.

Mommy's eyes and the frown on her face communicated to me without a single word, "You Are Mine... When We Get Home!" She politely thanked Principal Dohler for his hard work and guidance during my two years at Poly, and we walked out of his office and Baltimore Polytechnic Institute.

I started my eleventh grade school year at Southern High School in South Baltimore City, Maryland. This was my zone school, a school for general education. I spent the next two years relearning what I had already learned in the eighth and ninth grade. I decided to make the best of a non-challenging academic time at Southern High School. I played and became the captain of the varsity football team. In my eleventh grade year, our football team made it to the Baltimore City championship game; however, we lost to City College in the championship. By my twelfth grade year, I became involved in the student government, and I was the key person in rallying the crowd at our school's basketball games. Southern High School's basketball team was ranked very high in the State of Maryland each year. I graduated in the top 5% of my graduating class.

In the middle of my twelfth grade year, I also became a teenage father. However, even though I graduated in the top 5% of my graduating class, the birth of my daughter was a defining point in my life. It was one thing for me to be chaotic with my own life, when it was just me; on the other hand, I made up my mind that I wasn't going to be chaotic with the life of my daughter. I was going to be everything that my father wasn't for me.

So, I boldly stood up within myself and made the confirmed decision to change and grow.

For me, this decision was non-negotiable! It had to happen. I had to break the self-sabotaging cycle. I had to identify and break away from my deeply rooted rage and weapon of choice: "I wouldn't be this way if I hadn't spent time in foster care...if my father was in my life...if I had friends in school who didn't think I was weird because I didn't talk, walk, or act like them!"

I not only had to do this to begin living my life to the fullest, but if I wanted my daughter to live to her highest potential as well, I had to do this. I made an agreement with God and myself when I was about 15-years-old that if I ever fathered a child in this world, I would not be an absentee father and that no one would ever prevent me from being a vital and active part in my child's life. I didn't plan her birth to happen when it did; however, now I had to step up and deliver on my promise to my Higher Power, my daughter, and myself.

It was time for me to change and grow.

For anyone to boldly stand up within to change and grow, that person must learn and give power to the following learning principles:

1) See Change as an Opportunity

> *"The need for change bulldozed a road down the center of my mind."*
>
> — Maya Angelou

In the movie *Remember the Titans*, the main characters come together when their classmates and loved ones will not. It takes place in suburban Virginia, where schools have been segregated for generations, in sight of the Washington Monument over the river in the nation's capital. One black and one white high school are closed, and the students are sent to T.C. Williams

High School under federal mandate to integrate. The year is seen through the eyes of the football team where the man hired to coach the black school is made head coach over the highly successful white coach. Based on the actual events of 1971, the team becomes the unifying symbol for the community as the boys and adults learn to depend on and trust each other.

Change is not something to be feared. Rather it is something we should welcome—for without change, nothing in this world would ever grow or blossom, and no one in this world would ever move forward to become the person they want to be.

When you decide to "see change as an opportunity," a few of the opportunities that were evaporating right before your eyes due to your resistance to change may once again reappear.

2) Realize You Have Two Real Options in Life

Option # 1) You can allow life to tie you up, and subsequently, you sit on the shore hoping for your ship to someday arrive.

or

Option # 2) You can put yourself in the captain's seat of your own ship, steer, and enjoy the ride.

One of Aesop's Fables: The Seaside Travelers

SOME TRAVELERS, journeying along the seashore, climbed to the summit of a tall cliff, and looking over the sea, saw in the distance what they thought was a large ship. They waited in the hope of seeing it enter the harbor, but as the object on which they looked was driven nearer to shore by the wind, they found that it could at the most be a small boat, and not a ship. When however it reached the beach, they discovered that it was only a large bundle of sticks, and one of them said to his companions, "We have waited for no purpose, for after all there is nothing to see but a load of wood."

Moral of the Story: Our anticipations of life outrun its realities.

When you decide to put yourself in the captain's seat of your own ship, steer it, and enjoy the ride, you put yourself in a position to take more risks, to stretch, to learn, to grow, to meet people, and more importantly, to discover the true potential you have inside.

3) Find Solutions, Not Faults

"The real fault is to have faults and not amend them."

— Confucius

There once was a woman who woke up each day to her many faults. Her skin was too pale. Her makeup never went on right. Her stockings were always the wrong color. Her contact lenses barely made it into her eyes. She proclaimed this was happening because she wasn't born with the perfect body, the perfect smile, or with the perfect head of hair.

One morning she woke up and all her faults were gone. "How could this be?" you ask.

The night before that morning her husband finally replaced the two blown light bulbs in the bathroom.

When you decide to take a look around your area or mind to see if the faults you say you have are real, often, you will be surprised to learn that your faults are not really faults at all. They are exaggerated mishaps that you've given dramatic residence to in your life. However, if you do think or discover that you do have a legitimate fault, seek a second opinion, ask caring friends, or visit a professional doctor to find a possible solution. I believe an empowered life finds solutions, not permanent faults.

4) Literally Say Aloud, "NO MORE!"

"Every spoken word arouses our self-will."

— Johann Wolfgang Von Goethe

Several years ago, I was watching the Oprah Winfrey Show, and poet and novelist Maya Angelou was a guest on Oprah's show. Maya Angelou and Oprah were discussing how women deal with and get past domestic violence and abuse. Maya Angelou explained to Oprah that there comes a point in time when a woman makes the choice to say aloud, "NO MORE!"

"NO MORE! NO MORE will this continue to happen to me! NO MORE will I live my life like this!" Maya Angelou commanded in her thunderous voice.

On that day, I, even as a man, learned the power and the innate movement of saying aloud, "NO MORE!"

When you decide to "boldly stand up within to change and grow," you can give lion-like power to your stance when you say aloud, "NO MORE!" Bold and courageous words like "NO MORE" claim and command the essence of your being to halt... assess...remove...adjust...and take action. Try it and experience the power that comes from it.

5) Choose to Be Green and Growing

"Are you green and growing or ripe and dying?"

— Dr. Wolf Rinke

When I first decided to pursue my passion of being a professional motivational speaker, I joined the local chapter of the National Speakers Association in Washington, D.C. (NSA-DC). As a new member of the association, I decided to apply for and take part in the Fast Trackers Program. I was approved and was assigned to my mentor, Dr. Wolf Rinke.

Dr. Wolf J. Rinke is America's Business Success Coach, CSP (Certified Speaking Professional), an internationally recognized keynote speaker, widely published author, media personality, management consultant, executive coach, and management professor.

As my mentor, Dr. Rinke and I would talk at least twice a month about my development in the speaking business, my career status, and my overall family and life in general. He would begin every conversation we had by asking, "Ty, are you green and growing or ripe and dying?"

Dr. Rinke taught me early in our relationship that a person who is green and growing is a person who wakes up to each new day looking to change and grow. A person who is ripe and dying has reached a point in life where he or she has made the decision that they have no more reason to change and grow. They completely lack the desire or vision to do more, achieve more, or become more.

To get the results you're looking and hoping for out of your Untie the Knots journey, you need to choose to be green and growing through this entire experience.

When you decide to choose a green and growing attitude about life, you put yourself in a position to learn, change, grow, and make your desired possibilities accomplished goals.

Let's start with you saying it aloud with me three times, right now, "I'm Green and Growing! I'm Green and Growing! I'm Green and Growing!"

Thank you. Didn't that feel good?

This journey will be a green and growing experience. Stay the course! Stay committed! And I assure you that you will begin to experience real-life green and growing results.

Chapter Conclusion

So now you know a little more about Ty Howard and how my knots multiplied throughout the early stages of my life. I will share more personal stories with you as your journey continues, so you will continue to learn and grow in an inspiring and engaging way. In addition, you have proven principles that can help you to boldly stand up within to change and grow. The practice of these principles will work equally well to improve your business habits and those in your personal life. I encourage you to re-read learning principles 1 thru 5 of this chapter at least two more times before moving onto the next chapter. Only when you commit to learning and applying these principles to your daily routines will the true benefits become clear and real. Just keeping information in your head is short-lived. I want you to experience a transformation—in your results and in your lifestyle.

I want you to **Boldly Stand Up Within to Change and Grow!**

Chapter 5

THE NINE-STEP UNTIE THE KNOTS PROCESS

"Strategy without tactics is the slowest route to victory. Tactics without strategy is the noise before defeat."

— Sun Tzu

I think of the Untie the Knots Process as a cycle; if you put it into practice properly, the last phase in the cycle will lead you back to the first phase. That's when the cycle kicks in, and that is when the Untie the Knots Process can become a way of life for you. The changed and improved YOU will exhibit a life with fewer toxic habits, choices, people, and relationships. That will mean you're living a happier, healthier, significant, and prosperous life.

I also like the fact that the Untie the Knots Process breaks down neatly into nine steps. Everyone can remember nine steps, can't they? Committing to memory these nine steps is no more difficult than memorizing the digits in your telephone number.

The nine steps I cover here are an overview of what you will find in the chapters in Units 2, 3, and 4 (Chapters 7 through 15). Each step is equally valuable to you. Rarely will you be able to skip a step and still successfully "identify and untie a knot." Each step plays a critical role and, if done properly, will lead you to the next step in a natural, flowing manner.

Step #1: Identifying and Untying Your Knots

By practicing *self-awareness*, you will learn the 50 most common types of knots tying most people today. You will discover how to assess your life's current state by identifying the toxic barriers holding you back and find the solution needed to break away and move forward. You will look at the underlying causes of your toxic knots and discover how to turn tragedy into learning and continuous prosperity by taking a Knots Investigation Assessment.

Step #2: Deciding to Do YOU

You will discover the keys to self-empowerment by using the power of *definite decision*. When you decide that true freedom and life are what you want, and then decide to go where you can produce results, that's when you will become better prepared to handle the toxic habits of life. I will offer you the benefits and rewards of what could happen when you commit to "doing you" 100% of the time, regardless of what the world throws your way.

Step #3: Acknowledging and Pushing Through Your Fears

One of the greatest challenges to identifying and untying the knots that tie up your life is *fear*, whether it's fear of the unknown, fear in a relationship, or fear of your economic status. We will look at the benefits of a *delayed-but-rarely-denied* attitude when acknowledging and pushing through your fears. You will also learn the characteristics of the fear process, the three ways individuals respond to fear, and seven strategies to shatter and push through fear.

Step #4: Setting Unstoppable Goals

Once you've identified the obstacles that have been holding you back, it's time to look ahead and chart where you want to go. You will mark where you currently are, update yourself on where you truly want to be, then set *green-and-growing written goals* so you can chart and execute your revised Personal Life Plan. I will explain the strategy and benefits of creating a goal-monitoring sheet and a Personal Life Plan that can be easily updated and easy-to-follow daily.

Step #5: Quit Marking Time—and Move Forward

Nobody makes it anywhere in this world if they're literally marching in place. If you are doing the same activities day-in and day-out, yet expecting different results, you will never get anywhere. We all need a command and a plan of action to keep us moving persistently towards our destination. In this chapter, I will help you to create a set of *self-empowerment commands* that will aide you in managing both the smoothest of times and the most challenging of times. I will explain how to build willpower so strong that each time you want to move forward, you will move.

Step #6: Defeating Toxic Habits, Choices, People, and Relationships

A life suffocated by toxic habits, choices, people, and relationships can be transformed into a life of happiness, better health, productivity, and constant prosperity. You will discover the power of *detecting and removing* clutter, confusion, and unwanted stress from your life daily. You will also learn how to rid yourself of self-sabotaging habits by identifying the three Ds that cause self-sabotaging results.

Step #7: Making a Commitment to Life

To transform your green-and-growing attitude into action, you must make a commitment to monitor your inner self-talk. We will look at the power of *personal commitment* and how the relationship with your personal commitment will determine your happiness and shape your success. I will offer you strategies for standing firm to whatever the world throws your way by showing you how to monitor and manage your *personal commitment* to your improved life.

Step #8: Rewarding, Assessing, Managing, and Persisting

In this step, you will learn the importance of *rewarding* yourself after each "untie the knots" success you generate, no matter how big or small the accomplishment. You will learn how to prepare yourself for times when toxic habits, choices, people, or relationships threaten to delay or derail your new route to accomplishing your goals and living your dreams. You will learn that even with a green-and-growing attitude, determination and focus, an unshakable plan, and constant steps of action, your life will never become 100% knots free. There will always be obstacles, frustrations, delays, and problems. By developing an "untie the knots" approach to life, you ensure that you are better prepared to reward, assess, manage, and persist in the face of life's great challenges.

Step #9: Leaving a Lasting Legacy: Creating a Life of Significance

You can be successful without having a significant life, but you cannot have a significant life without being successful. Success without significance is hollow. In this chapter, you will learn the importance of *living a significant life* so you can *leave a lasting legacy*. You will learn why your Untie the Knots journey shouldn't only be about you but about a cause, purpose, or the improvement of some aspect of society. You will need to step back, think, identify, commit, and then move forward to creating and leaving your positive mark in the world. That mark should leave a lasting legacy that can advance your family, friends, community, or a cause forward for the betterment of society—a mark of great significance. Yes, this step will be your greatest challenge to accept and fulfill; however, when you decide to move, walk, and live a significant life, everyone wins. Your accomplishment of this step could be your repayment for the time your determined Higher Power has given you here on Earth. That's definitely powerful and worth pursuing. So, expect to find you and your significant life repeatedly back at phase one of the Untie the Knots Cycle.

Chapter Conclusion

Like all successful habits, learning to fit in, develop, and master them takes daily effort and discipline. Remember, to "untie your knots" successfully is an ongoing process. It's not a one-time Band-aid or quick-fix approach. Here is the nine-step process at-a-glance:

Step #1: Identifying and Untying Your Knots

Step #2: Deciding to Do YOU

Step #3: Acknowledging and Pushing Through Your Fears

Step #4: Setting Unstoppable Goals

Step #5: Quit Marking Time—and Move Forward

Step #6: Defeating Toxic Habits, Choices, People, and Relationships

Step #7: Making "A" Commitment to Life

Step #8: Rewarding, Assessing, Managing, and Persisting

Step #9: Leaving a Lasting Legacy: Creating a Life of Significance

DO THIS REPEATEDLY AND YOU WILL REWARD YOUR LIFE WITH BETTER HEALTH, BALANCE, SIGNIFICANCE, HARMONY, POTENTIAL, AND PROSPERITY, GUARANTEED!

Chapter 6

MAKING THE UNTIE THE KNOTS PROCESS YOUR HOBBY

"People rarely succeed unless they have fun at what they are doing."

— *Dale Carnegie*

Dictionary.com defines the word "hobby" as a noun that means, "an activity or interest pursued for pleasure or relaxation and not as a main occupation."

Not long ago, while I was speaking to an audience of 500 managers, directors, and executive professionals about their current jobs, I stopped to ask, "How many of you, when you were children, had a hobby?" About 98% of the audience raised a hand. I then asked them to keep their hands in the air if they still have a hobby today; about 80% of the 98% kept their hands raised.

Then I asked them on the count of three to yell out their current hobby. When I got to number three, it was like a sonic boom hit the conference ballroom. You heard: "crafts, fishing, gardening, pottery, skiing, reading books, boating, running, poetry, hiking, stamp collecting, playing an instrument, singing, magic, rock collecting, martial arts, trains, exercising, knitting, shell collecting, playing sports, walking, mountain climbing, writing, acting, electronics, rockets, coin collecting, crafts, jewelry making, sewing, genealogy, dolls, swimming, board games, model plane collecting, wine tasting, puzzles, drawing, birding, photography, computers, woodworking, motorcycle riding, volunteering, and more."

I spent the first 10 minutes talking to them about their jobs, and you could have literally heard a pin drop in the room. Then, when I switched to talking about their hobbies, whoa, what a difference! In a rare moment, I had triggered something bright and youthful inside each of them as they yelled out their passions and the things they did for relaxation, recreation, fun, and pleasure.

Hobbies benefit people in many ways. Because they are expressions of personal accomplishment and a means of self-discovery, they help build self-esteem. Hobbies are educational tools as well. For example, a person who becomes interested in rocketry -- one of the most popular hobbies, by the way -- learns about propulsion and aerodynamics. By working on hobbies, children and adults learn to set goals, make decisions, and solve problems. Hobbies often mature into lifelong interests and even careers.

Hobbies are connected to our inner emotions, which tell us that what we're doing is interesting, what we're doing is fun, and what we're doing is something we're actually good at. That's why we often find ourselves still enjoying and doing them well into our adult years. We love them so much that we're willing to share and teach them to our children and then our children's children.

If you do not currently have a hobby, still continue to read and get the most out of this chapter, because this chapter is designed to also help those without a current hobby to identify and begin enjoying a new hobby. It may first require you to practice and enjoy the Untie the Knots Process as your hobby. This will free you to have the time, money, and passion for additional hobbies.

So, how does one transfer this same level of passion and emotion into making the Untie the Knots Process a hobby?

It's not going to be easy; however, just like you carefully chose and learned about your current hobby, you have to now choose and learn about a new hobby that is equally fun and rewarding: an exploring hobby that you can do along with your current hobby. It's the hobby of "identifying and untying your toxic knots." This hobby can also bring you relaxation, happiness, and pleasure.

To transfer the very same level of passion and emotion you currently have for your general hobbies to the Untie the Knots Process, learn and apply, repeatedly, the following five strategies:

1) Transfer Your Emotion and Passion for Your Current Hobbies to Your Untie the Knots journey
2) Force Yourself to Get Out of Your Comfort Zone and Face New Challenges
3) Become a Lifelong Student
4) Be Prepared for the Challenges That Hinder Any Learning Process
5) Enjoy Falling in Love With the New YOU!

Let's explore each of the five above strategies individually.

1) Transferring Your Emotion and Passion for Your Current Hobbies to Your Untie the Knots Journey

Here's a quick look at three hobby comparisons and their benefits:

Hobby Comparison #1	Benefit #1	Benefit #2	Benefit #3
Fishing	Relaxation	Nature	Problem Solving
Untying the Knots	Relaxes you even more while fishing because you have fewer worries and fewer obstacles.	Helps you to create the free time to fish and explore nature.	Prepares you to quickly assess and untie your fishing line when it gets tangled.

If fishing is your hobby, when you add the Untie the Knots Process to your list of hobbies, it will help increase your opportuni-

ties to go and enjoy fishing. This will in turn increase your number
of opportunities to relax, enjoy nature, and problem solve more
effectively when challenges come your way while fishing. This is
why fishing is interesting, fun, and pleasing. Remember, a life with
fewer knots becomes a significant life with greater potential.

Hobby Comparison #2	Benefit #1	Benefit #2	Benefit #3
Shopping	Gets you out	Catch the sales	Buy new things
Untying the Knots	Gets you out to shop; however, as a consumer with smarter shopping habits.	Educates you about the importance of living within your budget.	Empowers you to set a more controlled shopping goal to only buy the things you truly need vs. the impulse things you want.

If shopping is your hobby, when you add the Untie the Knots
Process to your list of hobbies, it will help you become a smarter
shopper who only buys things that you need instead of using
the toxic habit of chaotic impulse buying that increases financial debt and problems in your life. When shopping becomes
toxic, it's normally done as an outlet to take your mind off other
toxic challenges you're dealing with (I will discuss how to defeat
the toxic habit of impulsiveness in greater detail in Chapter 12).
Smart hobbyists like antique, coin, stamp, train, or art collectors
shop every day with positive shopping habits that allow them to
enjoy and get the most from their hobbies. So, if you enjoy getting out, catching sales, and buying new things, learn to make it
interesting, fun, and pleasing by using your new hobby of untying the knots to support your hobby of shopping. Remember:

a life with fewer knots becomes a significant life with greater potential.

Hobby Comparison #3	Benefit #1	Benefit #2	Benefit #3
Playing Sports	Exercise	Competitive	Team building
Untying the Knots	Encourages exercise to lead to better health.	Conditions your mental attitude to allow you to be competitive in a controlled and healthy manner.	Increases your awareness to see and take on positive opportunities for you to develop skills that will help you succeed.

If playing sports is your hobby, when you add the Untie the Knots Process to your list of hobbies, it will help you increase the benefits of enjoyment and sportsmanship one can gain from playing a sport. You will increase your number of opportunities to play in a healthy and positive way. Sports hobbyists who play sports to exercise, compete, and build quality team-building skills gain more positive development from their sport when they play without anger, conflict, and selfishness. This positive style of sportsmanship makes playing sports interesting, fun, and pleasing. Remember: a life with fewer knots becomes a significant life with greater potential.

To successfully transfer that same emotion and passion you have for a current hobby to the Untie the Knots Process, it will require you to use the power of your positive mental attitude. Once armed with a positive mental attitude, you can then choose to make the Untie the Knots Process your hobby for continuous positive change, development, and growth.

2) Forcing Yourself to Get Out of Your Comfort Zone and Face New Challenges

Want to be successful?

Get out of your comfort zone and face new challenges! Start a new business. Stretch your life. Take a few new risks that you haven't taken before. Make untying your knots your new hobby.

When I started my professional speaking business 11 years ago, it was definitely a new challenge and leap out of my comfort zone. I had fears, uncertainties, and toxic knots in my life that I had to deal with. My fears and uncertainties stemmed from my worrying constantly, "Do I have what it takes? Who is going to listen to me? What if I fail?"

The primary toxic knot that I had in my life at that time was overwhelming financial debt. When I decided to start my professional speaking business, I was drowning in credit card debt. I had so many bill collectors calling my house that my family and I cringed at the thought of having to answer the telephone when it rang.

My internal sense of drive commanded me to STRETCH myself outside my comfort zone even more. It forced me to sit down and think about the main message and principles I was sharing with my audiences. I couldn't speak right and walk left. So, I sat and I thought. I thought and I wrote. I spoke to my mentors and advisors.

Then it hit me like a ton of bricks!

The very message "Untie The Knots That Tie Up Your Life" I was speaking about to each and every audience had to become part of my DNA. I had to own it, embody it, and live it daily. Not in a reserved and reluctant way, but rather in a fun, enthusiastic, and pleasing way.

To step out of my comfort zone and experience significant success, I had to make the Untie the Knot Process my hobby. For six years, I worked consistently to learn and master this process. I worked to harness it. I worked to challenge it. I worked to strengthen its vulnerable areas promptly. I spent countless hours journaling to discover and define me. And today, I'm proud to say that it is one of my hobbies, along with writing, exercise, theater, amusement parks, and collecting unique cufflinks. This process as a hobby, like all my other hobbies, is fun, relaxing, and pleasing.

It became a hobby for me when I made the decision to step out of my comfort zone to face a few toxic life challenges.

When was the last time you've stepped out of your comfort zone to face a new challenge?

Most of us have in our homes thermostats that regulate room temperature. When it gets too warm, the air conditioning kicks on to bring the temperature down to an acceptable range. When the temperature drops below a comfortable point, the heater comes on to bring the room temperature up. The "comfort zone" is the range of temperature that's not too hot and not too cold—just comfortable.

Our personal comfort zone is where we are comfortable with what we are doing in our personal and professional lives. It's when we experience no feelings of risk or anxiety. Some call it being comfortable. Some call it a rut. Some call it a no-fail zone.

Each of us has our own personal comfort zone. We possess built-in thermostats that regulate our levels of anxiety, fear, and discomfort. In the areas of our knowledge, skills, habits, and attitude, when we step outside our existing comfortable boundaries, we begin to feel nervous. Our natural tendency is to pull back.

Try this: Remove your right shoe and leave your left shoe on. Now walk around your home or business office for the next two minutes with just the one shoe on. How did that make you feel? Were you at first reluctant to try it? Were you nervous or worried about who may see you? Felt a bit unnatural, didn't it? When we try something new, we often feel uneasy and frequently pull back. That's why we usually stay within our comfort zone. The security feels good.

The downside is that always staying in our comfort zones can be limiting. The world passes us by as we refuse to stretch and grow. Complacency, in our fast-paced competitive world, can be fatal to our personal and professional growth. If you are not learning, trying new activities, and growing, your personal and professional life will begin to deteriorate. Toxic knots will begin to smother and delay you from accomplishing your goals and living your dreams.

Here are four simple methods to help you step out of your comfort zone:

a. Make a conscious effort to experiment.

- o   Drive home a different route.
- o   Shop at a different grocery store.
- o   Order something from the menu that you've never tried before.
- o   Volunteer to give a presentation at work or in your community.

b. Focus on what you want to positively have happen.

Too many times people fail to step confidently out of their comfort zones because they create dragons in their minds that horrify them into believing the outcome of their efforts will be disastrous. When you focus on the negative, your outcome is negative. When you focus on the positive, more often than not, your outcome is positive.

c. Ask yourself and write the answers to these questions: "What's the worst that could happen if I fail?" and "What two ways can I celebrate when I succeed?"

Whenever you find yourself in a position where you feel stuck or paralyzed in your comfort zone because of fear or self-doubt, ask yourself and write down the answer to the two above questions.

After you have your two detailed answers written, move forward boldly until you succeed. Look forward to your celebration.

d. Set a goal to take three new risks and accomplish them by December 31st of that year.

Many of us have heard this advice at one time or another: "The best way to eat an elephant is one bite at a time." The same applies to gradually pushing and moving yourself out of your comfort zone. If you consistently set three new risk-taking goals each year that you commit to accomplishing by year-end, you will feel great about yourself and your accomplishments as the years pass. You will definitely find a way out of your comfort zone in three, five, or ten years!

The important thing to remember here is that if you're going to accomplish anything of any significance, you absolutely have to take a chance. That means that you must get out of your comfort zone. You can start first by learning, practicing, and making the Untie the Knots Process your new hobby.

3) Becoming a Lifelong Student

"Develop a passion for learning. If you do, you will never cease to grow."

— Anthony J. D'Angelo

As a full-time professional motivational speaker, I also consider myself a full-time teacher, coach, and student. The term I prefer to use is *"lifelong student."* If the role of student wasn't placed on me by life's work, I think I would be still be a lifelong learner. I love to learn. The universe is such a large and diverse place and even our small corner of it is so complex and varied that you can find a new challenge in any direction you look. I love learning big lessons, small lessons, and even pocket-size lessons.

I love to read. Eight years ago I set and accomplished the personal goal of reading two books each month. I'm an enthusiastic watcher of the History, Biography, Health, Discovery, Art, Investigative Science, and other learning channels on satellite television. I'm like a sponge when it comes to the investigation and discovery involved in the process of learning. Sometimes, simply the process of learning interests me without worrying about the end result.

Three good reasons for becoming a lifelong learner include expanding your brain's ability, giving your life a sense of purpose, and empowering your financial security. Any one of these reasons should be enough, but all three combine to form a powerful motivation to learn.

Oliver Wendell Holmes put learning into perspective when he explained the brain's ability by stating, *"Once the mind expands to accept a new idea, it will never revert back to its original shape."* When you make it your commitment to continuously move through life as a lifelong student learning and absorbing one idea, lesson, principle, strategy, tip, or insight after another, you literally cause your brain's ability to expand and grow.

Albert Einstein proclaimed, *"The significant problems we face cannot be solved at the same level of thinking we were at when we created them."* To stand up to and defeat our challenges, problems, and toxic knots, we must first increase our awareness and knowledge of what has to happen.

Finally, there is the financial incentive for learning. Suze Orman, American personal finance author and television personality, stated this in an article to readers of *O Magazine* in February 2003: *"It's better to do nothing with your money than something you don't understand."* People who know more not only earn more money but also know how to use it as a tool to build their financial resources. No matter what your income or age, it is never too late to begin learning how to better manage your money.

Here are five sure ways to put you onboard with the many other lifelong students of the world:

1) Enroll in a course or earn a degree or certification from a college, university, or trade school.
2) Read books, magazines, and newspapers.
3) Watch the learning channels on television.
4) Listen to learning or motivational tapes and CDs or view videotapes and DVDs.
5) Attend seminars and workshops that provide you with learning and take-home value.

It is important to retain the aspirations of being a lifelong student. Learning continually throughout your life is vital if you plan to successfully and productively make informed choices about where you are headed. Lifelong learning is especially important if you plan to use and make the Untie the Knots Process your hobby.

4) Being Prepared for the Challenges That Hinder Any Learning Process

As with anything in life, being a lifelong student committed to the learning process comes with its challenges. The top three challenges that affect, discourage, and derail most people from being and remaining lifelong students are -

1) Poor Time Management Skills

Example: You're a person who wants to be a lifelong student; however, every time you plan to take a course at the college or finish reading a book about a topic you have a strong interest in, you cannot find the course or book due to poor time management skills.

<u>Suggested Solution</u>: Before you enroll in a course at the college or university, check your current personal schedule and the confirmed commitments you've already made during the semester to make sure you have the required time to commit to the successful completion of the course. Once you enroll in the course, commit to it 101%. Do not allow any time management conflicts, outside of a true emergency, to interfere with your plan of attending class on time and successfully completing the course to the end.

Before you purchase the book you feel is a must read, check your current schedule and the confirmed commitments you have made to make sure you do have time to successfully complete the reading of this book. Consider your reading speed, and schedule a window of time each day or every other day to read the portion of the book you commit to reading during your scheduled reading time. Once you schedule your reading times, put them in writing in your personal organizer, and commit to your reading time 101%. Do not allow any time management conflicts, outside of a true emergency, to interfere with your goal to successfully read this book based on your reading speed and scheduled times for reading.

2) Harmful Distractions

Example: You're a person who wants to be a lifelong student of health and fitness; however, every time you join the gym to keep up with your health and fitness you lose your commitment to constantly exercise. So, after only a few weeks of dedication, you stop going altogether because of harmful distractions. Harmful distractions may include choosing to go to happy hour after work with your co-workers, choosing to make it home in time to watch a reality television show, or choosing to do anything else imaginable so you have an excuse to not visit the gym for your scheduled exercise session.

<u>Suggested Solution</u>: Before you join a gym, check your current and projected schedule (at least three to six months into the future), and then make sure you have the required time to commit to successfully making it to the gym at least two or three times a week. Write in your personal organizer the day and period of time you will make it to the gym. Once you schedule your days and times at the gym for exercise, commit to them 101%. Do not allow any distractions, outside of a true emergency, to interfere with your goal of making it to the gym for your exercise session on your scheduled days and time.

3) Mediocre Participation and Application

Example: You're a person who wants to be a lifelong student of arts and crafts; however, every time you enroll in an arts and crafts course you find yourself halfway involved and turning in half-completed projects. You come to class five to ten minutes late, and you are often not prepared. You try to convince yourself that you're very interested and committed to learning what this class has to offer, but deep down inside, this constantly eats at you because you know that you can be a much better student. Still, you choose to settle on being a mediocre student who participates and turns-in average work.

<u>Suggested Solution</u>: Before you enroll in an arts and crafts course, check your current and projected schedule, and then make sure you have the required time to commit to successfully participating and turning in your best work. Write in your personal organizer the days and times this class meets. Once you put in your days and times to be at the arts and crafts class, commit to them 101%. Make it your goal to purchase all the necessary supplies to come prepared for each and every class. Also, make it your goal to participate and turn in your best work. Do not allow yourself to become a mediocre student. You will feel much better when you know that you are committed to, engaged in, and taking full advantage of everything your arts and crafts class offers.

Use the words of Terry Bradshaw, Super Bowl champion quarterback of the Pittsburgh Steelers and NFL Hall of Fame Inductee, to inspire you to become and stay a lifelong student:

"When you've got something to prove, there's nothing greater than a challenge."

When you commit to becoming a lifelong student, you're not only proving to yourself but to the world that you're courageous enough to continuously absorb and learn from whatever the world provides you.

You accept the challenge to keep you and your mind updated and on the cutting edge of life.

5) Enjoying Falling in Love with the New YOU!

"You cannot belong to anyone else, until you belong to yourself."

— Pearl Bailey

We enjoy our hobbies because we feel our hobbies are interesting, worthy, fun, and pleasing. To some degree, our hobbies complete us. They complete our character, complete our personality, and complete our desire to continuously learn something. More importantly, our hobbies complete our emotional craving and passion to connect with, enjoy, and fall in love with ourselves.

My mother always told me when I was going through the most challenging parts of my life and was filled with anger and frustration, "Ty, if you can't enjoy and love the one you're with all day, how are you going to learn to enjoy and love anyone or anything else?" In short, Mommy was passionately encouraging me to learn to enjoy and fall in love with me so I could move courageously through my day without being toxic or hazardous to myself. She taught me to do this with respect and a calm spirit.

Your current hobbies, including your new hobby of "Untying the Knots," offer you the same opportunity to learn, enjoy, and fall in love with YOU.

The new you, with the Untie the Knots Process as one of your hobbies, will find yourself enjoying the opportunity to identify and untie one toxic knot after another.

Chapter Conclusion

In this chapter, I explained the way people usually approach their hobbies and helped you find a way to approach the Untie the Knots Process in the same way. I explained how you might transfer the same emotions and passions for your current hobbies to your Untie the Knots journey. I shared with you the power of choice and the benefits of getting out of your comfort zone so you might get the most out of life and hobbies. I supplied you with simple strategies to assist you along the way when moving out of your comfort zone. I explained the value and benefits of becoming a lifelong student and how to combat methods of dealing with the many threatening challenges you may encounter while committed to the learning process. And I gave you a few ideas about how to enjoy and fall in love with you for ultimate *FUN*. As I've mentioned in previous chapters, attitude and passion are a huge part of success — in the Untie the Knots Process and in life — and in this chapter I let you know about both so you can put them to work for you.

Unit Summary

THE TIME IS NOW

There is no better time than the present to boldly stand up within yourself to begin identifying and untying the knots in your life. We change because it's required to grow. We grow because we struggle to learn. And we learn because it enables us to overcome.

Chapters 4, 5, and 6 were written to 1) encourage and launch your boldness from within; 2) introduce you officially to the Untie the Knots Process; and 3) have you look at, learn, and practice the Untie the Knots Process, not as a grueling job or punishing series of tasks, but as a fun, exciting, and rewarding journey to a better, healthier, and significant you.

Let's recap the three chapters that make up Unit 2, Part 1: THE TIME IS NOW:

Chapter 4: Boldly Standing Up Within to Change and Grow

Chapter 5: The Nine-Step Untie the Knots Process

Chapter 6: Making the Untie the Knots Process Your Hobby

We've encountered the following **Infusers** *(Freedom Break Away Tools)* that were explained in the introduction of this book:

Infuser #1: Reinstate a Positive Attitude
If you are serious about breaking free and away from the knots that tie up your life, you will be required to put into place a positive mental attitude. You will have to be committed to developing and working constantly with a positive attitude, regardless of your past experiences or current situations or circumstances.

Infuser #2: Refocus
How are you going to change the direction of your life if you're not aware of what direction you're currently going in?

Infuser #3: Choose
Decide true freedom and life is what you want and then go where you can produce those results.

Infuser #4: Identify
To successfully break away from anything that has delayed or derailed you in the past, you must summon the bold confidence to now identify it as a toxic habit, choice, person, or relationship.

Infuser #5: Simplify
Remove clutter, confusion, unwanted stress, and sabotaging distractions from your life daily, and watch new desirable opportunities appear.

Infuser #6: Believe
It takes your strong will and unshakable faith to make the impossible possible.

Infuser #7: Move
Don't just stand there filled with knowledge...do it! Quit procrastinating and making excuses. My ultimate goal is to inspire, teach, and empower you to create an updated personal life plan, boldly face your fears, and move forward daily in executing your new personal life plan.

Infuser #9: Persist
How strong do you want what you now see? No more excuses... no more procrastination...no more string of bad and unproductive days! Stay the course!

Infuser #10: Leave a Mark of Significance
It's one experience in living to simply have come and gone. It's another experience to have purposely decided to create and live a life of significance. A life that will enable you to leave behind a lasting legacy that will contribute to your family's heritage and that will also allow many others who come after you to learn and grow from your efforts.

This unit (Chapters 4 through 6) was quite energizing. Wasn't it? Make sure you read it more than once because the material in this unit is meant to uplift your mind, body, and spirit to continue if and when the thought of exhaustion or quitting enters your mind during your Untie the Knots journey.

Remember: As long as you keep identifying and working through your knots of delay, the answers and solutions will come.

Freedom, happiness, balance, harmony, significance, and prosperity await your arrival.

So, stay connected to the empowering thought that one day soon "My family, my friends, and my co-workers will bare witness to a big and positive change in my character—a significant change in my life!"

Time OUT!

Just to recap some of the major concepts you've read about thus far, find and write in your journal the answers to the following questions:

• What does it mean to be "green and growing"?

Refer to the "Choose to be Green and Growing" section in Chapter 4 for the answer.

• Why does Ty encourage you to say aloud, "NO MORE!"?

Refer to the "Literally say aloud, 'NO MORE!'" section in Chapter 4 for the answer.

• What are the first five steps of the Nine-Step Untie the Knots Process?

Refer to the first three pages of Chapter 5 for the answer.

• What can a life suffocated by toxic habits, choices, people, and relationships be transformed into?

Refer to the "Step # 6" section in Chapter 5 for the answer.

• What are two strategies you can use to force yourself out of your comfort zone?

Refer to the "Force Yourself to Get Out of Your Comfort Zone and Face New Challenges" section in Chapter 6 for the answer.

• What are the four reasons why we enjoy our hobbies?

Refer to the "Enjoy Falling in Love With the New YOU!" section in Chapter 6 for the answer.

"Science is organized knowledge. Wisdom is organized life."

— Emmanuel Kant

PART 2

YOU'RE MORE THAN WORTHY

My Personal Contract
The Beginning of Self-Mastery Starts Right Where You Are

Step 1—Identifying and Untying Your Knots
Your Mind Is Your Biggest Asset

Step 2—Deciding to Do YOU
Your Destiny is a Matter of Choice—You Become What You Do

Step 3—Acknowledging and Pushing Through Your Fears
Your Heart Functions Best When It's Bold and Resilient

In Part 2...

You will discover that self-worth comes from two realities—1) when you think that you are worthy, and 2) when you take the necessary steps to reach new levels of positive Personal Mastery. In this part, you will find information about how to identify and untie your knots and learn about the 50 most common toxic knots tying people up today. You will also gather some great tips for acknowledging, shattering, and boldly moving through your fears to a life that is more manageable and prepared for significant success.

My Personal Contract... Before I Journey Ahead

Today's date: _____

Print your name: _____

At this point, I am 100% decided and committed to learning, practicing, and making the Untie the Knots Process a way of life for the following three reasons:

1) _____

_____

2) _____

_____

3) _____

_____

I commit myself to making the three following necessary changes in my current daily behavior, right now, to help ensure my success in **Identifying and Untying The Knots That Tie Up My Life**:

Behavior change #1: _____

_____

Behavior change #2:_____

_____

Behavior change #3: _____

_____

By signing my signature below, I accept and agree to—

❖ Enthusiastically reading, learning, practicing, and mastering the steps and principles of the Untie the Knots Process;

❖ Eagerly completing all the tasks, exercises, and assignments given to me throughout my experience and journey through the Untie the Knots Process;

❖ Consistently mark all important insights, dates, principles, and learning outcomes in both my personal organizer and daily journal as I move through the Untie the Knots Process; and

❖ Diligently maintaining a relentlessly positive attitude and insatiably open mind to put me in the position of a lifelong student throughout my journey through the Untie the Knots Process and beyond.

My Personal Commitment to Untying the Knots Success,

_____

(Write your signature on the line above)

By committing yourself to a tougher and more persistent standard of developing, managing, and performing, you will remove toxic habits, choices, people, and relationships. Mastery is the next goal, and mastery is built on excellence—the gradual result of always wanting to make your best better. Aristotle stated many years ago, "You are what you repeatedly do. Excellence is not an event—it is a habit." Mastery demands an honest awareness of the present moment, followed by repeated steps of excellence to bring forth an individual's best effort and potential. I not only want you to learn and practice the nine steps of the Untie the Knots Process, but I want you to master them. In obtaining mastery, you apply the Process, which will become a new natural habit. Mastery of the concepts and process will become your un-shakable foundation to identify and break away from one toxic knot after another. Mastery is as emotional as it is mental. You can't attain mastery and neglect morale, and morale isn't simply desire. It is sparked by your trained and focused self-discipline to constantly reach for new levels of excellence daily.

Read on and you will see and experience what I mean!

Chapter 7

Step 1: IDENTIFYING AND UNTYING YOUR KNOTS

"Self discipline is when your conscience tells you to do something and you don't talk back."

— Tiger Woods

Getting Real with Yourself for Empowered Results

As I humbly stated in my personal anecdote at the beginning of Chapter 4, "Even though I graduated from high school on time with a high school diploma, I made the decision to boldly stand up within to change and grow. This was mainly due to the fact that I had to step up my responsibility as the teenage father of a new born daughter." This major event in my life caused me to get real with myself.

My fears of whether or not I would be an absentee father like my father was to me and my siblings often paralyzed me to a point of wanting to give up on life. Conversely, when I would hold my daughter, my baby, in my arms, the essence, smell, and look in her eyes would propel new determination within me to move forward in doing whatever I could to never disappoint or let her down. This relentless determination would bring empowering thoughts of inspiration to me. Whenever thoughts of quitting or giving up on life emerged, my inspiration forced those negative thoughts away.

I turned to the more positive aspects in my life at that time. I looked to my hard working and nurturing mother, who believed in her children so much that she would often work two or three jobs to provide us with the best life she could offer. My mother believed in getting the best education possible, so she would make us read the dictionary when we came home. She would discipline us when we were being disrespectful or disobedient. She would also discipline us when another adult in the neighborhood brought us to her for doing something wrong. She was a mother who inspired and taught me at a very early age that education, hard work, determination, and a clear sense of direction were the best way out of the ghetto.

Late one evening, at the age of 18 and in my senior year in high school, I found myself sitting up in the middle of my bed thinking about what changes had to happen to create better opportunities for my daughter and me. In that defining period of solitude, the following ideas surfaced:

1) I identified the negative toxic knots that were delaying me from truly getting what I wanted from life. My toxic knots at the age of 18 were a negative attitude, poor choices, excuse making, self-pity, denial, anger, fear, conflict, being unforgiving, confusion, self-sabotage, refusing help, complaining, pride, bitterness, imitating others, a lack of direction, and not wanting to let go of the past. As you can see, I was tied up in more knots than just a few. THIS HAD TO CHANGE!

2) I made the decision that if I was going to make a definite change for the better, I had to escape the toxic community I was currently living in, Cherry Hill. It had been said many times around Baltimore "that the only things known to come out of Cherry Hill are drug dealers, robbers, rapists, drug addicts, losers, prostitutes, high school dropouts, gang members, and future prison inmates." The stigma lurking over Cherry Hill was thick, and I decided I was not going to be represented by the toxic outcomes that plagued this community.

3) On that night, I pulled out of my book bag a few brochures that were handed to me by a military recruiter while walking through the halls in high school that day. I reviewed them and decided that joining the U.S. Navy

would get me out of Cherry Hill and teach me the discipline I needed at that time. The Navy would give my life a better sense of focus and direction to improve the quality of life for me and my daughter.

There were plenty of other positive options for me in the world at that time; however, the three aforementioned decisions were mine. My decisions were equally positive and productive for the improvement and empowerment of my soon-to-be changed life.

"Getting Real" with yourself promotes the skills of self-awareness and self-respect. It focuses on combining thoughts, feelings, and behavior in a way that can lead you to powerful and meaningful life changes. When it comes to learning and practicing the Untie the Knots Process, the "communicator" is you.

When a person chooses to "Get Real," there are normally two types of responses that emerge:

1) Defensive responses
2) Intimate responses

The defensive responses in "Getting Real" are self-denial, attacking, getting intellectual, getting righteous, avoiding, and joking.

Defensive responses often feel good immediately during and after using them. However, they often provide a false sense of well being.

For example, defensive responses sometimes

1. Increase feelings of control but ultimately result in the loss of influence;
2. Increase a sense of short-term power but result in a loss of long-term power;
3. Increase a short-term sense of safety but result in a long-term loss of relationship and security; and
4. Increase a short-term sense of pride but result in a long-term loss of self-esteem.

Defensive responses decrease trust, respect, and our positive influence with others. When we are defensive, we lose the opportunity to learn about ourselves from others, which results in low self-awareness, low self-improvement, and low potential for growth.

The intimate responses of "Getting Real" are the open, honest, and respectful sharing of thoughts and feelings.

Intimate responses often feel very discouraging, painful, and regretful after using them. However, they often provide a true sense of self-cleansing and well-being.

For example, intimate responses bring forth
1. Increased feelings of control that ultimately result in the continuous growth of influence;
2. Increased self-empowerment that eventually results in long-term power;
3. Increased safety that results in long-term healthy relationships and security; and
4. Increased self-confidence that after some time results in long-term high self-esteem.

Intimate responses increase trust, hope, respect, and our positive influence with others. When we are accepting, aware, and forgiving of our toxic habits, we increase our opportunities to learn about ourselves and from others, resulting in elevated levels of self-awareness, self-improvement, and continuous growth with significant potential.

When I followed the passions and determination of my intimate responses, powerful things began to happen in my life. I developed a better sense of direction, trust, respect, and positive influence with others. Doors and opportunities started to open that were previously being closed. I was not clinging to a failing life that was connected to the toxic life support machine of my previous defensive responses. I became committed to living my life to its greatest potential, and this positive behavior put me on the path to creating a life of significance and prosperity.

Which response, "defensive" or "intimate," are you clinging to right now in your life?

As you continue reading this chapter and the rest of the book, I want you to "Get Real" and "Keep It Real." Be open, honest, and respectful of your thoughts and ideas. During the next several minutes, hours, days, weeks, and months, focus on using intimate responses, and you will begin experiencing better health, influence, happiness, and growth. Go back to your Personal Untie the Knots contract that you signed at the beginning of this unit and read it before you begin reading every chapter from this point forward.

As you journey forward, you may discover or acknowledge current toxic knots in your life that are very discouraging and painful; however, focus on what your intimate responses bring you: elevated levels of self-awareness, self-improvement, continuous growth, and more importantly, increased self-worth. The changed and revised version of you is definitely worth the time you spend while successfully learning and practicing the Untie the Knots Process.

Remember: A life with fewer knots becomes a significant life with greater potential.

So, "Get Real" and "Keep It Real"— you will begin to experience an empowered life with positive results.

The Personal Toxic Knots Investigation Assessment (PTKI Assessment)

The PTKI Assessment is not a pass or fail assessment tool. The PTKI Assessment will help you assess where your life currently is regarding toxic knots. Be honest, have fun, and look to grow even more as a result of this self-assessment.

Select Yes or No with a "check mark" for each question.

1. I go to sleep and wake up most mornings looking forward to each new day.

_____ Yes   _____ No

2. I have at least a year's living expenses in the bank or in a money market fund to handle an unexpected change or emergency in my life.

_____ Yes   _____ No

3. I don't spend time around anyone who stresses, discourages, or uses me.

_____ Yes   _____ No

4. I am both pleased and content with my spouse or partner or I am happy being single.

_____ Yes   _____ No

5. I take at least three vacations a year.

_____ Yes   _____ No

6. I could die this evening with no regrets.

_____ Yes   _____ No

7. Life is easy; conflict, clutter, and confusion rarely enter my daily routine.

_____ Yes   _____ No

8. I am spending my leisure time enjoying my hobbies; I am rarely bored.

_____ Yes   _____ No

9. I am on a financial independence track or already there.

_____ Yes   _____ No

10. I have a circle of friends who encourage and empower me without effort.

_____ Yes   _____ No

11. My career is both fulfilling and rewarding to me: I rarely leave work drained or upset.

_____ Yes   _____ No

12. I love my home and its location, style, furnishings, lighting, feeling, décor, and energy.

_____ Yes   _____ No

13. I tolerate very, very little; I rarely get caught up in foolishness, drama, or nonsense.

_____ Yes   _____ No

14. I am living my life on my terms and not on the terms given or forced on me by other people.

_____ Yes   _____ No

15. I always pay my bills on time; my line of credit looks great today and will improve more in the future.

_____ Yes   _____ No

16. I don't have to work on keeping a positive attitude; being kind and positive is my way of life.

_____ Yes   _____ No

17. My wants have been satisfied; there is little I want.

_____ Yes   _____ No

18. My personal needs have been satisfied; I am not driven or motivated to purchase objects just because everyone else is buying them.

_____ Yes   _____ No

19. On weekends (or other days off), I am able to spend most of the day relaxing or having fun.

_____ Yes   _____ No

20. I have more than enough energy and enthusiasm to get me through the day: I rarely feel drained or burnt out halfway through the day.

_____ Yes   _____ No

21. I am mindful of my language and behavior around children: I have never experienced a moment where I discovered a child learned a toxic habit from me.

_____ Yes   _____ No

22. I am a lifelong student; I read books, enroll in courses, and make it a purpose to learn at least one new lesson each day.

_____ Yes   _____ No

23. There are few problems I am not facing head-on; there are no fears currently blocking my future.

_____ Yes   _____ No

24. I have designed, and am living, the perfect lifestyle for me right now.

_____ Yes   _____ No

25. I schedule and am examined by both my family doctor and dentist twice a year.

_____ Yes   _____ No

26. When I carry bags of groceries or boxes from a car into my house, I never find myself out of breath or in pain while doing so.

_____ Yes   _____ No

27. Who I was and what I experienced in my past does not stop me; I am 100% pleased and satisfied with who I am today.

_____ Yes   _____ No

28. My self-talk is positive and healthy; I choose to use words that edify and uplift my self-esteem.

_____ Yes   _____ No

29. I have connected my life to a cause or purpose to improve the world on some level; I chose to do this to advance my family, my friends, my community, or myself forward.

_____ Yes   _____ No

30. I am too blessed to be stressed; procrastination and excuse making doesn't exist in my life.

_____ Yes   _____ No

Now, add up your "YESs" to see your results.

Your "Yes" **Total:** _____

This assessment evaluated the following seven areas of your life:

1. Social relations / support systems
2. Money / economics
3. Activities of daily living
4. Occupational satisfaction
5. Psychological well-being
6. Physical health
7. Life satisfaction

Check your results by reading the rating scale below for your total "YES" score. Identify the area you need to improve, and refer to the relevant sections in this book to develop and improve your skills.

Results Rating:

26 - 30 YESs   GREAT! You are definitely a *Green and Growing Person*! Congratulations for such a high score and for living such a great life. If you have been honest with your responses on the assessment, you are already leaving a lasting legacy and living a significant life. Even if you scored a perfect 30, know that your life can always get better. Remember: We are never 100% knots free.

21 - 25 YESs   You are doing well. A score of 21 - 25 is very good. A life of significance is well within reach. Stay the course! Don't get distracted! Continue learning and practicing the Untie the Knots Process.

16 - 20 YESs   You are doing okay. You're about half way there. You see and experience more "A" days than most people. Make the Untie the Knots Process your hobby and you can reduce the number of knots in your life to move you confidently to the next two higher levels of "untie the knots" success.

11 - 15 YESs   Yes, there is work to do. Consider reading Chapters 1 through 9 a second time before moving onto Chapters 10 thru 18 to help you move your life (and your score) forward. Continue to invest in you by investing the necessary time to learn and master the Untie the Knots Process. Make it your way of life, and you will marvel over the new levels of success, potential, and achievement that will come your way. Remember: Your habits become your future!

0 - 10 YESs   You are not alone. It takes time and desire to raise the quality of your life. Use this assessment as a blueprint and your motivation to transform your checked "NOs" into checked "YESs" by continuing to learn and practice the Untie the Knots Process. Practice the principles and strategies shared within the Process often, and the payoff will be obvious. I'm looking forward to the day you retake this assessment and your score is in the 20 to 30 range.

Are you living the life you want? Is there something more ur-gent you now want to change, add, or improve in your life as a result of completing this assessment? You can get started right here, right now, today.

Start by pondering the words of Ralph Waldo Emerson, who said, "Life is a succession of lessons which must be lived to be understood." Then start learning and living wholeheartedly the principles and lessons of the Untie the Knots Process.

The 50 Most Common Toxic Knots Tying People Up Today

Read the 50 toxic knots listed in the table below. Then answer this powerful question:

Do you know someone who is tied up in any of them?

Procrastination	Excuse making	Self-pity	Anger	Pride
Financial problems	Addiction	Matching or trying to be like others	Fear	Pessimism
Conflict	Confusion	Stress	Clutter	Low self-esteem
Self-doubt	Lack of direction	Materialism	Distractions	Laziness
Misery	Unforgiving	Never finishing	Negative attitude	Toxic relationships
Poor health	People pleasing	Refusing help	Unfulfilling job	Passing judgment
Greed	Listening to negative people	Mediocrity	Worry	Toxic choices
Perfectionism	Denial	Regret	Stuck in the past	Negative self-talk
Complacency	Self-sabotage	Lying	Complaining	Staying in the presence of toxic people
Breaking promises	Cheating	Poor time management	Teaching negativity to others	Toxic self-respect

*** *To gain immediate access to a practical, comprehensive, step-by-step guide that will help you break free of the 50 Most Common Toxic Knots, visit the fol-lowing link on the Internet, right now:*
http://www.tyhoward.com/KnotsFree_SpecialGuide.html
(Or turn to Appendix C for more information about the Knots Free Special Guide.)

Albert Einstein said it best: "Only those who attempt the absurd will achieve the impossible." When one takes a look at the 50 toxic knots listed above, it can become very discouraging to understand and grasp how someone may have allowed his or her life to get tied up in such a big mess. The feeling can quickly become overwhelming, burdensome, and even absurd for a person to think it's possible to break free from more than a few toxic knots. It's POSSIBLE! And YOU can do it!

If you want to change, if you want to grow, and if you seriously want to *Untie the Knots That Tie Up Your Life*, you must confront "absurdity" head-on! Why? Because it was ridiculous toxic habits, illogical toxic choices, silly toxic people, and strange toxic relationships that put you in the position your life is currently in. Acknowledge the toxic knots, learn from your toxic knots, accept your toxic knots, forgive yourself for these toxic knots, and move forward to "untie your toxic knots."

Remember one thing though, before you read ahead: your toxic knots didn't develop overnight, so you will not be able to untie them completely in one day. It will require patience, learning, practice, and continuous work. They're your toxic knots and now your responsibility to untie.

Accepting, Learning, and Forgiving Yourself So You Can Move Forward

Life is full of choices, and every choice we make will either take us in a positive life-fulfilling direction or rob us of the opportunity to create a significant life of purpose.

The energy it takes to harbor anger, hatred, self-pity, and resentment towards yourself is draining. Every bit of energy we give to negative thoughts and activities makes another deposit into our bank account of personal regret.

The reality is that you cannot change what has happened to you in your life. You cannot press rewind to go back to a point in your life before a particular situation happened. However, you can begin a new journey right were you now stand. It will start with you 1) accepting what has happened, 2) learning from what has happened, and 3) forgiving yourself for what has happened.

Accepting, learning, and forgiving yourself do not let you off the hook. Accepting, learning, and forgiving yourself do not justify what you have done, and these qualities are not a sign of weakness. Accepting, learning, and forgiving yourself are positive choices that take courage and strength, and they give you the opportunity to persevere rather than remain a victim of your current toxic knots.

First things first; repeat after me, *"I Control Myself. I Accept and Forgive Myself for Any and All Toxic Knots That I Now Have in My Life!"* You need to hear yourself forgive yourself! There is great power in the spoken word. This time, let's say it aloud and with lion-like boldness, *"I Control Life! And I Forgive Myself!"* Thank you for giving voice to your current "untie the knots" situation.

Too many times we hang out in victim mode, taking whatever the world dishes our way because we feel helpless and hopeless. The toughest part with what I'm saying is stepping up and stepping out to admit that this is you, right where you currently stand, and right where you currently are. Toxic knots come into our lives as a result of toxic habits, choices, people, and relationships—not by mistakes.

There are no mistakes in life; only lessons. What this means is that whenever something happens, there is always a lesson to learn. If you can learn to accept your mistakes, shortcomings, and unwanted events as opportunities for learning and personal growth, then you will feel less stressed and fearful. You will be more confident and self-assured, and your experiences will be more rewarding and fun.

From this point forward, when you identify and discover that a toxic knot has come into your life, apply the proven four methods to manage it so that you acknowledge the toxic knot, accept the toxic knot, learn the lesson, forgive yourself, work through and remove the knot, move on from it, and grow stronger in the process. These methods are outlined below:

1) Be open to the fact that no one will ever be 100% knots free.

There will always be frustrations, disappointments, obstacles, and negative people in this world. Accept that you're human and that each of us will do things we regret. Each of us will take a wrong turn, hurt someone's feelings, or make a bad choice. When you open to learning from your toxic experiences, you will be able to accept, forgive, and move on rather than wallow in regret and disappointment.

2) Be aware.

Look for areas of improvement. Be on the look out for "toxic knots" and ways to strengthen your character and self-esteem. Be aware of what you are doing, why you are doing it, how you feel, and how it makes others feel. This way of thinking is about being proactive and seeking to avoid unnecessary future blunders.

3) Accept full responsibility for yourself and your life.

Accepting responsibility is liberating. Yes, it's hard to admit you were wrong. However, it demonstrates strength, courage, and commitment to personal change and excellence. It's respectful. By doing so, you demonstrate that you care about yourself and the other people you encounter each and every day.

4) Make it a habit to look for solutions and possibilities, rather than faults.

Some people refuse to accept the fact they did anything wrong. It was someone else or it was the system. This is known as a victim mentality. When you discover you've done something to attract or bring a toxic knot into your life, make it your new productive habit to find positive solutions and possibilities. The positive solution and possibility you find and use to combat your current toxic situation can be the needed strategy that cuts you free from what you are holding against yourself.

Accepting, learning, and forgiving yourself can and will change the direction of your life. It will take time to practice and fully understand the rewards and benefits of this process; however, you are worth it!

The best time to start taking those steps is right here and right now!

Chapter Conclusion

In this chapter, you were given the tools and strategies to help you assess, identify, and begin to work through and untie your toxic knots. I explained to you the importance of "Getting Real" and "Keeping It Real" for honest and productive results while learning and practicing the Untie the Knots Process. I shared with you the 50 most common toxic knots tying up most people today. And I gave you four strong methods explaining how to learn to accept, learn from, and forgive yourself for the toxic knots in your life, so you can move on to living a life of improved health, significance, potential, finances, harmony, and prosperity. Remember: life's challenges can often be its gifts.

To gain immediate access to a practical, comprehensive, step-by-step guide that will help you break free of the 50 Most Common Toxic Knots, visit the following link on the Internet, right now:

http://www.tyhoward.com/KnotsFree_SpecialGuide.html

(Or turn to Appendix C for more information about the Knots Free Special Guide.)

Chapter 8

Step 2: DECIDING TO DO YOU

"Your ability to use the principle of
autosuggestion will depend, very largely, upon
your capacity to concentrate upon a given
desire until that desire becomes a burning
obsession."

— *Napoleon Hill*

The power of substance and constant accomplishment comes from being who you are—no matter what. In short, deciding to be and do you!

How would you act today if you were the successful person you deeply desire to become?

How would you prioritize your time?

How would you speak to and interact with your immediate community?

How would you pick and choose your social circle?

How would you serve the "cause" you care for most?

What's stopping you from pursuing these goals today?

If you're not living life, right now, on your own terms, nine times out of ten, your current belief system is stopping you. You can prioritize confidently, serve your community confidently, pick and choose your social circle confidently, and serve your cause confidently, at any point in time.

It starts with you *"Deciding to Do YOU"* - win, lose, or draw. Confidence comes from not only knowing where you've been. It

also comes from knowing and believing in where you are headed.

When I decided to go after and create a better life for my daughter and me, I started with the strong belief that it was possible.
It was possible for me to change. It was possible for me to grow.
It was possible for me to constantly stretch for higher levels of
excellence and a healthier way of living.

I believed enlisting in the U.S. Navy on full-time active duty would
provide me with a strong and disciplined means to change and
grow. I took the necessary steps of action to begin developing
my journey. I delayed my entry into the U.S. Navy by one year
because my daughter's mother was one year behind me in high
school. I took care of my daughter during the day and worked
at McDonald's in the evening. This allowed her mother to continue attending school stress free and do her best to graduate on
time.

In the beginning of my journey, my greatest challenge was confronting the negative comments and disbelief from friends, people, and family members. It wasn't easy; however, I managed to
do it.

I stayed focused on my decision to enter the military by tough-
ening my belief system and taking an immediate assessment of
what I already knew about my life's journey up until that point.
The results became my self-empowering motivators to succeed
for both my daughter and myself.

I already knew how living in poverty—felt.

I already knew how living with a sense of hopelessness—felt.

I already knew how living with little to no direction—felt.

I already knew how living a life doing what everyone else told
me—felt.

I already knew how striving just to make ends meet—felt.

I already knew how working a job daily that made me literally sick—felt.

I already knew how following and listening to toxic people yet getting nowhere positive—felt.

I already knew how blowing ripe opportunities and wasting my gifts and talents—felt.

In a nutshell, I knew how being tied up in toxic knots and not doing "my" best—felt.

That was not and is not living life to its fullest on my terms!

During my struggle while living life on society's terms, I realized a powerful principle about life. That powerful principle is this: "The WINNERS in life understand that it's their actions and determination to do them at the highest level possible that creates their reality."

When I began to learn, internalize, and practice this principle, my persistent belief system for "doing me" became unshakeable. That was when my toxic way of thinking "Why me?" changed to my new empowering way of thinking "Try me."

My next phase of development was to learn through experience "What could my life be if I decided to do ME?" Through this developmental process, I began the teachings and creation of the "untie the knots" philosophy on life.

My belief in Mommy's principle about education transformed me into a lifelong student. At this stage in my life, I was an avid reader who read and absorbed everything. I was still sold and hooked on my mother's teachings about "Education! Education! Education! Once you put it in your head, no one can ever take that away!"

This positive and healthy habit brought to my life a compass with four sound principles to guide me toward continuously "doing me". These four principles are

1) What's the Worst That Could Happen;
2) Try Sacrifice Before Happiness;
3) Blocking Out the Pings and Blows of the Doubt Patrol; and
4) The Rewards and Benefits of Doing Me.

Let's now review and learn the power behind these four guiding principles.

What's the Worst That Could Happen?

"Great souls have wills; feeble souls have only wishes."
— Chinese Proverb

Too often, we are stuck in life behind our barriers and fears. These barriers and fears can become so toxic we never venture to discover and unleash our true potential. We learn and adapt to playing it safe throughout life. We play by everyone else's rules, and we do what is prescribed as safe and secure. Guess what? That's not living!

If you're the same person you were a month ago, you haven't changed or grown.

If you're the same person you were six months ago, you haven't changed or grown.

If you're the same person you were a year, three years, or five or ten years ago, you haven't changed or grown.

Which means—you are not living and you haven't Decided to Do YOU!

STOP.

Ask yourself, "What's the worst that could happen?"

You fail. You have to start over. You have to end a toxic relationship. You lose all your material gains. You have to find a new job. You lose all your money. You have to go back to school for more education.

Is that all you're stressing over and worried about?

Consider the following rewards and benefits you will bring to your life:

- When you fail, it gives you the opportunity to learn and do better the next time
- When you start over, it gives you the opportunity to start with a clean slate.
- When you end a toxic relationship, it gives you an opportunity to heal and repair yourself.
- When you lose your material gains, it gives you the opportunity to appreciate what you do have.
- When you have to find a new job, it gives you an opportunity to find a job that you will enjoy.
- When you lose your money, it gives you an opportunity to re-learn the value of money.
- When you have to go back to school for more education, it gives you the opportunity to once again learn and grow.

That's what "doing you" is about! Doing whatever it takes to create and live life on your terms.

Doing whatever it takes to claim and drive your life with fewer toxic knots towards a life of significance and prosperity.

We all have a certain amount of energy, so let's apply it to creating extraordinary relationships, advancing our careers, meeting our goals, and "untying our knots" instead of wasting that energy stuck behind our preconceived barriers and unfounded fears. Take action on what you have control over and minimize risks for what you don't. Then invest your energy wisely in purposefully moving your life continuously forward.

In doing something for the first time, imagine you have already done it in the past. Close your eyes, then vividly imagine succeeding beyond your expectations. The mind does not know the difference between something vividly imagined and something real. Make it as vivid as possible by involving all five senses: touch, taste, hearing, smell, and vision.

Ask yourself, "What's the worst that could happen?"

When "doing you" isn't positive, find someone who is doing what you want to do in a positive way. Model as many of their positive behaviors, attitudes, values, and beliefs as you can. How can you do this? Talk with them if you have access to them. Ask them questions like "What did you do to bring yourself to your current level of confidence? Who influenced you throughout life? What books have you read?" If you do not have access to your positive role model, research and try to collect as much information about them for you to model.

Use the "as-if" frame. I literally love this frame of mind. If you were doing you, how would you be acting? How would you be moving? How would you be speaking? What would you be thinking? What would you tell yourself inside? By asking yourself these questions, you are literally forced to answer them by going into a "doing you" state. You will then be acting "as-if" you are doing you. After a while, just forget you are acting and pretty soon you will develop this frame of mind into a positive and productive habit.

Ask yourself, "What's the worst that could happen?"

Remember, if you never venture out, you will never gain anything. To get what you want, ask for it. I fully believe that if I ask enough people for whatever I want, I will eventually get it. As you think about your goals and what you are striving for, how effective would it be to believe that all people out there want to help you succeed, if you only ask? Whether that is true or not in the "real world" does not matter. What does matter is that you adopt a new belief and venture out. Nothing ventured, nothing gained. Begin asking people for help.

Disarm the toxic, self-sabotaging internal voice. That negative internal voice will keep you stalled. To disarm the internal voice, imagine a volume control button and push that button continuously to make sure your toxic internal voice is off. The point is to disarm your toxic internal voice by minimizing the power it has over your mind. Continue to research and learn effective ways that you can use to disarm your toxic, self-sabotaging internal voice.

Ask yourself, "What's the worst that could happen?"

Are the challenges and fears you're currently facing stopping you permanently? Well, they shouldn't. Keep your challenges in proper perspective and this will help you to diminish your fears.

Try Sacrifice Before Happiness

"Great achievement is usually born of great sacrifice and is never the result of selfishness."

— Napoleon Hill

In a world today that is so caught up in instant everything, it's not shocking to find more people who are chasing instant happiness before making sacrifices. With television shows like *Who Wants to Be a Millionaire, American Idol, Survivor,* and *Real World*, it's no wonder why more and more people are beginning to look for the quick meal ticket to happiness instead of rolling up their sleeves and making the necessary sacrifice to manifest their dreams.

When I decided to delay my entry into the military for a year, I made that decision to give my daughter's mother the opportunity to successfully complete high school on time and earn a high school diploma.

I chose to make the necessary sacrifice to increase the potential long-term happiness for my daughter, daughter's mother, and me. This didn't mean I was unhappy; it meant I was being responsible and accountable for my previous actions.

There were times when I wanted to hang with the guys but chose not to because my daughter and her well-being were my priority. In the evenings, I worked so I could continue to buy the necessities she needed, such as Pampers, formula, food, medicine, lotion, wet wipes, clothes, bibs, hygiene products, blankets, etc.

The entire time I was caring for my daughter, I continued to establish my personal plan about how I would make more sacrifices early in her life to improve her opportunities later in life. I didn't want to just join the military for four years to say, "I was in the military." I researched the different schools and programs the U.S. Navy offered. I visited the schoolyard in my neighborhood to jog long distances to get myself in shape. I wanted to enter the Navy in the best shape possible. I wanted both my mental and physical toughness to be at their peak.

There were many times while taking care of my daughter, working at McDonald's, and running around the schoolyard track in preparation for the military where I grew frustrated and wanted to quit. Then I would think, "That's NOT an option! This is the sacrifice that I have to make for both my daughter and I, a sacrifice that will bring us more opportunities and happiness later in the future." And I stuck to it faithfully.

Happiness is a good feeling, and we all want and pursue it daily. However, happiness can distract us from completing our tasks. The pursuit of constant in-the-moment happiness can tie people in many toxic knots as they become complacent and content with a superficial sense of well-being.

If you want to buy a house but have bad credit, you must make sacrifices. If you're in a shaky relationship but want it to improve, you must make sacrifices. If you want a promotion at work but your supervisor said you need to obtain a higher level of education, you must make sacrifices. If you want to take you and your family to the next level as a family, you must make sacrifices.

It has been said, "The only place success comes before work is in the dictionary."

Yet, most people today will still choose in-the-moment happiness instead of making the necessary sacrifices that will improve and move their life productively forward.

I spoke at a local university, and posed the following scenario to an audience of 100 students in attendance:

> You've found on campus an old, dirty lamp. You take it back to your dorm and begin to polish it. Suddenly, from the lamp rises a puff of smoke and out pops a Genie. This Genie, however, is not of the "three-wishes" variety; instead, it makes you the following offer. He is willing and able to increase either your general level of intelligence or your general level of happiness. The price is an equal reduction in the other's attribute. How much of your intelligence are you willing to sacrifice to gain greater happiness? Or would you wish to give up some of your happiness for the promise of greater intelligence?

I told them to mark their answers on the piece of paper I provided, to remain anonymous, and to quickly pass their papers forward. The results were interesting. Take a look:

Votes	Answers
41	I would sacrifice a lot of my intelligence if it guaranteed a lot more happiness.
25	I would sacrifice some of my intelligence if it guaranteed some more happiness.
17	I like the balance of my happiness/intelligence the way it is.
12	I would sacrifice some of my happiness if it guaranteed some more intelligence.
3	I would sacrifice a lot of my happiness if it guaranteed a lot more intelligence.
2	Other

As you can clearly see in the table above, many of the students elected to "sacrifice" a lot of their intelligence to gain a lot more guaranteed happiness. None of the students asked me if the happiness was instant, in-the-moment, or long-lasting. It didn't matter.

Some of you may even think, "Hey Ty, the students did make a sacrifice."

Yes, the majority of the students did make a "sacrifice"; however, the students who chose to "sacrifice" a lot or some of their intelligence did not improve or move their life forward in a productive way.

How would you have answered the same questions asked by the Genie?

Yes, working through sacrifices does take much longer to reach happiness; however, when you accomplish your ultimate goal, you will celebrate your achievement with a greater level of happiness. Your celebration will show that you've done something worthwhile. Sacrifice adds to your life, and the pursuit of "constant, in-the-moment" happiness subtracts from your life.

The choice is yours. I hope in this case, by choosing to learn, practice, and master the Untie the Knots Process," you choose sacrifice over happiness. I hope you choose to undertake the necessary tasks and pursue the necessary work that is needed to accomplish your goals and dreams. When you do choose sacrifice before happiness, you will experience in the days, months, and years to come a higher level of long-term happiness.

All because you chose and endured your sacrifices for a brighter future of happiness.

Blocking Out the Pings and Blows of the Doubt Patrol

"Doubt can only be removed by action."

— Johann Wolfgang Von Geothe

We experience the Doubt Patrol (the toxic critics) each and every day. The Doubt Patrol can be external and internal. They send constant pings and blows to remind us of the toxic challenges in life.

The Doubt Patrol represents the people, images, and voices that try to tell you what you can and cannot do. They tell you what is for and not for you. They help to remind and keep you connected to your past.

The Doubt Patrol represents the toxic assassins whose sole purpose is to take out your dreams, your hopes, your goals, your energy, your positive beliefs, and you. They think they are saving you from pain and disappointment; however, they prey on you because they themselves are not taking any meaningful risks in life.

Watch out for them!!!

The one feature of Doubt Patrol members is that you can see them coming or recognize them once they are in your presence.

The internal Doubt Patrol is you, that little voice or internal view projector that constantly works on you.

The external Doubt Patrol member can be removed from your life in the following ways:

-   Only share your goals, hopes, and dreams with people who you know care about you.
-   Distance yourself from toxic people. They will zap and work hard to kill your positive mental attitude.
-   If you have a toxic person in your family or place of work, try your best to minimize your interactions with them.
-   Strengthen your belief system daily by feeding it with positive thoughts and information.
-   When you realize that an external Doubt Patrol member has made it past your sensor barrier, defuse and remove yourself from them immediately.

External Doubt Patrol members can only do damage if you let them in and keep them in your life.

The internal Doubt Patrol member, YOU, takes more effort and practice to silence. To tone down the toxic inner voice, try the following:

-   Smile often, and refuse to listen to and give in to your internal toxic words.
-   Create a personal collage or scrapbook of your accomplishments. Hang the collage up or keep the scrapbook in your bedroom to remind you that you are a good person who is making your life's goals happen.
-   Create a list of five positive features about yourself each morning and read them to yourself every four to six hours within the day.
-   Ask a friend, mentor, or family member to tell you at least two positive statements about you each day.

Your internal Doubt Patrol can do much more damage than the external Doubt Patrol members because the internal patrol knows how to shut you down. Don't allow this to happen.

When you Decide to Do YOU, you also make a stand to boldly and confidently disallow the external or internal Doubt Patrol members to crush you or your hopes, dreams, or goals.

The Rewards and Benefits of Doing YOU

*"One important key to success is self-confidence.
An important key to self-confidence is
preparation."*

— Arthur Ashe

The rewards and benefits of Doing YOU are powerful.

1) You're now living life on your terms. Now you're pursuing the goals, dreams, and purpose for your life relentlessly.

2) You've empowered yourself to determine how long a negative experience will affect you. There will still be challenging situations; however, you now can masterfully determine how long these periods will last. As time passes, you make them shorter due to your mastery of the Untie the Knots Process.

3) You've put yourself in a better position to identify and untie your toxic knots. When you Decide to Do YOU, you put both you and your mental attitude in a better position for change, growth, and awareness. Now you're looking for areas to work on and improve daily.

4) Your belief system now expects a happier, healthier, harmonious, and prosperous life. When your belief system and a higher level of confidence begin to work together, you can achieve powerful results.

5) You bring yourself one step closer to creating and living a significant life. Deciding to Do YOU says, "I want to create and leave a lasting legacy, a legacy that will leave this world a little better than the way I came into it."

Through continuous preparation, practice, and self-confidence, you will position and find yourself enjoying the benefits and rewards of Doing YOU.

Here's a poem for you written by me for everyone to enjoy. This poem communicates how challenging yet simple and rewarding making the decision to "do you" can be.

Decide to Do YOU

Two glasses sat on the table before me,
Both filled to the rim.
This was a major life decision,
On this day, only one glass could win.

This test represented my life's quest,
As I sat there all alone.
I had to make a choice,
Not just a grunt…or a groan.

Up until this point,
I took life somewhat day-by-day.
I didn't see future victories,
Why should I…new success never came my way.

In the past, I had sipped from both individual glasses,
And swished the fate in my mouth.
Today, I had to choose a single winner,
Without question…and without doubt!

Underneath each glass there was a note…

The note under the glass on the right read:
"Choose me, YOUR LIFE'S PURPOSE, and you will be freed!"

The note under the glass on the left read:
"Choose me, NO NEW RISKS, and you will remain the same."

Which clearly communicated to me,
If I win or if I lose in life,
I have only me to blame.

Then, I stood up from the table...
Proud and determined by my choice!
This was a powerful decision,
My life's new direction and voice!

On that day and each day forward,
I choose to do ME,
Without question or hesitation,
I choose to live FREE!

Decide to Do YOU!

Staying Committed to Doing YOU Every Day

Whether you are one who has been unsuccessful in Deciding to Do YOU, hasn't yet Decided to Do YOU, or is sticking to it so far, you can still benefit from a few tips to help you stay committed to Doing YOU every day.

1) Stay focused. Stay the course. And Do YOU!
2) Keep a positive mental attitude and belief system.
3) Learn and practice the four main principles I shared with you in this chapter.
4) Remember that preparation, practice, and self-confidence will be your ultimate key to Do YOU.

Nothing can equal the sense of accomplishment that comes from getting the results you desire, plan, and actualize. When you decide to take the necessary steps of action to do and be you, you will transform your faith, hopes, and belief system into real and undeniable results. And there is no better time to begin your journey than today.

You are awesome and worthy. Decide to be you. Decide to go after your personal dreams, goals, and aspirations…no matter what! The world is awaiting the arrival of the genuine and gifted person you know you are. Make today the day you decide to start acting like a success by identifying and lessening the number of toxic knots in life. And before long you will be living life 100% on your own terms. All because you Decided To Do YOU!

Chapter Conclusion

In this chapter, I explained to you the power people ignite and obtain when they decide to do and be themselves 100% of the time. With the four guiding principles of this chapter

1) What's the Worst That Could Happen
2) Try Sacrifice Before Happiness
3) Blocking Out the Pings and Blows of the Doubt Patrol
4) The Rewards and Benefits of Doing YOU

you now have a sound compass leading you to direct and empower your belief system, confidence, and life. Put these key principles among your notes, and review them often. You've invested your hard-earned money in my book, but now will you decide to do you and own my concepts? Will you invest the time and effort that's required to make them yours? It's your life and your decision. I hope you make the right one. Decide to Do YOU!

Chapter 9

Step 3: ACKNOWLEDGING AND PUSHING THROUGH YOUR FEARS

"The habit of doing one's duty drives away fear."

— Charles Baudelaire

WHAT IS it for you? Fear of public speaking, asserting yourself, making decisions, being alone, making mistakes, parenting, passing a test, financial problems, intimacy, commitment, the past, change, hearing results, building relationships, large groups, repeating a bad experience, being hurt, losing material objects, discovering the real you, failing, or succeeding?

We all have fears. Fear is often based on the uncertainty of change and lack of positive self-image. Fear is crippling. It can be stifling and self-sabotaging in our lives.

When I was working at McDonald's during my one-year delay of going into the military after graduating high school, I had many reckless fears.

I had fears that challenged and questioned my uncertainty of change.

Would I really become the responsible and involved father for my daughter that my father wasn't for my siblings and me?

Would going into the military truly offer me a new and better sense of direction?

Maybe I'm getting into something that's over my head by doing this military thing, having to learn and adapt to a more structured way of behaving. This will be too difficult for me.

What do I know about surviving anywhere else than in the small toxic community of Cherry Hill? I hadn't been outside the State of Maryland, other than amusement parks in Richmond, Virginia and Hershey, Pennsylvania. Now, I was going to San Diego, California for the U.S. Navy's Basic Training Program. The only real family I knew lived in Baltimore, Maryland.

I had self-image fears that were equally if not more stifling and crippling.

How can I raise a child when I'm still a child myself?

What if the military finds out that I spent time in foster care?

What if the military finds out that I was raised by a single mother, who suffered from a period of alcoholism due to the fact that she had to constantly struggle to make ends meet?

Do I even have what it takes to successfully enter and complete 13 weeks of basic military training?

Who am I to step out of the ranks of my immediate family to break the cycle of complacency with the hope of improving the future for my daughter and me? I come from the ghetto, so maybe I'm supposed to stay and live in the ghetto.

Did you know that we are born with only two real fears? The fear of falling and the fear of loud noises; everything else is a learned behavior.

My fears were undoubtedly the uncertainty of change and lack of a positive self-image. During my year of delay into the military, I knew I had to definitely acknowledge, confront, and push through fears. I had to formulate a course of action to overcome the fears that stood before me in my life. My course of action was simple; however, it was difficult because it took courage. I had to learn to be bold and resilient.

During my simple yet difficult course, I learned what fear was. I learned about the causes and effects of fear and that there was healthy and unhealthy fear. I learned to acknowledge and confront my fears, to shatter and push through my fears, and what to do when I arrived on the other side of my fears.

Before I began my quest to shatter my fears, I recalled an empowering affirmation that my grandmother taught me when I was struggling in high school. After being expelled from Baltimore Polytechnic Institute and feeling down on myself, my grandmother said, "Grandson, you have to know that in life you may be delayed, but you're rarely denied." My grandmother was an ordained deaconess in her church at this time, and her words "You may be delayed, but you're rarely denied" spoke power into the core of my being. Grandma Bland explained to me, "Just because you experience a bump or pothole in the road doesn't mean that is the end of the road. And boy, you're much too bright to be giving up so soon because of uncertainty and a bruised self-image. Pick yourself back up, and face and push through your fears."

Let me tell you something: when Grandma Bland told you something, you did it without hesitation and without questions. It was done, fears or no fears.

Follow me as I guide you through my course of action. You will enjoy this journey because I'm confident this process will also have you acknowledging, confronting, and successfully pushing through your fears.

What is Fear?

Dictionary.com defines "fear" as "a distressing emotion aroused by impending danger, evil, pain, etc., whether the threat is real or imagined; the feeling or condition of being afraid."

Susan Jeffers, author of the groundbreaking self-help book *Feel the Fear and Do It Anyway*, says, "Fear is false evidence appearing real."

I believe fear is our <u>F</u>alse <u>E</u>motions <u>A</u>cting <u>R</u>ecklessly™. As expressed in the definition of "fear" from Dictionary.com, fear occurs when our false (aroused) emotions begin to introduce danger, evil, pain, and stress over us, whether real or imagined; fear creates reckless feelings that often become hazardous and toxic to our lives.

Let's take a look at the "<u>F</u>alse <u>E</u>motions <u>A</u>cting <u>R</u>ecklessly" illustration below.

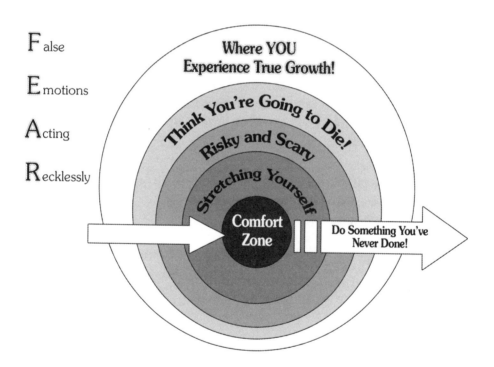

The Fear Zone Reduction Model™

As we look at the layers within the "Fear Zone Reduction Model," it becomes apparent that our reckless emotions can force us to stay snug and cozy within our comfort zone.

To take control of your fears, your "<u>F</u>alse <u>E</u>motions <u>A</u>cting <u>R</u>ecklessly," you must do something you've never done before: 1) acknowledge the fear that is keeping you inside of your comfort zone, 2) confront your fear by taking it head on while stretching yourself outside of your comfort zone, 3) take on the new risks that are required for you to push through this fear, 4) endure the feeling and thought that you might die, and 5) experience and celebrate your new growth once you arrive on the other side of your fear.

By acknowledging and pushing through our fears we begin to take on greater risks; however, as you can see in the illustration above the reward in the end is much sweeter on the other side of our fears than what we get when we choose to stay tied up by our fears, trapped in our comfort zone.

Causes and Effects of Fear

> *"I can stand what I know. It's what I don't know*
> *that frightens me."*
> — Frances Newton

There are many causes of fear:

1. Irrational beliefs about how an object, event, or feeling will result in negative, disastrous, life-threatening, disturbing, or unsettling consequences for you.
2. Underlying motives behind many of your actions or lack of action that block your thinking, problem solving, and decision-making abilities.
3. Negative self-scripts you have either given yourself or were given to you about how you will suffer dire consequences if you involve yourself in certain activities, behavior, or events.

4. Disabling beliefs you carry that prevent you from living a productive, healthy, and growth-enhancing life.
5. An underlying foundation of a weak self-image and self-concept; they keep you from fully asserting yourself, and that hinders your quest for self-actualization.
6. "Comfort Zone" ways of acting and responding. Because of your habitual and well-established nature, fears can become second nature; therefore, they make you extremely resistant to change.
7. The basis of your negative belief system. If you were no longer the recipient of the negative consequences that fears predicted, you would have to take off your "mask" and become authentic.
8. Excuses people hide behind to avoid change or growth. To rid yourself of your fears is to rid yourself of the life-long reasons for avoiding personal growth.

There are many effects of fear:

Fears can—

1. Immobilize decision-making.
2. Prevent you from overcoming your insecurity, prevent you from trusting in others, and prevent you from becoming vulnerable to grow.
3. Prevent you from being willing to release old habits or ways of thinking to change.
4. Make you resistant to all offers of help from others.
5. Terrify you and make you unwilling to venture into the world, making you a prisoner in your home.
6. Stifle your motivation to pursue an education or a career.
7. Keep you locked in self-destructive behavior.
8. Prevent you from believing in your chances to become a fully functioning, healthy individual.
9. Be the reason why you find yourself tied in old beliefs and old behaviors.
10. Be the roadblock to your desires to change and grow.

When people are tied up in the toxic knots of fear, they can be paralyzed from living life to the fullest. Fear can infect our relationships, our career prospects, our parenting skills, and our social lives. It is not always easy to grasp the cause of our deep-seated fears, but in most cases, there are ways to unlearn our reactions to fear and learn more positive ways of coping with it.

There Is Unhealthy Fear and Healthy Fear

"You can set yourself up to be sick, or you can choose to stay well."

— Wayne Dyer

According to Buddhist philosophy, there is unhealthy fear and healthy fear.

When we are afraid of something that cannot actually harm us - such as ghosts - or something we cannot avoid - such as old age or being struck down with Parkinson's Disease or being run over by a truck - then our fear is unhealthy, for it serves only to make us unhappy and paralyze our will.

However, when someone gives up smoking because they are afraid of developing lung cancer, this is a healthy fear because the danger is real and there are constructive steps they can take to avoid it.

We have many fears such as a fear of terrorism, fear of death, fear of being separated from people we love, fear of losing control, fear of commitment, fear of failure, fear of rejection, or fear of losing our job. The list never ends!

Many of our present fears are rooted in what Buddha identified as "delusions" — distorted ways of looking at the world around us and ourselves. If we learn to control our mind and reduce and eventually eliminate these delusions, the source of all our fear—healthy and unhealthy—can be managed and reduced to a level that no longer hinders our ability to change, grow, and continuously succeed.

However, we need the healthy fear that arises from taking stock of our present situation so we can identify our toxic knots, push through any fear we have, and successfully untie our toxic knots. For example, there is no point in a procrastinator fearing being stuck unless there is something he or she will do about it such as choosing a task, starting it, blocking out all distractions, and working it through until completion.

If a procrastinator has a sufficient fear of staying stuck and never getting where they want to be in life, they will take steps to untie the toxic knots of delay. If they prefer to ignore the danger of staying stuck in chronic procrastination, they will prolong their internal discomfort and suffer.

Here are three powerful ways to respond to fear:

1) Admit you have a fear.
2) Choose to fight—don't run away.
3) Continue the process shared in this chapter on a regular basis until you have defeated your fear.

Until you have removed the causes of your vulnerability to fear through identifying and untying your knots, you will be bound down, wedged between the emotional recklessness of unhealthy fear.

Acknowledging Your Fears

"If you listen to your fears, you will die never knowing what a great person you might have been."

— Robert Schuller

Step 1: In your journal, list the fears you believe are active in your life. Be 100% open and honest with yourself. Once you've listed the fears, rank them in order of greatest intensity, with #1 being your greatest fear.

Step 2: Once you have ranked your fears, explore your level of motivation to confront these fears by answering the following questions in your journal:

1. How real are these fears?
2. How much power in my life do these fears have?
3. How do these fears explain past or current actions in my life?
4. How do these fears determine my self-image, self-concept, or self-esteem?
5. How do these fears disable me?
6. How do these fears inhibit me?
7. What emotions do these fears block?
8. How long have I had these fears?
9. What have I done to overcome these fears?
10. How convinced am I of the need to confront these fears?

Step 3: Once you have explored your motivation for confronting your fears, convince yourself of the need to address these fears. On a separate sheet of paper, answer these questions:

1. How do my fears influence my decision-making process?
2. How do my fears heighten and make worse my sense of insecurity?
3. How do my fears keep me from making a change in my life?
4. How do my fears influence my response to offers of help from others?
5. How have my fears kept me chained down and locked in?
6. How have my fears influenced my educational, career, and work pursuits?
7. How have my fears contributed to my self-destructiveness?
8. How have my fears affected my belief in a healthy future?
9. How have my fears kept me from growing as a person?
10. How have my fears contributed to an unhealthy lifestyle?

Step 4: Now that you are motivated to confront your fears, address the following issues in your journal: (These issues need to be addressed before you can proceed to Pushing Through Your Fears.)

1. What new behavior do I need to develop to confront my fears?
2. What beliefs block my desires and attempts at confronting my fears?
3. How willing am I to try out new behavior?
4. How willing am I to use some of the "tools" available to overcome fears?
5. What new beliefs do I need to confront my fears?

When you acknowledge and confront your fears, you turn your fear and indecision into confidence and action.

Pushing Through Your Fears

"In time we hate that which we often fear."

— William Shakespeare

Once you are committed to acknowledging and confronting your fears, use tools found in the "Shattering Your Fears Tool Box" to identify strategies to assist you in pushing through each fear. For each of your fears, list the tools you will use to push through them.

The Shattering Fears Tool Box

Tool #1: Handling Irrational Beliefs.
Change the way you think and you change the way you act. You can control your thoughts. Since you're only able to consciously think about one thought at a time, only allow positive thoughts to go through your mind. Whenever a negative thought or fear enters, simply choose to stop it right in its tracks and immediately change that thought to something positive.

Tool #2: Self-Affirmation.

Think about your positive attributes. Take stock of yourself by making an inventory of your best qualities, abilities, or attributes. Are you gorgeous? Write it down. Are you a hard worker? Make note of it. Write each quality down in a short sentence, starting with "I" and using the present tense: "I am beautiful," for example, or "I am generous". These statements are affirmations of who you are. We rarely focus on those features that we like about ourselves, instead choosing to dwell on traits we'd like to change. An inventory will help you break that cycle, and using these affirmations to help you appreciate who you are will give you the confidence you need to accept your affirmations of who you want to become.

Tool #3: Handling Guilt.

Face your guilt. Don't block it out; it will only make it worse. Arrange a time of the day to think about it. Could you have made a better choice? How can you fix it? Spend as much time as it takes to confront the guilt. You will know it when it's done. Everyone faces his or her own guilt a different way, so do it your way.

Tool #4: Building Trust.

Create a list of courageous statements about why you want to finally confront and successfully push through this fear. It doesn't have to be a large list. Then beside each statement write two reasons why you will trust yourself to commit, follow through, and shatter this fear. Increased self-trust and self-confidence can knock over walls when pushed meaningfully.

Tool #5: Handling Insecurity.

Tell yourself you're not insecure. Think about what in particular makes you feel insecure and beside it, jot down three or four qualities about you that help you to overshadow your insecurity. You don't have to be insecure; it's a state of mind enhanced by the word. If someone said you are, dismiss it, because it's usually them reflecting their "insecurities" on you! Don't become so absorbed in your "insecurities" that you don't realize when someone is being mean to you. If someone chooses to intentionally hurt your feelings because they don't like you, which will happen occasionally to all of us, realize it's their problem, not yours!

Tool #6: Letting Go.

Visualize yourself acting and doing activities as you move forward and leave your fears behind. Use the techniques of visualization and self-affirmation to help you with this tool. Focus on what it feels like once you've let go.

Tool #7: Stress Reduction.

Stress can cause many mental, physical, and emotional problems in your life. One of the major causes of stress is worrying about things that are recklessly, emotionally false. Get some alone time. If you spend your whole day surrounded by people, it may cause you stress. Spend some time in your bedroom reading a book or feeding your belief system with positive, calming music. Take up Yoga as a weekly routine for relaxation.

Tool #8: Spirituality.

Having a connection to a High Power is an excellent way of confronting and pushing through your fears. It doesn't matter what faith you believe in. Prayer or meditation are great for calming yourself and improving your self-image.

Tool #9: Becoming a Risk Taker.

Pursue the required steps of action despite the fear that you may not overcome your fear the first time. Do not feel guilty or disappointed; it's a part of the shattering your fears process. Get back up, dust yourself off, and try again. You'll get through. Your fear-shattering success starts with you believing, choosing, and taking the necessary risks to confront and push through.

Tool #10: Accepting Change.

The key to accepting change is to have an open mind and accept the fact that change is necessary and required for constant growth. If you do not understand something, ask and pay attention to the answers you receive: you just may be enlightened how others have acknowledged, confronted, and pushed through their own fears.

Once you have identified the tools for each fear, use them, addressing your highest ranked fear first.

Use Steps 1 thru 4 under Acknowledging Your Fears and the Shattering Fears Tool Box to help you acknowledge and push through your fears or reduce their impact on your life. You will need to be bold and resilient in confronting your fears. If, however, you lose faith and become discouraged, return to Step 1 under Acknowledging Your Fears and begin again.

Do not attempt to face the fear if it is one that could possibly hurt you or someone else. For example, do not use these steps if your fear is "fear of needles," etc.

If you come to a point where you feel these strategies are not working, consider seeing a health specialist trained in dealing with human emotions. They will take you through steps to unravel the source of your fears and create new ways of coping.

Remember: Action Delayed = Fear Shattering Denied!

What to Do When You Find Yourself Through Your Fear

"The more you praise and celebrate your life, the more there is in life to celebrate."

— Oprah Winfrey

Your life will soon communicate passionately, "I may have fears, but my fears do not have me!" Say that one time with me, please, **"I may have fears, but my fears do not have me!"** The Untie the Knots Process wants to bring you to the point where you learn, practice, and believe each word of that statement: "I may have fears, but my fears don't have me!"

There is definite empowerment and liberation in those words. If you don't believe me, you will think differently after reading the following story:

Anna Mae was a 70-year-old widow who decided she needed something to keep her company. So, Anna Mae went to the pet store to purchase a parrot. She was unaware that she had purchased a talking parrot.

On the way home, the parrot, in his covered cage, started talking. He stated a few times that his name was Poly. So, Anna Mae began to call him Poly through the cloth covering his cage.

When Anna Mae got Poly home, she sat his cage on a stand and took the cover off his cage. Once she took the cover off, Poly began to curse and swear. Anna Mae was both shocked and offended by Poly's words and actions.

Anna Mae quickly opened the cage, grabbed Poly, walked him into the kitchen, opened the freezer, and threw Poly in. After five minutes, she grabbed Poly, walked back to his cage in the living room, opened the door, and placed him back on his perch.

Then, Anna Mae looked inside the cage at Poly and stated, "Oh, Poly! I won't have that language in my house! Each time you choose that language, I will throw you back into the freezer and your time inside will get longer and longer! Poly, you have to promise me that you will no longer use such language."

Poly first looked at Anna Mae, then he looked at the freezer, then he looked back at Anna Mae, then he looked back at the freezer, then he looked at Anna Mae, and he said, "Squawk! Before I give you my answer, I have one question to ask."

Anna Mae asked, "What's your question Poly?"

"What did the TURKEY do?!" Poly asked.

We shouldn't create fears based on what has happened to others because when we do we bring into existence reckless emotions and unjustifiable fears. To successfully shatter and push through your fears, you must bring yourself to realize this: while you may have fears, your fears don't have you.

Sometimes, our fears are self-inflected, and other times, other people or circumstances impose them on us. Regardless of how your fears emerge, they should not control you in such a way that your life becomes paralyzed or stagnant. You can learn to identify, confront, manage, and push through your fears.

Say it with me one more time, "I may have fears, but my fears do not have me!"

Now that we have shared a quick laugh or chuckle, let me explain to you exactly what to do when you have successfully shattered and pushed through your fears.

1. **Celebrate.** When you have accomplished a significant goal like shattering and pushing through your fears, you must stop to celebrate. Regardless of whether you pushed through a small or big fear—celebrate. It's a great accomplishment, and you've earned it. A fear confronted is a hazard punted from your life and hopefully forever.

2. **Create a short list of goals you want to accomplish now that you've removed this fear.** Create a list of one to three goals you can pursue in the direct area of the fear you removed. Do it again, make it happen, and prove to yourself that this fear is definitely removed and under your control.

3. **Always go back to do preventive management.** One of the most challenging aspects about life is we often rid ourselves of a toxic behavior and accept it as being completely gone never to surface or bother us again. Then, three to five years later, we're dealing with that same toxic habit again. Do the required preventive management. As you are learning, practicing, and mastering

the Untie the Knots Process, make returning to do preventive management on your list of fears a part of the process. Look for potential setbacks or for the fear disguised as something else.

4. **Identify, confront, and push through another fear.** We will never be 100% fear free. Once you have acknowledged, confronted, and pushed through a fear, move to the next fear to be conquered. This positive behavior is the mark of a pro-active manager.

5. **Once you've successfully pushed through your next fear, repeat Steps 1 thru 5.**

Your habits will become your future. I hope now you will choose a future where you continuously acknowledge your fears, confront your fears, manage your fears, and shatter your fears.

Remember: You may have fears, but your fears do not have YOU!

Chapter Conclusion

In this chapter, I shared with you the definition and crippling effects of fear. I explained how I formulated a course of action for conquering fear in my life. My answers are simple; however, my course of action is difficult only because it requires courage. I explained how fear is based on the uncertainty of change and the lack of a positive self-image. I avoided a bunch of theoretical jargon and included easy-to-follow strategies that can help you to acknowledge, confront, and push through your fears, starting today. The Shattering Fears Tool Box gave you additional tools to help you work through your fears. My message in this chapter is reassuring: fear represents your false emotions acting recklessly, and however you choose to handle your reckless emotions will determine your future. I addressed the fundamental causes of fear and encouraged you to embrace the belief that "I may have fears, but my fears don't have me!"

Continue courageously and fearlessly forward in your Untie the Knots journey with a bold and positive mental attitude like that of Ralph Waldo Emerson, who said, *"Do the thing you fear, and the death of fear is certain."*

Unit Summary

YOU'RE MORE THAN WORTHY

Your value, whether tied up in toxic knots, not living your best by doing you, or trapped in fear, is still priceless and worthy of striving to obtain a life of better health, balance, harmony, significance, potential, and prosperity. The worth of our lives comes not in what we do or who we know, but by WHO WE ARE.

Chapters 7, 8, and 9 were written to 1) increase your awareness of toxic knots and fear; 2) inspire you to "do you" and begin living your life on your own terms; and 3 increase your understanding that toxic knots and fears may have caused you to delay and derail your life; however, you now know that in life, "You May Be Delayed, But You're RARELY Denied!"

Let's recap the three chapters that make up Unit 3, Part 2: YOU'RE MORE THAN WORTHY:

Chapter 7: Identifying and Untying Your Knots

Chapter 8: Deciding to Do YOU

Chapter 9: Acknowledging and Pushing Through Your Fears

We've encountered the following **Infusers** *(Freedom Break Away Tools)* that were explained in the introduction of this book:

Infuser #1: Reinstate a Positive Attitude
If you are serious about breaking free from these knots, you must adopt a positive mental attitude. You must be committed to developing and working constantly with a positive attitude, regardless of your past experiences or current situations or circumstances.

Infuser #2: Refocus
How will you change the direction of your life if you're not aware of what direction you're currently in?

Infuser #3: Choose
Decide true freedom and life is what you want and then go where you can produce those results.

Infuser #4: Identify
To successfully break away from anything that has delayed or derailed you in the past, you must summon the bold confidence to now identify it as a toxic habit, choice, person, or relationship.

Infuser #5: Simplify
Remove clutter, confusion, stress, and distractions from your life daily, and watch new, desirable opportunities appear.

Infuser #6: Believe
It takes your strong will and unshakable faith to make the impossible possible.

Infuser #7: Move
Don't just stand there filled with knowledge: Do it! Quit procrastinating and making excuses.

Infuser #9: Persist
How strongly do you want what you now see? No more excuses…no more procrastination…no more wasted and unproductive days! Stay the course!

Infuser #10: Leave a Mark of Significance
It's one experience in living to have simply come and gone. It's another experience in living to have purposely decided to create and live a life of significance: a life that will enable you to leave behind a lasting legacy that will contribute to your family's heritage and also allow the many others who come after you to learn and grow from your efforts.

This unit (Chapters 7 through 9) was a definite wake up call and classroom filled with useful strategies, tools, and information for your journey. Make sure you read it more than once because the material in this unit is meant to inspire, educate, and elevate your awareness so you can courageously and confidently drive the Untie the Knots Process to your new life of living significantly.

You are special! You are more than worthy! And don't YOU ever forget it!

Time OUT!

Just to recap some of the major concepts you've read about thus far, find and write in your journal the answers to the following questions:

• What were Ty's toxic knots at the age of 18?
> *Refer to the "Getting Real with Yourself for Empowered Results" section in Chapter 7 for the answer.*

• What are 10 toxic knots tying people up today?
> *Refer to "The 50 Most Common Toxic Knots Tying People Up Today" section in Chapter 7 for the answer.*

• What's stopping you, nine times out of ten, if you are not living life, right now, on your own terms?
> *Refer to the first two pages of Chapter 8 for the answer.*

• Who do the members of the "Doubt Patrol" represent?
> *Refer to the "Blocking Out the Pings and Blows of the Doubt Patrol" section in Chapter 8 for the answer.*

• What is Ty's acronym for the word "Fear"?
> *Refer to the "What is Fear?" section in Chapter 9 for the answer.*

• What's the 3rd step in acknowledging your fears?
> *Refer to the "Acknowledging Your Fears" section in Chapter 9 for the answer.*

"Only when we are no longer afraid do we begin to live."

— Dorothy Thompson

PART 3

YOU MAY HAVE BEEN DELAYED, BUT YOU'RE RARELY DENIED

My Personal List of Empowering *Untie the Knots* Affirmations
The Second Step of Self-Mastery Is Changing and Becoming

Step 4—Setting Unstoppable Goals
If Your Goal Forces You to S-T-R-E-T-C-H, Then It's a Goal Worth Pursuing

Step 5—Quit Marking Time—and Move Forward
Your Movement Creates Momentum and Energy to Succeed

Step 6—Defeating Toxic Habits, Choices, People, and Relationships
Your Habits Become Your Future

In Part 3...

When you're real and honest with identifying and beginning to untie your knots, you can turn your attention to charting your new course of direction and moving forward. In this part, you will find information about setting unstoppable goals so you can put you and your life in the best position to move forward. You'll also discover how to quit doing the same negative activities daily to bring positive life results. Finally, you will receive great tips on how to defeat toxic habits, choices, people, and relationships, so you can begin to pursue, work, and live in your life's purpose.

My Personal List of Empowering
Untie the Knots Affirmations

- I am healthy, happy, and wise.
- I embrace change and growth as motivators for my life.
- My life is more significant each day.
- The Untie the Knots Process brings me energy daily.
- I study and comprehend quickly.
- I am green and growing.
- My positive attitude brings me peace and clarity.
- I am calm and relaxed in every situation.
- I control my thoughts.
- I radiate love and happiness.
- I choose continuous determination, focus, and action to empower myself each day.
- I remove toxic habits, choices, people, and relationships from my life immediately.
- I bring constant freedom and prosperity to my life.
- I have good and loving relations with my family, friends, neighbors, and co-workers.
- I have a wonderful, satisfying job.
- I am successful in whatever I do.
- Everything is improving daily.
- I have positive and resourceful friends.
- I am always respectful of myself.
- I'm a good listener.
- I ask good questions.
- I'm full of good ideas.
- My confidence and self-esteem are bold and fearless.
- I can do anything I set my mind to.
- I am confident; I CAN DO IT.
- I believe in myself.
- Reading is fun and rewarding to me.
- I'm good at identifying, working through, and untying the toxic knots that come into my life.
- Every problem has an answer.

- I FEEL HAPPY.
- I'M GOOD AT BEING ME.
- People are happy when they see me.
- I am unique and special.
- I am courageous and strong.
- My body is my best friend.
- I FEEL GREAT.
- Every day in every way I strive to make my BEST better.
- I feel calm and relaxed in challenging and toxic situations.
- I make people feel better and happier when they're in my presence.
- I will step outside my comfort zone today.
- No matter what you do or say to me, I'm still a worthwhile person.

Affirmations can be used to destroy bad habits and create good ones. Affirmations can help you simplify your life and stay focused. Affirmations can help you stay committed to accomplishing your goals. Affirmations can keep you balanced and calm. Affirmations can change your life. Affirmations can help you live the life you want.

The key is that you need to know how to use them. It is important to first understand what affirmations are about. In short, they are everything positive that you think, say, believe, feel, and do. If you've ever recited affirmations that didn't manifest themselves in your life, it's likely because you chose not to believe in the power and effectiveness that positive words can have on your state of mind.

Once you understand what affirmations are, you need to know how they work. Understand that quality affirmations relate directly to our energy. Our energy directly relates to the universe. The universe relates back to us. So in other words, our affirmations work because of who we are.

Are you starting to notice a common thread? Affirmations really have no power in the universal scheme; it is you that has all the power. Affirmations are simply a tool for influencing you. And you, by way of your energy and actions, influence the universal flow as it relates to your life.

Affirmations are extremely powerful; however, they are one of the most overlooked techniques for personal growth. This is because most people do not understand how they work. Your assignment in conjunction with reading the following three chapters is to research and learn more about the power of affirmations and how to use them properly.

When you put quality affirmations and their principles to work in your life, you will see your life change in ways that will make you feel happier, more empowered, and more motivated to achieve one new goal after another.

Your life of greater potential and significance is ahead! Let's journey on.

Chapter 10

Step 4: SETTING UNSTOPPABLE GOALS

"A good goal is like a strenuous exercise—it makes you stretch."

— Mary Kay Ash

Have you found yourself pumped up at the beginning of the year to set new goals? You can't wait to start the New Year so you can strive to be ten times more productive and successful than you were in years past. But weeks later, you're still doing the same old activities. Where did your excitement disappear to? What happened to your goals?

News FLASH! You're not the only person who experiences this shift in personal drive.

Answer the following questions:

Are you a visionary? Does your mind continuously identify new ideas and projects you want to pursue, and yet, nothing really happens?

Do you manage goals with details yet find yourself struggling to meet deadlines due to your mismanagement of time?

Do you wait until the last minute to start a goal, only to find there are many factors you didn't consider, which consequently results in losing interest in pursuing the goal altogether?

Have you pursued a goal and been hit by life's many distractions which caused you to abandon your pursuit of the goal permanently because you had no clear record of where you were when you stepped away?

Do you plan your schedule in your mind every morning with a nice mental "to-do list"? Do you keep everything in your head, and by the end of the day, feel tired and worn out because you couldn't finish or remember your accomplishments?

Do you stop in the middle of pursuing a goal because the thought of possible failure or a new level of success scares you to death?

If you answered "yes" to at least two of the above questions, you can definitely benefit from setting and accomplishing unstoppable goals.

In the early 1990s, I made an investment in myself by purchasing an audiocassette series by world-renowned motivational speaker Zig Ziglar titled *Goals: How to Set Them, How to Reach Them*. I purchased this series after Mary, a shift manager at the McDonald's I worked, strongly recommended it. I shared with Mary my life's plan for my daughter and me, and she encouraged me to write my plan on paper and take actions toward actually achieving my plan and goals. My plan was worthless, she suggested, if it was only in my head. I always heard goals were important; however, I didn't have a clue about how to effectively identify my goals and work them through to accomplishment. Ziglar's tapes began this journey and lesson for me.

In this audiotape series, Zig states repeatedly and passionately, "Without clearly defined written goals, you simply cannot achieve the success you want!" He guides people through a clear, beautifully organized "success trip." Along the way, I learned how to recognize and set my goals. I learned techniques for finding extra time I didn't think I had and for reducing huge, complex goals into easy-to-handle, practical goals. I learned how to set goals, monitor them, and accomplish them.

Here are a few additional nuggets, strategies, and principles that I learned from Zig Ziglar's tapes:

1) 97% of people today do not have clearly defined written goals.
2) Most people don't set goals because of fear and because they haven't been sold on setting goals.
3) You have to see your target, spell out exactly what you need to hit that target, create a specific plan of action, and set a deadline for reaching that target.

I learned, practiced, and am still learning to master the art of effective goal setting and accomplishment. What I learned from Ziglar's tapes has evolved and matured since the early 1990s; however, many of his universal principles and strategies have become a positive part of my goal-setting and continual-success process.

I'm about to give you the inside scoop on goal setting that can change your life. It is THE secret formula for personal and professional success.

This formula is for people who are committed to the Untie the Knots journey and who truly plan to use that journey to improve their lives.

Are you ready?

Here it is...The Proven Formula to Having the Significance and Freedom You Deserve.

Vision + Processes = Unstoppable Accomplishment

That's it! There's no other hidden secret. Yes, it's THAT simple.

Successful people know how to answer the following two crucial questions:

"What do I want?" and "How am I going to get it?"

Before you read further, stop and ask yourself those two questions right now.

The Bible states, *"Without a vision the people shall perish."*

Regardless of your spiritual beliefs, your personal vision statement guides your life. Your personal vision statement provides the direction necessary to guide your course and choices. Your personal vision statement is the illuminating lantern that guides and helps you find your way.

Write your personal vision statement as the first step in focusing your life - for your goals, accomplishments, contributions, happiness, significance, and legacy.

An Exploration to Help You Prepare to Write Your Personal Vision Statement

Use these questions to guide your thoughts.

- What are ten activities you most enjoy doing? Be honest. These are the ten activities without which your weeks, months, and years would feel incomplete.
- What three tasks must you complete every day to feel fulfilled at work?
- What are your five or six most important values?
- Your life has a number of important facets or dimensions, all of which deserve some attention in your personal vision statement.
    - Write one important goal for each of them: physical, spiritual, work or career, family, social relationships, financial security, mental improvement, and fun.
    - If you never had to work another day in your life, how would you spend your time instead of working?
    - If your life were to end right now, what will you regret not doing, seeing, or achieving?
    - What strengths have people identified about you and your accomplishments? What strengths do you see in yourself?
    - What weaknesses have other people identified about you and what do you believe are your weaknesses?

Craft Your Personal Vision Statement

Once you have thoughtfully prepared answers to these questions and others that you identify, you are ready to craft a personal vision statement. Write in the first person tense and make statements about the goals you hope to achieve. Write the statements as if you are already making them happen in your life. Some experts recommend 50 words or less, but I would rather see you fully articulate the vision you want than be limited by a word count.

Ziglar also stated in those tapes, *"You generally accomplish your written goals, dreams, plans, and vision. Writing them down makes them real for you and increases your commitment to their accomplishment."*

Keep in mind that your personal vision statement can change over time, depending on what is happening in your life. You will be amazed, however, at how many components remain consistent over time. I wrote my first written vision for my life in 1995; this personal vision statement guides my life to this day.

My Personal Vision Statement

My own personal vision statement includes such items as "doing me" every day; creating better life opportunities for my daughter and me; letting go of the past; valuing family relationships; building healthy quality friendships; being aware and in control of my attitude at all times; living daily a life dedicated to integrity, character, commitment, growth, change, humility, and faith; working continuously on better managing my anger and negative responses to life; being aware of my environment and the people in it at all times; striving to have a positive impact on every person I come in contact with; working out consistently to maintain a healthy mind, body, and spirit; stopping more frequently to smell the roses, taking a break to enjoy non-work related fun; doing something different twice a month outside my comfort zone; eliminating my credit card debt and putting myself on the path to financial independence; crafting a life story worth re-membering and sharing; watching plays and movies; going on long travel vacations; minimizing my worries and increasing my hopes; starting and operating a very successful business; becoming a steward, humanitarian, and philanthropist within my community; writing and publishing books; and always being an active, reliable, influential, and positive role model to my daughter, family, friends and co-workers.

As I live and experience the components of my personal vision statement, I feel happier, healthier, more balanced, worthwhile, victorious, and inspired to continue my life's journey. Your personal vision statement can have the same impact for you. Take the time to formulate answers to the above questions, and write your personal vision statement over the next two to four days. Then, pay close attention to how you begin to drive your life forward and block out toxic distractions.

Processes

Now that you have an updated, written vision in place, it's time to focus on the importance of processes.

A clear written vision guides your life while processes drive your vision. One supports and fuels the other.

When you connect your personal vision and processes to one of your ideas that has the potential to become a personal goal for you, you put your new goal on the path to Goal Accomplishment.

I looked the word "process" up in Webster's English Thesaurus and the following words were listed beside it: *procedure, course, development, progression, method, route, practice, course of action, manner, and means.* Back your personal vision with the necessary action of those words, and you will make your life more powerful, driven, and successful.

To get ideas actualized and accomplished takes processes that will help you extract the necessary information, help you clarify that information, tell you what to do with the clarified information, and guide you to your desired results. We live in a world of processes. Successful people know that and use them; mediocre people ignore the importance of following a process.

Choose to acknowledge and use processes to drive your personal vision, and you too will be prepared and ready to set and begin accomplishing unstoppable goals.

What Are Unstoppable Goals?

"It's not what the vision is—it's what the visionary does."

— Author Unknown

Unstoppable goals are unblocked, never tiring, specific, time managed, organized, planned, purposeful, attainable, bold, and loveable experiences. That's what makes them unstoppable.

1) **U**nblocked.	These are goals that are unblocked by toxic habits, choices, people, or relationships, guided by a clear personal vision, and driven by processes.
2) **N**ever tiring.	These are goals that are resilient and distraction-proof that do not simply fizzle out or lose their appeal. Unstoppable goals are designed to withstand time and distance.
3) **S**pecific.	These are goals that are clear and exact. If you want to be a scientist, what type of scientist? If you want to obtain an undergraduate degree, what college or university will you enroll in? What major are you going to pursue?
4) **T**ime managed.	These are goals that have deadlines and schedules to effectively guide your journey. Ask yourself, by or on what date will you commit to accomplishing your goals?

Write this date on your Unstoppable Goal Worksheet.

5) **O**rganized.

These are goals that have been clearly thought out and organized into long-range, mid-range, and short-range goals. The more organized both you and your goals are, the more you assure success.

6) **P**lanned.

These are goals that have been researched and given a clear course of action about how you will achieve them. It has been frequently said, "Fail to plan and you plan to fail." Unstoppable goals are always planned entirely and put in writing.

7) **P**urposeful.

These are goals that have personal meaning to YOU and no one else. When an unstoppable goal is created because it has great meaning to you, that goal becomes personal and purposeful. When your goals reach this level of design, they are definitely backed with personal passion and a strong commitment towards achieving them.

8) **A**ttainable.

These are goals that are realistic and believable enough to reach, based on your current habits and actions. They are reachable. They are goals you have control over when success or failure depends on what you and you alone can do. It's good to have lofty goals because they make you stretch; however, it is more rewarding to create a string of attainable goals so you can start a string of successes (small wins) that will build your confidence and lead you to your ultimate goals.

9) **B**old.

These are goals that are realistic yet firm and challenging. Always aim high but be practical. Be willing to stretch yourself and be fearless about the goals you plan to pursue when you prepare and position yourself to create and live a significant life. It will take courage for you to live a significant life and leave a lasting legacy.

10) **L**oveable.
These are goals that force you to get involved and take constant steps of action to get you excited and enthusiastic about accomplishing them from beginning to end. When these emotions are present, they cause you to fall in love with your goals.

11) **E**xperiences.
Goal setting and accomplishment is a journey and an enduring experience. If you choose a journey that's not interesting and inspiring or filled with passion and fun, most likely you will not see that journey through to the end. Unstoppable goals are goals that are carefully planned, organized, and set in motion to generate positive, fun, and productive experiences.

When you begin setting personal goals with the above qualities and characteristics, your goals will become meaningful, powerful, and UNSTOPPABLE! So prepare yourself for the next level of real-life results as they pertain to accomplishing unstoppable goals in the future.

Why Set Unstoppable Goals?

"Success is neither magical nor mysterious. Success is the natural consequence of consistently applying the basic fundamentals."

— Jim Rohn

You should set Unstoppable Goals for three good reasons:

1) *Goals can provide motivation, positive results, and fulfillment.* Most significant accomplishments are riddled with obstacles, struggles, and failures. It is estimated that Thomas Edi-

son failed over 1,000 times before he finally discovered a way to make the light bulb work. It is rare for something important to be accomplished successfully on the first try.

If you want to achieve anything significant, it is likely you will struggle and fail many times before you reach your target. High achievers keep picking themselves up after each fall and continue working steadily toward their targets until they reach their goal. Struggle and failure are often a part of the price you must pay for high achievement.

As you can see, any major accomplishment requires motivation and persistence. Where does this motivation come from? It comes from your desire and purpose, from the reasons why you want to accomplish it.

It has been said that a person with a big enough "why" can bear almost any "what" or "how." When your "why" is big enough, you find a way to reach your targets, even if you struggle and have to try many different alternatives to get there.

One of the main reasons why people give up so easily in the face of failure is they lose sight of their "why." Goals can help you remember your "big why" when you need to pick yourself up and continue moving in the face of adversity.

2) **Goals can help you establish priorities.** You will find many forks in the road between where you are now and where you want to be. Instead of just going with the flow and letting the "current" or other people's opinions determine where you end, you have to consciously decide which way to go.

Goals and the missions, visions, and dreams that inspire them provide a natural framework to help you identify and establish your priorities and make the "right" choices based on the long-term view of what is most important to you.

3) ***Goals can provide a roadmap to take you from where you are to where you want to be.*** A well-crafted strategy with an accompanying set of intermediate goals provides a framework to reach far away targets. One of the best ways to deal with large or seemingly "impossible" tasks is to break them up into a series of intermediate, achievable steps and work on each piece. As Brian Tracy says, *"By the yard it's hard, but inch by inch it's a cinch!"*

Your intermediate goals give you valuable feedback: they tell you whether you are making progress or not and can warn you if you're off course.

In almost any endeavor, you will need to make adjustments to your plans and overall strategy as you learn from your mistakes, face and overcome obstacles, and experience unexpected setbacks. As the old adage states, "No plan survives first contact with the battlefield."

You will need to change and adapt your strategy based on the situations and circumstances you experience.

Six Reasons Why Most People Don't Set Goals

> *"Most people are other people, their thoughts are someone else's opinions, their lives a mimicry, their passions a quotation."*
>
> — Oscar Wilde

It is estimated that only 10% of people bother to think about their goals on a regular basis, and only 1% to 3% have clearly written goals. If goal setting is such a powerful tool, why don't more people use it?

1. ***They don't have a good reason to set goals.*** A steady pursuit of your goals can help you get what you want, but they won't help you figure out what that is! You have to be clear about what you really want before you can use goals to help you obtain it.

2. *They don't know about it.* Another reason people don't set goals is they don't realize the power and value of goal setting as a tool for success and high achievement. Maybe they were never introduced to goal setting. After all, it is not something usually taught in our school system. Logically, if you don't know about a tool, you can't use it.

3. *They don't know how to use it.* Many people think they have goals, but what they really have are just wishes. You ask them what their goals are and they say something vague and generic like "I want to be rich," "I want a better job," or "I want to be healthy." Those are good dreams to have, but they are not goals.

Others say they tried goal setting and concluded that it doesn't work. They tell you something like "I tried setting a New Year's resolution a few years back, but it didn't last a week!" What they don't realize is that most New Year's resolutions are vague wishes, not real, specific goals. People almost never write them down or prepare a plan for achieving them.

Imagine someone trying to use a power drill without knowing that you have to plug it in and then claiming power drills don't work! Goal setting is a tool that helps you achieve what you want step by step, but you must know how to use goals properly or you won't obtain or learn anything from them.

4. *Fear.* Fear is a powerful emotion that can help us in many circumstances, but it can also be destructive and paralyzing. Goal setting often requires people to overcome several deep rooted-fears: fear of failure, fear of rejection, and fear of the unknown. Failing to overcome these fears leads to mediocre goals that produce mediocre results, or worse still, no results at all.

5. *They are too busy and disorganized.* A common reason why people don't set goals is they are too busy and disorganized to even consider taking on new challenges. Subconsciously, they reject the notion and find excuses for why they can't set goals. They can't fool themselves into believing they will be able to achieve their goals when they already feel stressed and overwhelmed just trying to cope with their current demands.

One common excuse is, "I'll set goals someday, when things settle down a bit, and I get more time," but those people never actually find the time. You have to make time for goal setting. Once you become an experienced time manager, you can schedule time for goal setting just like you do for your other projects.

6. *They get overwhelmed.* Many people are inspired to try goal setting because they read about it or hear it on the news. They want to be more successful and achieve better results, and they understand goal setting can help them.

A large number of them fall into the common trap that quickly leads them to feeling overwhelmed and frustrated, and they often abandon goal setting before they even begin. The trap I'm talking about is trying to set a large number of goals for every aspect of life. They grab a piece of paper, write the word "Goals" on it, and then struggle to come up with anything to put down. They try to mentally juggle everything they want in all the different areas of life before committing to any one area or goal. Or they identify too many goals for each area of life and quickly realize there is no way they can handle all of them.

Think of goal setting as a muscle. Like any muscle, the more you use it, the stronger it gets, but you have to be gradual about it. What would happen if you walked into the gym and tried to bench-press too much weight? You would strain or tear your chest muscles. To get stronger, muscles need gradual increases in resistance.

Goal setting is the same way; you have to start small and gradually build up. New goal setters should limit themselves to one small "warm-up" goal they can pursue from beginning to end in a matter of a few weeks. After completing their first goal, they can increase the resistance by pursuing one or two larger goals.

Eventually, most people can simultaneously pursue one or two large goals in every important part of their life without feeling overwhelmed. They just have to get there gradually to avoid straining their goal-setting "muscles."

When to Start Setting Unstoppable Goals?

"When you do things from your soul, you feel a river moving in you, a joy."

— Rumi

When should you start setting Unstoppable Goals?

Now!

Start working towards your goals today. Ask yourself, "What can I do today to get one step closer to achieving my goals?"

Be passionate. Striving towards a goal without passion is like a fire that slowly runs out of fuel to burn. Get excited; this will mean you will love what you are doing. Methodically check your behaviors against the dreams you developed as a child. Always share the child within you among your peers. This ignites the Law of Attraction that shapes childhood dreams into the creative forces of the adult.

Focus your attention. Don't get swayed easily by toxic distractions. Put your attention on what you are trying to achieve. Remember, you control the discomforts and difficulties of your goal-pursuit journey.

Seek help. Find the information, skills, and knowledge that you need from other people, books, and audio or video programs. Read inspirational stories of people who have achieved extraordinary goals. Speed up your learning process by emulating what other successful people have done. This will ensure that you save time and get results faster.

We can all learn from the following Unstoppable Goals Achievers who made history by being passionate, focusing their attention, and seeking help when necessary:

Unstoppable Goals Achiever #1: Heading into the 1972 Olympic games in Munich, Mark Spitz was a cocky 22-year-old swimmer who had failed to win a single individual gold medal in the 1968 games in Mexico City (although he did get two team gold medals). Nonetheless, Spitz bragged he would win six gold medals in Germany. He didn't. He won seven--the most anyone has ever won in a single Olympiad--and broke seven world records in the process. Spitz's career total of 11 medals ties him with fellow swimmer Matt Biondi as the two most decorated U.S. Olympic athletes in history.

Unstoppable Goals Achiever #2: Rita Dove, former Poet Laureate of the United States and the first ever African-American to hold the position, responded in 1993 to this question by a reporter:

Reporter's question: "When did you first know what you wanted to do?"

Dove's reply: "It was a gradual thing. It really wasn't until I was in college. When I was in college, I took creative writing courses, and I began to write more and more, and I realized I was scheduling my entire life around my writing courses, and I said, 'Well, maybe you need to figure out if this is what you want to do.' That was the point. I loved to write when I was a child. I wrote, but I always thought it was something you did as a child, then you put away childish things. I thought it was something I would do for fun. I didn't know writers could be real live people, because I never knew any writers. The first inkling that maybe it was a possible thing happened in my last year of high school. I had a high school teacher who took me to a book-signing by an author, John Ciardi, and that's when I saw my first live author."

3) Unstoppable Goals Achiever #3: Barack Obama graduated

from Columbia University with a degree in political science in 1983 and moved to Chicago in 1985 to work as a community organizer in some of city's toughest neighborhoods. In 1991, he graduated magna cum laude from Harvard Law School where he was the first African American editor of the Harvard Law Review. Obama taught for many years at the University of Chicago Law School. He spent seven years in the Illinois State Senate, always putting working families at the top of his agenda. In 2004, he made a successful bid for the U. S. Senate, becoming only the third African-American elected to the U.S. Senate in more than a century.

Remember: you can do anything if you put your mind to it and chart your course with clearly defined, written unstoppable goals.

How Do You Set Goals?

> *"Happiness is when what you think, what you say, and what you do are in harmony."*
>
> — Mahatma Gandhi

STEP 1: Dream a little: What do you want to do, see, accomplish, and experience? Look at a wide range of areas while you're mulling over your life and values, including your career, the arts, tangible achievements, finances, education, and public service.

STEP 2: Ponder more personal goals: How do you want to feel? Do you want to have a family? Create a stronger one? Would you like to change your attitude or how you relate to people? Improve a core relationship? Go back to school? Start a new career? Be truthful.

STEP 3: Review and reprioritize your goals until they reflect the life you want to live.

STEP 4: Set your lifetime goals. Establish goals for 10 years from now, five years, three years, one year, six months, and one month.

Now prioritize them.

STEP 5: Break each goal into subtasks that need to be completed. For example, if a financial goal is to be debt-free in two years, you might decide to establish a budget plan, spend less than you make, and refinance your mortgage to lower your monthly payments. Set a time frame and priority for each subtask.

STEP 6: Use your daily "to-do" list and personal organizer to reach your lifetime goals. Now that you've divided your goals into achievable tasks, incorporate those tasks into your list and personal organizer, and pick them off, one at a time.

STEP 7: Review and reprioritize your goals regularly. This will prepare you for when you suffer inevitable setbacks. You may also find your goals change over time, and you may have to list and keep track of certain objectives as you place them on hold while working on others.

STEP 8: Keep in mind your goals may affect loved ones. You might have to do some work together. If you have children or a spouse or significant other, bring them into the loop and fully consider their opinions. If an objective is to spend more time together as a family, and one solution is for you to work only part-time, ask family members what material goods they'd be willing to surrender to spend more time with you. You might be surprised.

STEP 9: Commit to carrying out your plan of action. You've already journeyed further than most. Stay focused on the process, and reward yourself as you attain each individual unstoppable goal.

Where to Aim Your Unstoppable Goals?

Dr. Benjamin E. Mayes, former Morehouse College President, minister, and author, once stated profoundly, *"The tragedy of life doesn't lie in not reaching your goal. The tragedy lies in having no goal to reach. It isn't a calamity to die with dreams unfilled, but it is a calamity not to dream. It is not a disgrace not to reach the stars, but it is a disgrace to have no stars to reach for. Not failure, but low aim, is a sin."*

So, aim your goals high; however, don't aim unrealistically high. Also, be careful not to set goals too low. Aim for attainable goals that will put you on a higher plane and position in life, a plane that will enable you to 1) give back to your community, and 2) contribute to the betterment of society.

When you accomplish one unstoppable goal, you will begin to create victorious and courageous momentum to move to your next unstoppable goal.

Sample - Setting Unstoppable Goals Worksheet

- One goal I would like to accomplish is _____

    _____.

- It is an important goal because _____

    _____

    _____.

- Here are some specific ways I can reach my goal:

    _____

    _____

    _____

    _____.

- I will know I have achieved my goal when _____

_____

_____.

- The following people can help me achieve my goal: _____

_____

_____.

- What resources or training will I need to accomplish my goal? _____

_____.

- When I reach my goals, I would like to reward myself and celebrate in the following way:

_____

_____

_____.

I, _____, will try my hardest to reach the goal I have set for myself.

Today's date is _____, and I hope to reach my goal by _____

_____

Your Signature

_____

Trusted Support's Signature

Staying on Track

"I'd rather be a failure at something I love than a success at something I hate."

— George Burns

Here are a few additional tips you can consider to accomplish your Unstoppable Goals.

The most important step is to create an Unstoppable Goals Worksheet that will work:

- Break big pieces of the goal into small steps.
- Be sure you've listed all relevant obstacles.
- Write down the tasks needed to overcome those obstacles.
- Assign realistic timeline dates. Adjust them as necessary.
- What is a great goal? Sure, making more money, earning university degrees, getting married, or having kids are great goals. However, asking "that" person on a date, getting a part-time job, or coping with depression are great goals too. Goals don't have to be huge. It's the achievement in itself that matters.
- Read the timeline every day and write down benefits you will earn from doing this.
- Find faith in yourself. A person, song, or quote will not give you lasting motivation. Only you can give yourself lasting motivation because that must come from within.
- Set reminders to keep you on track. Place notes in your personal organizers on specific dates to notify you of specific tasks, times, or reminders in reference to your goals.
- Write and repeatedly read any "notes" you put on your Unstoppable Goals Worksheet. These become helpful and useful tips for keeping you on track.
- Think of your unstoppable goal plan as dynamic; it should be changed as necessary. Add, rename, or delete obstacles and tasks as the situation warrants.

Here are a few defense tips against toxic influences:

- Solicit the encouragement of supportive family members and friends.
- Avoid the discussion of your goals with naysayers and toxic people.
- Don't stop, even if you get sidetracked or discouraged. Just get back on track and keep plodding forward.
- If you feel discouraged, it's probably the result of not meeting your own expectations. Ask yourself, "Was the expectation realistic in the first place?" If not, you have no reason to feel discouraged. Simply create a new goal or task you feel is realistic and keep on going.
- If you pursue a goal but don't succeed, then it's a learning experience for which you are probably a better person with more knowledge and skill than before—all the better equipped for the next attempt.
- The best way to ensure your success is to simply keep on going. The accumulation of many small steps equals significant progress, and the further you go, the easier it gets.

Chapter Conclusion

In this chapter, you learned the importance of having a personal vision and process to guide and drive your unstoppable goals. You learned the difference between an average goal and an Unstoppable Goal. I shared with you reasons why 97% percent of the people in society today don't have goals and gave you nine steps, with a sample Setting Unstoppable Goals Worksheet, to put you in the 3% of society that set clearly defined, written goals. I explained to you when, why, and how to set goals so you can achieve the best unstoppable goals success possible. Unstoppable Goals are written goals with deadlines. Taking the time to plan and set your unstoppable goals can give you a new sense of direction and purpose.

Speaking of purpose and goal accomplishment—by reading this chapter you just fulfilled one more unstoppable goal that now brings you one step closer to learning, practicing, and mastering the Untie the Knots Process. Congratulations, and keep going!

Chapter 11

Step 5: QUIT MARKING TIME— AND MOVE FORWARD

"You have much more power when you are working for the right thing than when you are working for the wrong thing."

— Peace Pilgrim

Finally, the day came to leave for sunny San Diego, California in September 1990, to begin the U.S. Navy's Enlisted Basic Training Program. I was excited, ready, and afraid. I was excited about leaving my community of Cherry Hill and traveling on an airplane for the first time in my life. I was ready physically because I had trained and conditioned myself for military basic training by running and doing sit-ups, push-ups, and lightweight training. I was afraid because I still had some self-doubt and fear about what awaited me once I arrived on the U.S. Navy's Basic Training Base.

I arrived on base around 1:00 a.m. It was dark, cool, and filled with much yelling from instructors who welcomed us once we arrived. There were about 90-100 men in civilian clothes who looked excited, ready, and afraid, just like me: men from all races, walks of life, and ranging in age from 18 to 35. We were taken to a facility and given clear instructions about where we were headed and what our plans were later that day, which officially began bright and early at 5:00 a.m. At 2:30 a.m., we were taken to our barracks and told to select a rack for sleeping.

Bright and early, like we were told, we woke to the sounds of loud, constant banging on steel trash cans as two male instructors demanded that we "GET OUT OF YOUR RACKS! SHOWER! SHAVE! AND GET DRESSED IN 20 MINUTES! MOVE! MOVE! MOVE! NOW!"

I was definitely in the military now. On this day, my military experience began and so did the lessons of the U.S. Navy. I was quickly learning about new cultures. The firm molding and conditioning of a new way of discipline and life were already taking root.

One of the most profound lessons I learned in basic training came on the third day of my 13-week training program. My platoon of 90 men was on the grinder (a large open asphalt area like that of a school yard) with one of our company commanders. We were being taught how to march in ranks as a company.

We were learning how to "mark time." Marking time happens when a company is marching along and the command MARK TIME, MARCH is given as either foot strikes the ground. The company takes one more 24-inch step with the right (or left) foot. Then the company brings the trailing foot to a position so both heels are in line. Alternately raising and lowering each foot continues the cadence. The balls of the feet are raised four inches above the ground. Normal arm swing is maintained. And marching in place begins.

To resume marching, the command FORWARD, MARCH is given as the heel of the left foot strikes the ground. The company takes one more step in place and then steps off in a full 24-inch step with the left foot.

A halt could also be ordered while "marking time" if the company commander orders COMPANY HALT. Then the company raises and lowers first the left foot and then the right. Then a quick time halt is executed. Marching stops completely, and the company is now at a stand still and in the full standing at-attention-position while still in ranks.

We also learned on that day that we would mark time for one of three reasons:

1) To learn how to practice and improve our marching skills;

2) To allow another company to go by, and

3) To allow a vehicle or VIP sedan to go by.

Our company was on the grinder marching along when the company commander ordered the company to MARK TIME, MARCH. We all started marking time (marching in place). Then I stopped, without any command or instruction, and walked out of ranks while the other 89 recruits continued marking time.

Before I explained my strange action, I have to explain why I joined the Navy: 1) to get away from my mother because she was constantly telling me what to do; 2) to create and find better opportunities for my daughter and me; and 3) to receive the much needed discipline and direction I needed in my life.

At the moment when I walked out of rank, I was made aware of two guarantees: 1) yes, I escaped my mother; however, I now inherited two big, muscular and hairy mothers with tattoos of Navy anchors on each arm; and 2) I would no longer need to seek or ask for discipline and structure in my life.

When my company commander noticed me walk out of ranks, he blew a gasket! The company was still marking time when he dashed to me and aggressively stood eyeball-to-eyeball in front of me like a raging bull. Then he yelled at and berated me like no one had ever done before. His exact words were, "RECRUIT, WHY ARE YOU OUT OF MY RANKS! DID I TELL YOU TO STOP? DID I TELL YOU TO QUIT? ARE YOU STUPID? ARE YOU MISSING YOUR MOMMY ALREADY? PLEASE, TELL ME YOU'RE CRAZY! BECAUSE I BET YOU, RIGHT HERE AND RIGHT NOW, I'M GOING TO OUT DO YOU! SO, WHAT'S YOUR MALFUNCTION, NUT?"

I was literally shaking and terrified at this point. While standing at-attention with my knees knocking, I squeaked in a muffling whisper, "Sir, I didn't join the Navy for this…to mark time."

My company commander barked back at me, "WELL, EXCUSE ME RECRUIT. WHY DID YOU LEAVE YOUR PLUSH LIFE-STYLE TO COME AGGRAVATE ME?!"

Still terrified and scared like never before, I squeaked another reply, "Sir, my recruiter told me when I come into the Navy all I would experience is palm trees, beaches, and women."

My company commander barked back at me once again, "WHAT?! WHAT DID YOU SAY RECUIT?!"

I once again squeaked my nervous reply, "Sir, my recruiter told me that when I come into the Navy all I would experience is palm trees, beaches, and women."

My company commander barked firmly back with clarity and rage, "RECRUIT, IF YOU DON'T GET BACK IN MY RANKS WITHIN TWO SECONDS, I'M GOING TO UNLEASH A WORLD OF HURT ON YOU TO A POINT WHERE YOU WON'T KNOW IF YOU'RE COMING OR GOING! YOU'VE GOT A HALF A SECOND TO MOVE!"

At that point, I was motivated. I broke a speed record that day. I was back in the company's ranks before that half-second was up. The company was still marking time, so I joined them. Moments later, the company commander ordered the company to FOR-WARD, MARCH. We stepped off on our left foot and continued with our marching drill lessons for that day.

Later that evening, after we returned to the barracks from chow (dinner), our company commander ordered the entire compa-ny into the barracks learning area. This was an area where we would come each night during our 13 weeks of training for ad-ditional teaching and learning from our company commander or selected company leaders.

Our company commander began by saying, "What happened between Recruit Howard and I today will never happen again!"

He continued by saying, "Let me explain something to you men: The skills I will teach you over the next 13 weeks are skills you can use not only to get you through basic training and when you're out in the fleet, but you'll be able to use them repeatedly to drive and empower your life. First, let me explain to you what's going on with people who aren't in the military and don't learn what you all learned today. Every morning a large majority of civilians in the world wake up and begin marking time. They wake up stressed out, unfocused, and unmotivated for life. They often hit the snooze alarm three to ten times before they frantically get up out of their bed when they realize that they are running late. They get the children ready for school, get themselves ready for work, and then head to a job they wish they could stay away from. After completing their 9 to 5 responsibilities, they come home stressed out and frustrated from work, prepare dinner, check the kids' homework, do a task or two around the house, get the kids ready for and in bed, then they prepare for bed and go to sleep. Then the alarm clock goes off the next morning, and they are still trapped and locked into marking time. Say hello to a life with no change, no fun, and no gratifying productivity."

"The one thing that you're going to learn here is how to mark time—how to give yourself the command to MOVE, FORWARD again and again. Whenever we mark time from here on out, know that you will always hear sooner or later the command FORWARD, MARCH. I want you to hear, understand, and value what I'm saying. I want you to not only learn the power behind this command from a marching perspective. I want you to learn and use this command to empower and drive you internally throughout the rest of your life. I will teach you how to never get stuck or mark time unproductively for the rest of your life."

"Ladies and gentleman, there is great value and power in learning how to give yourself the internal command to QUIT MARKING TIME—AND MOVE FORWARD!"

The Toxic Effects of Marking Time

"In ourselves are triumph and defeat."
— Henry Wadsworth Longfellow

There is little value and benefit to marking time. However, I will say there are times in life when it's best that we pause to look around, assess, and repair problems in our lives. Notice that I used the word "pause" and not "stop." When you literally stop, that's when challenges and problems become toxic because while marking time in a stop position you create dead space that invites discouragement, complacency, and doubt. In a pause position, your intentions are set for you to begin moving forward promptly once you've solved your problem.

Here is a quick list of potential results when a person unproductively marks time:

- ☹ You deny that a problem exists and that action needs to be taken.
- ☹ Your toxic habits begin to "cloud" your thinking.
- ☹ Your inability to solve your own problems increases.
- ☹ You lose support from others who have been assisting you in working on your problems.
- ☹ Your physical health declines.
- ☹ Your emotional health declines.
- ☹ You are ignored by others as you wallow in self-pity and chronic excuse-making.
- ☹ You feel stuck and unmotivated to move.
- ☹ You repel others with your lack of direction.

Growth is compromised by marking time and improved by learning and practicing how to give yourself and your life the command to MOVE, FORWARD.

What Causes People to Begin Marking Time?

"We may encounter many defeats, but we must not be defeated."

— Maya Angelou

What causes people to mark time? Why do people often react differently when challenging situations arise? The answer has to do with human emotions (mainly, FEAR = False Emotions Acting Recklessly). The better we understand our emotions, the more equipped we are to handle challenging circumstances that arise.

People who begin to mark time in toxic ways do so for the following reasons:

1. **Fear.** Some people get into their personal rhythm, and their fear to change and grow paralyzes them. Paralysis can also be due to the fear of failure, success, and not having all the details about what's ahead.

2. **Need for approval.** Some people will not move unless they gain approval from others about their choices. If they do not receive approval, they will not move.

3. **Lack of belief in self and others.** When people do not believe in their abilities or talents, they find it hard to trust and believe others who may see and believe in their potential.

4. **Desire to avoid conflict.** Some people choose not to move forward because they do not want to disrupt the status quo at work or home. So, they choose to "just continue with the way things are."

5. **Unwillingness to face problems honestly.** Some people discover and know they have to first deal with problems staring them in their face, and they elect to ignore them and pretend they don't exist. These individuals are marking time because they're hiding from themselves.

6. **Playing it safe.** Some people feel they must have steady security in their life. This causes them to not take risks as they opt to play it safe.

7. **A belief that life should always be fair.** Some people start marking time because of a few bad experiences in life. They believe that life should always be fair, and since they feel it currently isn't, they choose to no longer move forward.

8. **Avoiding change.** Some people start marking time because they're avoiding change. They are comfortable with their complacency and current routine in life and feel there is no need to change.

9. **Slow progress.** Some people experience longer periods of stagnation in life than others, so they decide to start marking time because they are not experiencing any significant gains.

10. **Inability to take personal responsibility.** Some people haven't been taught or coached how to take full responsibility of their life. Because of this lack of education or access to important information, they are unable to guide and empower their lives with positive forward motion.

11. **Over dependence on others.** Some people are pacified excessively. When they get around people who don't over protect and pacify them, they feel lost and begin marking time because nobody is willing to constantly hold their hand as they proceed.

12. **A chronic "Yes, but" attitude.** Some people stop themselves with chronic excuses that normally start with "Yes, but." When these excuses are articulated, they block progress and positive growth because your "but" is literally in the way.

13. **Playing the blame game.** Some people blame others for their complacency and marking time. They blame others mainly because they feel that others should help them solve problems they created themselves. So, the problem still exists and is becoming more toxic as time passes; still, this person has elected to mark time.

14. **Holding onto self-destructive, self-defeating toxic knots.** Some people are marking time due to their self-destructive or self-defeating behavior. Every time they attempt to take a single step forward, their toxic habits knock them two steps back. These individuals will not get ahead until they "Get Real" with themselves by acknowledging and learning to remove their self-sabotaging habits.

Now, congratulate yourself. Reading this chapter is another step toward assuring you won't surrender to the toxic effects and causes of marking time. Many people do not quit marking time because they get comfortable and locked into their own little rhythms. They think they will pick up and start moving forward again someday. Unfortunately, that someday never comes.

You are not made for marking time. You are significant and of the kind that is "RARELY denied". Do whatever it takes to learn, practice, and master the principles that will have you not marking time but moving forwardly continuously.

Five Power Strategies to Get You Moving and Marching Forward

"This is no time for ease and comfort. It is the time to dare and endure."

— Winston Churchill

Here are five power strategies to get you moving and marching forward in your life:

1) **Change your thoughts.** Your thoughts affect your behavior. By redefining the meaning of your emotions and experiences, you will generate a different attitude. Get inspired with powerful long-range goals. Powerful goals keep you inspired. You can't feel stuck or complacent when you are motivated to move your life continuously forward.

2) **Fire up your passion.** Write down ten activities you're good at. Then write down five activities from that same list that interest you most. Now, rank those five based on which ones will add the most meaning to your life right now if you started pursuing and doing them. Choose the activity that you ranked number one, and visualize where your life could go if you began engaging in this activity. Using your imagination to fire up your passion can create a powerful mental energy that will reconnect you to your desire to continuously move forward to fulfilling your goals and dreams.

3) **Put in motion your curiosity to assess what's happening inside and around you.** If your routine habits and activities have you feeling life is boring, try to look at and do them differently. Or try to create excitement for yourself with other options and possibilities that you listed on your "Fire Up Your Passion" list above.

4) **Create your own Quit Marking Time Power Word or Power Phrase that will constantly and effectively command you to move.** For example: Your power word could be "MOVE!," "GO!," or "Execute!" Your power phrase could

be "Quit Marking Time," "It's Time to MOVE!," "Let's Go, I've Been Here Too Long!," or "I've Been Delayed, But NOT Denied!" When you start using Quit Marking Time Personal Power Words or Phrases for all situations where you feel you've been at a certain point for too long, you realize it will become easier and easier to move. Remember, practice doesn't make things perfect. Practice makes improvements.

5) *Move.* Movement is a choice. Take control of your life. You control your destiny. When you find yourself at a point in your life where you know you have and want to move, move forward. Even if that movement just gets you out and about again so you can assess your life from the inside out. You will never be able to effectively assess, evaluate, or move your life while standing still. So MOVE!

We all get stuck and face challenges in our lives that trap us in periods of delay. From this point forward, when this happens to you, I want you to acknowledge that this has happened, assess it, review and revise your plan, and give yourself the command to MOVE, FORWARD.

Marching YOU Continuously onto Victory

"No matter how often you are defeated, you were born to victory."

— Ralph Waldo Emerson

The Untie the Knots Process does not make any claims that you will never again experience failure or defeat. It teaches you a process that will allow you to endure moments of failure, defeat, or challenge yet bounce back resiliently, expecting to learn from what happened, grow from what happened, and continue forward toward your ultimate victory of significant living.

To march yourself continuously forward to experiencing one victory after another with the Untie the Knots Process, you must start by making a commitment with yourself. A commitment to do whatever it takes to "untie the knots" that currently have you marking time. This positive action will require your unblocked honesty, and may also require help from others along the way.

Another requirement will be to constantly work on polishing your act. When I was in basic training, my company won every marching and inspection award a developing company could win. By the time our company graduated from the U.S. Navy Basic Training Program, we were the number one company within our division. Why? We worked constantly on polishing our act, and making our best even better.

We polished our act by using our time wisely. We focused on the tasks we had to complete first to make sure we would be sharp and ready for any inspection. Because of our high honors and accomplishments, we earned and created more free time to celebrate and have fun.

We polished our act by learning to make the right choices amidst many challenges. There were several times within ourselves when we wanted to quit, give up, and go home. And some of the guys in our company did just that. The recruits who remained with the company grew stronger emotionally and more confident in effectively blocking out our negative self-talk and the beliefs of the Doubt Patrol who didn't believe in our ability. As each day and week passed, we were able to accomplish several victories by reversing the negative, discouraging effects of our critics.

We polished our act by making it a constant habit to prepare today for tomorrow. In the civilian world, this means preparing your clothes, projects, presentations, to-do lists, homework, or anything you know you will need for tomorrow. It has been said, "The world belongs to those who show up prepared and expecting to succeed." How are you currently showing up for tomorrow? Are you prepared and expecting to succeed? Or are you constantly running late and leaving things behind?

Anyone who has experienced victory in any area or channel in life knows that discipline is key. It doesn't matter if you're in the military, on a sports team, in Corporate America, a part of a community effort, or in school inspiring or helping yourself to change and grow. If you want to be and want to experience constant victory, learn the discipline of your craft and victory will find you.

Marching you on to continuous victory is a matter of possessing staying power and a matter of choice. Choose to stay the course! Eliminate the toxic distractions! And from this point forward choose to command, guide, and drive your life continuously forward to your awaiting victories.

Chapter Conclusion

In this chapter, I shared with you one of my most powerful life stories and lessons that helped place me on the path I am on today. It was an experience filled with honesty and humility, and it is a lesson that has already inspired thousands to Quit Marking Time—and Move Forward. I explained to you the toxic causes and effects of choosing to needlessly mark time. I shared with you five power strategies to constantly have you marching and moving <u>forward</u> in life. You now know that marking time in life is a choice and that you have the power to choose and command yourself to MOVE, FORWARD. There is nothing sweeter than the taste of victory after struggle, change, growth, and commitment. Wouldn't you agree?

Here's a command for you to now learn and enjoy—FORWARD, MARCH.

Chapter 12

Step 6: DEFEATING TOXIC HABITS, CHOICES, PEOPLE, AND RELATIONSHIPS

"Your net worth to the world is usually determined by what remains after your bad habits are subtracted from your good ones."

— Benjamin Franklin

Some of you may have been reading enthusiastically to make it to this chapter, and some may have actually started reading this chapter first. Why? Because the title of this chapter carries a close connection to the subtitle of this guide: *A Practical Guide to Freeing Yourself From Toxic Habits, Choices, People, and Relationships.* You may also have an immediate need to find a sound practical strategy to guide you through untying a toxic knot in a key area of your life that has become out of control. However you arrived at this chapter, I want you to know that all 18 chapters of this guide were written to have equal importance in the Untie the Knots Process.

Before you begin to immerse yourself in the substance, guidance, and potential life-changing value of this chapter, allow me to inform you of two important points:

1. What my ultimate goal is for this chapter.

My ultimate goal for this chapter is: 1) to increase your awareness as it pertains to the effects toxic knots have on the quality of your life; and 2) to provide you with real-life scenarios and guidance that will help you better identify, control, and defeat the toxic habits, choices, people, and relationships that are hindering you and suffocating your life.

2. Where you can find more "detailed" information, strategies, and resources to assist you in slowing, controlling, blocking, and defeating toxic habits, choices, people, and relationships.

As stated in Chapter 7, Step 1: Identifying and Untying Your Knots, there are Appendices in the back of this guide that share the following information:

i.   Appendix A is a list of organizations and resources that you may call for additional professional help and guidance on your Untie the Knots journey to a life of better health, balance, harmony, significance, potential, and prosperity.

ii.   Appendix B is a list of suggested books to read for continual learning, growth, and development.

iii. Appendix C is your link to a practical, comprehensive, step-by step "special guide" that will help you break free of the 50 Most Common Toxic Knots.

Now that I have made you aware of my ultimate goals for this chapter and informed you about where to find additional information, strategies, and resources, let's move ahead on your journey to continuous Untie the Knots success.

It's time to learn how to defeat Toxic Habits, Choices, People, and Relationships.

While serving ten years in the U.S. Navy on full-time active duty, I changed, grew, and obtained the necessary discipline I needed to improve and empower my life. The Navy taught me many lessons; it taught me responsibility, respect, and restraint. It also taught me how to set and accomplish goals. The Navy's rigid demand for discipline taught me in a ten-year span how to defeat Toxic Habits, Choices, People, and Relationships.

The many lessons I learned, practiced, and mastered while in the U.S. Navy turned my otherwise out of control life around, directing me toward a more desirable and prosperous future.

As I developed and matured in the Navy, I realized two powerful facts from my journey: 1) toxic choices and habits are both internally driven. Our toxic choices eventually become our toxic habits over time if they remain unattended to or untreated; and 2) toxic people and relationships are both externally driven. The toxic effects and emotions we experience in this case come from an outside contributor half the time. The remaining half means that we are still responsible and accountable for what we allow to happen to and exist in our lives. Remember, people can only treat, and continue to treat you, the way you allow them to treat you.

Let's first look at defeating Toxic Habits and Choices.

Defeating Toxic Habits and Choices

"Each year one vicious habit discarded, in time, might make the worst of us good."

— Benjamin Franklin

What is a Toxic Habit?

A **"toxic habit"** is a self-destructive behavior where the power of self-control and reason are diffused by a person's chaotic and reckless emotions; if this negative behavior continues, the person's mental and physical health will decline, opening them to chronic disease, mediocrity, helplessness, and failure.

What is a Toxic Choice?

A **"toxic choice"** is a negative decision that becomes a threat or hazard to one's life, character, self-esteem, self-image, self-respect, health, hopes, goals, potential, and dreams.

Based on the two definitions above, toxic habits and toxic choices chip away at the life you could be living right now. They stifle your potential to create and live a significant life. They hold you back from enjoying rewarding personal relationships. And they prevent you from looking and feeling GREAT!

Can you put a price on the opportunities and potential your toxic habits and choices are holding you back from?

Of course not! Because your goals and dreams are priceless!

Life is NOT a dress rehearsal—it's a live show! You owe it to yourself to offer your best possible performance. And to do this, you need to "identify and untie the knots that tie up your life."

You must defeat your toxic habits and choices. Period.

Identify them...control them...defeat them...and manage your life so you have complete control over your future and well-being forever!

Short List of Toxic Habits and Toxic Choices

> *"What's going on in the inside shows on the outside."*
>
> — Earl Nightingale

The table on the next page is a short list showing how Toxic Choices can lead to specific Toxic Habits.

Toxic Choices	Toxic Habits
Negative mental attitude	Fear
Poor time management	Procrastination
Negative self-talk	Excuse making
Stress eating or over eating	Poor health
Trying to be like others, materialism, compulsive shopping, or poor budgeting	Financial problems
Excessive use of drugs, tobacco, the Internet, gambling, sex, nicotine, sugar, shopping, video games, etc.	Addiction
Not willing to accept help	Misery, hopelessness
Lying	Denial
Worrying	Stress
Negative self-respect	Low self-esteem, poor self-image
Listening to toxic people	Self-Doubt
Not letting go of the past	Unforgiving
Complacency	Mediocrity
No personal vision or written goals	Lack of direction
Being a workaholic	Neglecting your family

Buddha was correct when saying, "All that we are is the result of what we have thought. The mind is everything. What we think, we become."

What are your thoughts and choices today? What were they yesterday? Last week? Last month?

Toxic Habits and Choices are impulses, so if you don't control them, you are bound to repeat them.

The Untie the Knots Process will assist you in identifying, controlling, managing, defeating, and no longer repeating your Toxic Habits and Choices.

You Must Change the Way You Think Before You Can Change the Way You Act

"You are today where your thoughts have brought you; you will be tomorrow where your thoughts take you."

— James Allen

A teacher takes a bit of thread and wraps it one time around a student's wrists.

He tells the class, "This string represents the power of doing something one time. Can you break the string?"

The student easily breaks the thread with a small flick of his wrists. The teacher then wraps the string around the student's wrists many times and repeats the challenge to break it.

Despite repeated efforts, the thread is too strong to break.

His teacher says, "Now you see the power of repeated actions...habits. It takes more than mere will power and personal strength to break it. It takes a change in the way you think about the problem."

Toxic habits and choices prevent you from reaching your potential. They are self-inflicted hazards that drain you of motivation, time, potential, and money. And they hold you back from living the great life you can achieve.

The apparent satisfaction you gain from your toxic habits and choices is the reason you repeat them. Whether real or imaginary, it is the value you place on satisfaction that determines how successful you will be in defeating your toxic habits and choices. This then leaves you with a question that you must answer before you move further with this topic: "Are you prepared to pay the price?" You need to be prepared to not only give up the habit, but also the short-term "satisfaction" it brings. Remember, this requires you to change the way you think.

Here are some simple examples of invalid thoughts that some people use to justify their toxic choices:

1) <u>Complacency</u> - "It keeps me safe and protected in my own little world."
2) <u>Alcohol</u> - "It helps me to relax and unwind."
3) <u>Coffee</u> - "It wakes me up."
4) <u>Unforgiving</u> - "It gives me control."
5) <u>Compulsive shopping</u> - "It helps me take my mind off my troubles."

Such toxic choices cover up the damaging effects toxic habits may be having behind the scenes. In cigarette smoking, for example, the more immediate damage is to the lungs and that damage can eventually manifest into lung cancer.

If your will does not support freeing yourself from toxic habits and choices, then it means you are not prepared to do whatever it takes to break the habit or choice. I encourage you to take a hard look at your life and find the value and potential you possess deep within.

Are you still with me? Great. That tells me something about you. It tells me you are sincere. That you believe you have an urgent need to defeat your toxic habits and choices once and for all. It tells me that in spite of any "on the surface satisfaction" these habits may currently generate, you can see beyond that to the permanent damage they could cause if left unaddressed.

You see the value in changing the way you think, so you can change the way you act. You envision and can almost touch the kind of lifestyle you really want, the kind of person you really want to be.

Okay. Let's do it. Let's make that change. You've come with me so far, now let's pick up the plan and run with it.

Replacing Your Toxic Habits and Choices with a Positive Habit and Choice

"Never underestimate the power of dreams and the influence of the human spirit. The potential for greatness lives within each of us."

— Wilma Rudolph

Below are some strategies to help you stop, block, and slow down your Toxic Choices.

Potential Toxic Choice	A Positive Action to Stop, Block, or Slow Down Your Toxic Choice
Negative mental attitude	Choose a positive mental attitude.
Poor time management	Write out every hour of the day on a piece of paper starting with the hour you wake up. Then write in your tasks and commitments for that day. This will allow you to see your entire day at-a-glance.
Negative self-talk	Focus on solutions. Assume most problems have solutions, and ask, "How can I successfully get over this situation?"
Stress eating or over eating	Choose to listen to soothing music or read an interesting book when you find yourself wanting to constantly eat.

Potential Toxic Choice	A Positive Action to Stop, Block, or Slow Down Your Toxic Choice
Trying to be like others, materialism, compulsive shopping, or poor budgeting	Practice buying only the items you need versus the items you want.
Excessive use of drugs, tobacco, the Internet, gambling, sex, nicotine, sugar, shopping, video games, etc.	Seek professional help and family support.
Not willing to accept help	Seek and allow three people to help you over next three months.
Lying	Don't over-promise. Only promise what you can realistically do.
Worrying	Focus on what you can control in your life.
Negative self-respect	Keep your language clean and respectable. Think highly of yourself.
Listening to toxic people	Avoid people who don't have your best interests at heart.
Not letting go of the past	Accept and forgive yourself for past experiences.
Complacency	Make it a goal to do something outside your comfort zone at least once a week.
No personal vision or written goals	Define and write out a list of five personal goals with deadlines that you will pursue and accomplish within the next six months.
Being a workaholic	Refuse to bring work home or to stay at work after a full day. Do this two days each week. Dedicate and spend this freed up time with your family.

Below are a few strategies to replace Toxic Habits with positive actions.

Current Toxic Habit	A Positive Action to Replace It
Living in Fear	Only allow positive thoughts into your mind.
Procrastination	Get started whether you "feel" like it or not.
Excuse making	Restrict yourself to the goals you can accomplish.
Poor health	Exercise and eat healthy.
Financial problems	Pursue financial education and budgeting.
Addiction	Seek professional help and coaching.
Misery, hopelessness	Spend time with family and friends, have them make a list of your best qualities, and share that list with you.
Denial	Recognize when you are hiding behind a "safe" mask when discussing your problems, and remove it.
Stress	Organize and simplify your life.
Low self-esteem, poor self-image	Use positive visualization exercises.
Self-Doubt	Practice positive affirmation.
Unforgiving	Forgive yourself and others, and move on.
Mediocrity	Take new risks to move outside your comfort zone.
Lack of direction	Create a written personal vision.
Neglecting your family	Balance your time and schedule.

Toxic habits and choices are meant to be broken. Do not think in any way that your toxic habits and choices are permanent. Start working today, right now, by finding and replacing your toxic habits and choices with positive actions and strategies that will free your life and move it continuously forward.

12-Step Process to Defeat Toxic Habits and Choices

"Self conquest is the greatest of victories."

— Plato

As a child, I was angry and bitter at life because I had an absentee father and I spent time in foster care away from my biological mother. This anger stayed bottled up inside me and would erupt like a raging volcano whenever I got angry. I carried this uncontrollable toxic choice and habit with me until I was 25-years-old. My toxic choice to become angry at the drop of a hat later evolved into these two more toxic habits: self-destruction and self-sabotage.

This is how toxic habits and choices can have far-reaching effects. My toxic habit almost cost me my life when I was 24-years-old. I was driving from Baltimore, Maryland to Norfolk, Virginia to make it back to the Norfolk Navy Base to return to my ship for morning muster. It was 3:30 a.m., and I was driving 50 miles per hour, when out of nowhere, a car cut me off. I almost lost control. Rage began to build inside me, and while crazily honking my horn I began to chase behind the car that cut me off. I was upset and I wanted "cut off" revenge. I sped up to get in front of the car to cut the driver off. Suddenly, out of the woods two deer darted onto the road about 50 yards up the road. I was driving at that moment 80 miles an hour and I had to stop immediately. I frantically slammed on the brakes! The car swerved, and I lost control. I did not hit the deer, but I ended up in a ditch with a blown front passenger side tire. The entire time I was changing my blown tire, I said to myself, "This foolish and destructive behavior has to STOP!" For over 20 years, my anger and unforgiving spirit had trapped me in the prison of my toxic habits and choices. This way of toxic living had to stop! It wasn't productive, it wasn't rewarding, and it always created more problems for me as time went on. I had to get my life back on track, and I did.

How many toxic habits and choices have you allowed to damage or spoil your life? How many dreams have you said "No" to because of a toxic habit or choice? How much of life are you now missing because of a toxic habit or choice? How can you get your life back?

You can get your life back with a well-planned process and some persistence. It won't be easy to defeat your toxic habits and choices; however, your desired result in the end makes your objective that much more worthwhile. You too will be living and enjoying a life with fewer knots and greater potential and significance. I now am.

The following 12-step process will help you defeat your Toxic Habits and Choices once and for all.

1. **Recognize your toxic habit or choice is not acceptable.** One of the most powerful discoveries we can have in life is to assess ourselves and determine if something is good or bad for us. I bet you're reading this book because you feel the need to overcome a toxic habit or choice in life right now. Write down in your journal right now your current list of toxic habits and choices.

2. **Slow down the action.** Now that you have your list of current toxic habits and choices, write beside or underneath each one at least two positive actions you can use to slow down the toxic habit or choice so you can begin to control it.

3. **Stop or block the unwanted action so it can be edited and modified.** Now that you have two positive actions about how to slow down the action of your toxic habits

or choices, write down two positive ways you can stop or block the action. (If you need help finding positive strategies about how to slow down and block the unwanted action of your toxic habits and choices, turn to Appendix C in the back of this book).

4. **Find an opposite but acceptable positive habit.** Once you have found a reliable strategy that will stop and block the unwanted action of your toxic habit or choice, replace it with an opposite but acceptable positive habit or choice.

5. **Devise a plan of action to put in its place.** Once your new acceptable habit or choice is in place, create a written plan for how you will practice, maintain, and grow while using your new positive habit or choice.

6. **Think baby steps.** Your toxic habits and choices did not form overnight; do not expect them to go away overnight. Commit, persist, struggle, adapt, adjust, and persevere. Focus on one step and day at a time. Baby steps.

7. **Practice the new action.** Remember, practice makes improvements, not perfect. We do not want to create an additional toxic habit, that of perfectionism. Practice! Practice! Practice! For improvements.

8. **Control the acceptable habit.** Sometimes, our new positive acceptable habits and choices have the potential to become compulsive and out-of-control. Learn to control and manage your acceptable habits and choices so you never lose control.

9. **Reward yourself.** When you realize you have successfully defeated and replaced a toxic habit and choice with a positive habit and choice, reward yourself. Go out to a movie, treat yourself to a nice dinner, hang out with friends, or buy yourself something special.

10. **Set an "Achieve by Date."** When you set out to defeat a toxic habit or choice, set a written date for yourself for when you will defeat and replace it with a positive habit or choice. It is good to have a deadline in place because it helps you stay focused and committed to the process.

11. **Watch for signals.** Once you have your new positive habit and choice in place, watch for the signals. Now that you are aware of this process, you can perform "Re-Flash Watch." When you see characteristics of the old toxic habit or choice reappearing, you can recognize it for what it is because you can identify it and quickly stomp it out. Be on the lookout and always stay alert and attentive, but not to the point of obsession.

12. **After three honest and determined attempts, seek professional help and the caring support from family and friends.** Remember, we win in life with people, and you will mostly need the assistance and encouragement of at least one extra caring person to help you stay committed and focused on your Untie the Knots journey.

When toxic storms in your life come, you may be tempted to surrender. However, will power and process are two of the greatest tools one can use to destroy toxic habits and choices.

What Is Required of YOU for Continuous Defeat of Your Toxic Habits and Choices?

"Faith is not something to grasp; it's a state to grow into."

— Mahatma Gandhi

To confront and defeat anyone or anything in life takes confidence and trust in one's ability and plan; it takes faith. It has been said, "A strong level of faith and belief can move mountains."

When people add committed unshakable FAITH to a process, they have:

Focus.	A vision that guides them and keeps out unwanted and unnecessary distractions.
Attitude.	A positive life perspective that empowers them to stay on course and stay motivated.
Imagination.	A personal belief that allows them to see the impossible as possible.
Toughness.	A thick interior and exterior that significantly increases their threshold for pain.
Heart.	A courageous spirit that prevents them from surrendering to failure, self-doubt, struggle, or critics.

If you strive to maintain a higher level of FAITH through this process, I am sure you will soon find yourself living a happier, healthier, more rewarding and significant life. Remember, defeating toxic habits and choices requires you to change the way you think before you change the way you act.

Defeating Toxic People and Relationships

"No matter what, there are makers, takers, and fakers."

— Robert Heinlein

What is a Relationship?

Dictionary.com defines "relationship" as "an emotional or other connection between people: *the relationship between teachers and students."*

What is a Toxic Person?

A **"toxic person"** is an individual who possesses negative energy and projects negative, destructive emotions onto others.

What is a Toxic Relationship?

A **"toxic relationship"** is a relationship where the emotions and unpleasant conditions of that relationship have escalated to continuous, undesirable situations.

No matter where we go in life, we are always forming relationships: with family, friends, teachers, co-workers, neighbors, service organizations, doctors, hotel managers, flight attendants, or retail store employees. It's a known fact that we cannot avoid interacting with others. We need to improve how we build healthy relationships, relationships that can enrich and advance our life forward.

Toxic people and relationships slow down and diminish your quality of life. They can suffocate your ability to improve your health, hopes, and happiness. And if you allow them to exist in your life for too long—they can and will prevent you from living your dreams.

Toxic people and relationships threaten, weaken, and destroy self-esteem, character, and mental and physical health. Life is too short and too valuable to allow toxic people and toxic relationships to run down and ruin hopes, goals, and dreams. You owe it to yourself to only allow positive people and relationships to have space in your life. And to do this, you need to "identify and untie the knots that tie up your life."

You MUST defeat toxic people and relationships. Period.

Identify them...control them...defeat them...and manage your life in a way that does not give toxic people or relationships a front row seat in your life.

Short List of Toxic People and Relationships

"The quality of your life is the quality of your relationships."

— Anthony Robbins

The table below is a short list explaining how Toxic People can lead to Toxic Relationships.

Toxic People can lead to	Toxic Relationships
A cousin who passes negative judgment on you.	Toxic Family Relationship
A parent who reminds you in a negative way of who you used to be.	Toxic Parent Relationship
A brother or sister who makes it his or her purpose to stop or derail you due to envy and jealousy of you.	Toxic Sibling Relationship
A spouse or significant other who nags or attacks you continuously because you're choosing to pursue your dreams and not play it safe.	Toxic Spouse or Significant Other Relationship
A friend who talks and pressures you into doing negative and toxic activities.	Toxic Friend Relationship
A co-worker, supervisor, manager, or boss who stresses you out by making your time at work a living hell.	Toxic Work Relationship
A teacher, professor, or administrator who makes your hill a steeper hill to climb than for other students because of bias he or she may have with you or people of your culture.	Toxic School Relationship
A neighbor, church member, or community association member who continuously turns others against you because of personal reasons.	Toxic Community Relationship
A person who is working at an organization where you need help (Motor Vehicle Administration, state office building, hospital, or doctor's office) who decides to make you jump through hoops to get the service you need because he or she is having a bad day.	Toxic Service Organization Relationship
A waiter, waitress, or manager who treats you and others in your party in a negative way because of your race.	Toxic Restaurant Relationship

Toxic People can lead to	Toxic Relationships
A cashier, store employee, or manager who refuses to listen to or help you because his or her solution to your challenge is the only solution possible.	Toxic Retail Store Relationship
A front desk, maid, or hotel manager who does not fulfill your requests based on who they see asking for the request.	Toxic Hotel Relationship
A registration agent, ticket agent, or stewardess who makes your travel experience a bad experience because you had a disagreement with one another.	Toxic Airline Travel Relationship
A colleague, vendor, client, or business partner who does not pay you the money he or she owes you due to poor money management habits.	Toxic Business Relationship

It was Oprah Winfrey who once said, *"Never give up your power to another person."*

When you surrender your power and emotions to a toxic person or relationship, you have given up your power, and this course renders you powerless. It means you're not living life on your terms. It's time for you to clean house and regain control.

Two Reasons Why Most People Are Affected by Toxic People and Relationships

1) Clutter, Confusion, and Unwanted Stress

When your life is filled with clutter, confusion, and unwanted stress, it becomes a primary target for toxic people, relationships, situations, choices, and habits.

If you look at your life right now and all you see is clutter, I assure you that you're lacking direction and focus. When you cannot think effectively, toxic people and relationships slip in and begin their attack on your life.

If you look at your life right now and all you see is confusion and a whirlwind of negative problems and distractions, I assure you that you've been stringing together a long line of sleepless and worrisome nights. When you and your body constantly feel tired and drained, toxic people and relationships push you in whatever direction they choose. Why? Your level of awareness and control are not at their peak.

If you look at your life right now and all you see is unwanted and uninvited stress, financial debt, failing relationships, poor evaluations at work, and declining health, I assure you that you're not getting the desired results you truly want from life. When the hands of unwanted stress are strangling you continuously, you begin to feel hopeless, helpless, and overwhelmed.

Make today the day you begin to defeat and remove clutter, confusion, and unwanted stress from your life by organizing, controlling, and managing your space, mental state, and physical health. When you do this, you can begin to defeat and remove toxic people and relationships from your life.

2) The Three Self-Sabotaging Ds

When the Three Self-Sabotaging Ds exist in your life or in any situation you're involved in or connected to, toxic people and relationships are able to slip in and attack you.

The Three Self-Sabotaging Ds are "Disrespect," "Devaluing," and "Disregard."

Everything we do to ourselves internally will eventually reveal itself to the world on the outside.

Disrespect yourself internally and the world will soon see you as a person of poor character.

Devalue yourself on the inside and the world will soon see you as a person who considers themselves unworthy.

Disregard yourself on the inside and the world will soon see you as a person with a poor self-image.

Toxic people and relationships gravitate and cling to people with poor character, a low level of worthiness, and a poor self-image.

Make today the day you begin to defeat and remove self-disrespect, self-devaluation, and self-disregard from your life. You are more than worthy, and you should regard yourself as a person with a healthy self-esteem and positive character. When you do this, the defeat and removal of toxic people and relationships from your life will be liberating.

Replacing a Toxic Person and Relationship With A Positive Action

"You must take action now that will move you toward your goals. Develop a sense of urgency in your life."

— Les Brown

Whenever you discover or encounter a potential toxic person situation, whether it is a new person (someone you don't really know) or an established relationship, your first positive action to stop, block, or slow down the situation should be to inform the other person in a positive and cordial way that his or her actions are not acceptable.

Most "potentially" toxic people and relationships can be stopped or changed if you let the person involved know as soon a possible. Do not assume that the other person knows what they are doing to you; inform them. This may be a situation or relationship that can continue on a positive note.

If the toxic person or relationship continues to worsen, below are a few strategies to help you put a positive action in place of a current Toxic Relationship.

Current Toxic Relationship	A Positive Action to Replace It
Toxic Family Relationship	Limit the amount of time you spend with this person.
Toxic Parent Relationship	Deal with this parent respectfully but only when necessary. Let them know you care; however, don't let them beat you up or derail your life.
Toxic Sibling Relationship	Speak cordially to this person on occasion to let them know you care; however, don't allow them to run your life or have a front row seat in your life.
Toxic Spouse or Significant Other Relationship	Work cordially to change the toxic state of your relationship. If that doesn't work, seek professional help or leave the relationship.
Toxic Friend Relationship	Avoid and remove this friend from your social circle.
Toxic Work Relationship	Be cordial, remain positive and productive, and try not to turn a current toxic work situation into a more toxic job-threatening situation.
Toxic School Relationship	Sort positively through the negative emotions of the situation, and seek a professional person within the school to mediate the situation between you and the other person involved.

Current Toxic Relationship	A Positive Action to Replace It
Toxic Community Relationship	Cordially deal with the official community representative but do not focus on the nitpicky stuff.
Toxic Service Organization, Restaurant, Retail Store, Hotel or Travel Organization Relationship	Cordially ask to speak with a supervisor or manager.
Toxic Business Relationship	Cordially and professionally settle all open business, then bring closure to and get away from the toxic business relationship.

It can be a tough emotional battle defeating toxic people and relationships, especially when the person or persons are family members, spouses, friends, neighbors, business partners, or employers. In most cases, we still care for and even love the toxic person. However, toxic people and relationships add no real value or benefit to our life. The motivation behind such a task stems from one simple question: "If I allow this toxic person or relationship to continue projecting or bringing unpleasant hazards to my life, will I be able to move forward in peace?" If your answer is "No," decide to remove the toxic person or relationship—immediately.

Every minute you allow a toxic person or relationship to run rampant in your life, you lose 60 seconds of peace of mind and self-control.

10-Step Process to Defeating Toxic People and Relationships

"Put all excuses aside and remember this: YOU are capable."

— Zig Ziglar

At the nine-year point of my ten years served in the U.S. Navy on full-time active duty, I was faced with an important decision due to a once healthy relationship beginning to turn toxic.

After gaining control of my life around the six-year mark of my military service, I decided to begin pursuing my life's passion and purpose. This decision came about when my command participated in an Adopt-A-School Program in the Washington, D.C. area, where I was asked to be the guest speaker for a middle school's Black History Month Program. I spoke at the event, and it was a huge success; the principal, administrators, students, and parents enjoyed it thoroughly and were all inspired by the message.

A few weeks later, Captain Drew, a captain on staff within our command, shared with me information about the professional speaking industry. She handed me the information and ended our conversation by saying, "You might want to look further into the professional speaking business." I did just that, and my efforts ignited a new passion, focus, and purpose for my life. I wanted to share my Untie the Knots philosophy and message with the world.

First, I had to honorably separate from the U.S. Navy at the end of my second contract. At the seven-year mark, I felt my relationship with the Navy was beginning to grow toxic. The Navy had received everything it was going to get from me, and I had received everything I wanted from the Navy. I came to grips at that point that whenever I began to lose motivation and interest in something, and it began to feel toxic, I would make plans to quickly remove the toxic relationship.

The following 10-step process will help you defeat Toxic People and Relationships once and for all.

1. **Recognize the situation is unacceptable.** To confront and defeat a toxic person or relationship, you must first recognize the person or relationship is not acceptable. Allow yourself time to write on a sheet of paper what specifically is making this person or relationship undesirable. When you do this, what you express in your writing becomes more evident to you.

2. **Stop, block, or slow down the unwanted situation.** Now that you have recognized and identified the toxic situation as unacceptable, quickly identify a positive action to slow down, block, or stop the toxic person or relationship from attacking you.

3. **Find a positive and healthy plan of action to address the situation.** Once you have your positive choice of action, you have to place it into a sound plan. Think over your plan and write it down. Think about how you plan to implement your plan of action in a positive and effective way.

4. **Address the person or people involved in the situation.** One of the first steps in your planning process should be to address the person or people involved in a positive and encouraging way. Sometimes, making the person aware of his or her toxic behavior can begin the process of them making corrections. If this step doesn't work, continue to step number five.

5. **Change the condition or your position as a result of addressing the other person.** After you had your discussion with the person or persons, listen to exactly what they tell you. Watch their actions to see if the condition of the relationship changes for the better. If things continue as before, do not talk yourself out of it; change your position and defeat and remove the toxic relationship from your life.

6. **Practice and stay committed to your choice about how to handle this situation.** One of the most self-sabotaging and destructive things we as human beings do occurs

when we decide to remove a toxic person or relationship from our life: we turn around the next day and allow the person or relationship back into our lives. This is tough when you love and care about a person; however, it does you more harm than good to allow this person or relationship to bring your life down.

7. **Set a "Defeat by Date."** If the toxic person or relationship you've planned to defeat requires gradual time to remove them, set a written "Defeat by Date." This date will keep you focused and committed to the process of defeating this toxic person and relationship. The date will also prevent the person from festering like a toxic sore in your life.

8. **Reward yourself.** When you realize you have successfully defeated and replaced a toxic person or relationship with a positive action, reward yourself. Go out to a movie, treat yourself to a nice dinner, hang out with your friends, or buy yourself something special.

9. **Watch for the signals.** Once you have your new positive action in place, watch for the signals. Now that you are aware of this process, you can perform "Re-Flash Watch." When you see characteristics of an old or new toxic person or relationship trying to attack your life, recognize it for what it is, and quickly defeat and remove it. Be on the lookout and always stay alert and attentive, but not to the point of fear or obsession.

10. **After three honest and determined attempts, seek professional help and the caring support from family and friends.** Remember, we win in life with people, and you will most likely need the assistance and encouragement of at least one extra caring person to help you stay committed and focused on your Untie the Knots journey.

Do this and you will find yourself breathing better, thinking better, accomplishing more, having more fun, and improving your health, all because you chose to live freely by not allowing toxic people and relationships to occupy the front row seats of your life.

What Is Required of YOU for the Continuous Defeat of Toxic People and Relationships?

"Show me someone who has done something worthwhile, and I'll show you someone who has overcome adversity."

— Lou Holtz

To defeat and remove toxic people and relationships from your life takes confidence and boldness to stand firm on your decision—it takes DRIVE. It was Norman Vincent Peale who once said, "Enthusiasm releases the drive to carry you over obstacles and adds significance to all you do."

When people have committed themselves to defeating and removing Toxic People and Relationships from their life, they show up in the world filled with DRIVE.

Determined.   Determined to maintain positive health and well-being.

Responsible.   Responsible to do whatever they can to keep the level of toxicity in their life as low as possible.

Inspired.   Inspired to not allow toxic people and relationships to run their life down.

Victorious.   Victorious in defeating toxic people, relationships, and energy without hesitation.

Enthusiastic.   Enthusiastic in quickly identifying and defeating toxic people, relationships, and energy time-and-time again.

A person filled with DRIVE becomes a living example of what Mahatma Gandhi expressed in these words: *"Become the change you want to see in the world."*

When you begin regularly defeating and removing toxic people and relationships from your life, you will become the change you want to see in the world. You will also begin to experience and enjoy a life filled with better health, productivity, happiness, potential, and prosperity.

Chapter Conclusion

In this chapter, I shared with you two processes that can have you defeating one toxic habit, choice, person, or relationship after another. I explained to you how toxic habits and choices are internally driven and how toxic people and relationships are externally driven. I shared with you comparison tables that allowed you to see how toxic choices can lead to toxic habits and how toxic people can lead to toxic relationships. I explained that you first have to change the way you think before you can change the way you act. You also have to defeat clutter, confusion, and unwanted stress and avoid the three self-sabotaging Ds before you can defeat toxic people and relationships. I shared with you lists of positive actions to replace, slow down, block, or stop toxic habits, choices, people, and relationships in optimistic and gentle ways. As I've stated several times before, the defeat and removal of your toxic habits, choices, people, and relationships won't happen overnight; however, you are worth the effort.

Remember, *"You May Have Been Delayed, But You're RARELY Denied!"* When you learn to continuously and effectively "Defeat Toxic Habits, Choices, People, and Relationships," you too will find your life on a path toward healthier, significant, rewarding, and prosperous living.

To gain immediate access to a practical, comprehensive, step-by-step guide that will help you break free of the 50 Most Common Toxic Knots, visit the following link on the Internet, right now:

http://www.tyhoward.com/KnotsFree_SpecialGuide.html

(Or turn to Appendix C for more information about the Knots Free Special Guide.)

Unit Summary

YOU MAY HAVE BEEN DELAYED, BUT YOU'RE RARELY DENIED

To empower one's life takes an unstoppable vision, continuous movement, and the constant courage to confront and defeat toxic habits, choices, people, and relationships.

Chapters 10, 11, and 12 were written to: 1) inspire you to update your personal vision, and write your new personal course of action (your goals and life direction); 2) inspire you to learn a new technique, words, and phrases that can assist you in commanding yourself to move forward whenever you feel or see your life becoming stagnant or idle; and 3) provide you with practical and easy-to-apply processes that will plow and clear your path to Untie the Knots success. This is where you've charted your course and begun to command your plan to defeat your toxic nemesis on your way to a life of significance.

Let's recap the three chapters that make up Unit 4, Part 3: YOU MAY HAVE BEEN DELAYED, BUT YOU'RE RARELY DENIED

Chapter 10, Step 4: Setting Unstoppable Goals

Chapter 11, Step 5: Quit Marking Time—and Move Forward

Chapter 12, Step 6: Defeating Toxic Habits, Choices, People, and Relationships

We've encountered the following **Infusers** *(Freedom Break Away Tools)* that were explained in the introduction of this book:

Infuser #1: Reinstate a Positive Attitude
If you are serious about breaking free from these knots, you must adopt a positive mental attitude. You must be committed to developing and working constantly with a positive attitude, regardless of your past experiences or current situations or circumstances.

Infuser #2: Refocus
How will you change the direction of your life if you're not aware of what direction you're currently in?

Infuser #3: Choose
Decide true freedom and life is what you want and then go where you can produce those results.

Infuser #4: Identify
To successfully break away from anything that has delayed or derailed you in the past, you must summon the bold confidence to now identify it as a toxic habit, choice, person, or relationship.

Infuser #5: Simplify
Remove clutter, confusion, stress, and distractions from your life daily, and watch new, desirable opportunities appear.

Infuser #6: Believe
It takes your strong will and unshakable faith to make the impossible possible.

Infuser #7: Move
Don't just stand there filled with knowledge: Do it! Quit procrastinating and making excuses.

Infuser #9: Persist
How strongly do you want what you now see? No more excuses...no more procrastination...no more wasted and unproductive days! Stay the course!

Infuser #10: Leave A Mark of Significance
It's one experience in living to have simply come and gone. It's another experience in living to have purposely decided to create and live a life of significance: a life that will enable you to leave behind a lasting legacy that will contribute to your family's heritage and also allow the many others who come after you to learn and grow from your efforts.

This unit (Chapters 10 through 12) was an eye-opening and transforming experience filled with useful strategies, tools, and processes for your journey. Make sure you read it more than once because the material in this unit is meant to light your vision, direct your passion, build your confidence, and clear away the toxic weight that may have been weighing you down and keeping you from living the life you truly want.

Everything in your life has been leading up to this moment. Now is the time to fully experience and fulfill the life you were born to live.

Time OUT!

Just to recap some of the major concepts you've read about thus far, find and write in your journal the answers to the following questions:

- What does "Vision + Process" equal?
  Refer to the first four pages of Chapter 10 for the answer.

- What are Unstoppable Goals?
  Refer to "What Are Unstoppable Goals?" section in Chapter 10 for the answer.

- What are six factors that cause people to begin Marking Time?
  Refer to the "What Causes People to Begin Marking Time" section in Chapter 11 for the answer.

- What are the toxic effects of Marking Time?
  Refer to "The Toxic Effects of Marking Time" section in Chapter 11 for the answer.

- What are the 12 steps to defeating toxic habits and choices?
  Refer to the "12-Step Process to Defeating Toxic Habits and Choices" section in Chapter 12 for the answer.

- What are the 10 steps to defeating toxic people and relationships?
  Refer to the "10-Step Process to Defeating Toxic People and Relationships" section in Chapter 12 for the answer.

"Success consists of going from failure to failure without loss of enthusiasm."

— Winston Churchill

PART 4

NEVER QUIT! NEVER STOP!
DON'T EVER GIVE UP!

My Personal Creed for Continual *Untie the Knots* Success
The Third Step of Self-Mastery is Practicing and Managing

Step 7—Making "A" Commitment to Life
When Your Commitment to Life Is Deeply Rooted,
Then Life Will Give You Some Answers

Step 8—Rewarding, Assessing, Managing, and Persisting
Your Celebrations in Life Create Meaningful Reasons for You to
Continue Growing

Step 9—Leaving A Lasting Legacy: Creating A Life of Significance
Your Significant Life Will Leave a Lasting Legacy for All to
Remember You By

In Part 4...

When you've learned and embraced the principles and strategies of the concept that in life "You May Have Been Delayed, But You're RARELY Denied," you can then place yourself on a path that enables you to make "A" commitment to life and create a lasting legacy. In this part, you will find information about how to make "A" commitment to a significant life so you can make the Untie the Knots Process a permanent way of life. As you strive to master the Untie the Knots Process, you will learn the importance and benefits of taking the necessary time to celebrate, assess, manage, and persist with making your best efforts better. Finally, you will receive practical tips about how to create a life of significance so you assure you leave a lasting legacy that can advance your family, friends, or community.

My Personal Creed for Continual
Untie the Knots **Success**

Today, this new day, I am a successful person. Overnight, my mind and body have produced thousands of new cells to give me the greatest advantages possible. I am born anew, revitalized, and full of energy.

I am rare, valuable, and unique in the universe. I am nature's greatest miracle in action. I have unrestricted potential. I believe in my abilities, attitudes, and goals. I am worthy of greatness because I am the most important person in my world.

Today, I will push myself to new limits. I will use my skills and knowledge. I will begin the day and end the day with a success. My goals are reached every day, and I seek them eagerly.

I act positively and happily, fully accepting others and myself. I live to the fullest by experiencing life without limits. I embrace life. I control my life. I approach each person, each task, and each situation with enthusiasm, happiness, and joy. I thirst for knowledge. I look forward to reading and believing this creed each and every day.

Today, I will keep an open mind about all subjects and toward all people so I may rise above small-mindedness. I will look for good in others and teach myself to deal gently with their faults. I will avoid self-pity. Under all circumstances, I will seek stimulation to make my best effort better.

I believe I am a positive and successful person. I know each step I must take to continue to be that way. I am clear about my goals and see myself reaching them. I now realize my unlimited potential; thus, my problems lighten. I smile and laugh repeatedly. I have become the greatest person in the world.

Finally, my daily prayer will be for infinite wisdom to recognize and live my life in harmony with the overall purpose of the Creator.

People who fully believe they can attain success are the only ones who ever achieve success. They are convinced of one fact: "Whatever my mind can conceive and believe, my mind can achieve!"

They consciously work to develop belief in themselves and their capability to realize any goal they set for themselves. Edwin C. Barnes conditioned his mind to a single aim: to become the business partner of the great inventor, Thomas A. Edison. Barnes developed his tremendous power of belief by daily repetition of a creed. And one day he became the business partner of the great inventor.

Repeating the "Creed for Continual *Untie the Knots* Success" to yourself at least twice each day will help you realize your greatest wishes too.

The words will soak into your subconscious mind and make it part of your character. You will develop attributes that will help you develop a pleasing personality and significant character. A character that is designed to Never Quit! Never Stop! And Never Give Up!

Chapter 13

Step 7: MAKING "A" COMMITMENT TO LIFE

"Commitment is what transforms a promise into reality."

— Abraham Lincoln

After serving my country while on full-time active duty for ten years, I left the U.S. Navy for Corporate America. In Corporate America, I held and worked in positions like Human Resources Generalist, Senior Executive Support Staff Professional, Office Manager, Outside Sales Account Manager, and Sales Trainer.

Corporate America was definitely another culture shift for me. I quickly discovered the military had conditioned me to be pro-active, assertive, and focused about getting any job done. In the military, I was taught to accept a set of tasks and work them through to the desired results. Corporate America, however, had its own rules and pace.

I showed up to work ahead of schedule and often worked a few hours later than expected to complete the job. I took great pride in my work and professional image. My drive and commitment to perform at my peak, however, would begin to cause tension, jealousy, and dislike from a few co-workers, who began to attack my dedicated work ethic by saying, "Well, I guess if I had served in the military, I would be a dedicated worker like you. Ty, you do know that it's okay to not always finish a project or task ahead of time. Are you trying to show us up or make us look bad by performing the way you do?" I wasn't trying to show anyone up or make anyone look bad. My dedication and work ethic was who I was and how I performed.

All too often we find ourselves in life choosing to play small to fit-in, conform, or not reveal the lack of performance of others.

When you choose to play small, you choose to create and place a toxic habit in your life. You choose to give control of your life to someone or something other than you.

News Flash: THIS IS NOT LIVING!

At the three-year mark in Corporate America, I began to plan my exit strategy. I had to do me—I had to continue being me. I left the military because I took back control of my life, and I was not giving up control of my life to anyone else. My passion and purpose at that time was to speak to and inspire people to pursue their dreams and live their best. I was not a person who chose to speak right and yet walk left. I had to stand up within and become the example and my own standard.

Two years later, I tendered my resignation from Corporate America, and I started my own business as a full-time paid professional motivational speaker.

I took back control of my life by deciding to do me—by deciding to live! There is great power in personal commitment. Personal commitment can change the impossible to possible.

Taking Back Control of Your Life

"Moving to another city or state will not solve your problems. You still have to take you with you."

— Author Unknown

Taking back control of your life doesn't mean you or everyone must leave a current employer to start a business. Taking back control of your life means choosing to live and enjoy life on your terms. It means going after your life's purpose and passion wholeheartedly and without hesitation.

Taking back control of your life by making your own positive decisions and choices is essential in the Untie the Knots Process. It will help you feel better about yourself and will empower you more as you string together one successful accomplishment after another.

The way you think, the way you act, and the way you feel can make a tremendous difference in the quality of your life. These emotions and attitudes are all under your control.

There are several steps you can pursue to begin this process. You can achieve these steps in whatever way feels right. You may want to use a journal to list or write your thoughts and ideas to stay focused on what you want or as a way to motivate yourself and record your progress.

1. Think about what you really want your life to be like. Do you want to
   - Go back to school and study something of special interest?
   - Enhance your talents?
   - Travel?
   - Become more financially independent?
   - Have a different home or own your home?
   - Move to the country or the city?
   - Have a steady and supportive intimate spouse or partner?
   - Have children?
   - Work for a purpose or cause that you're passionate about?
   - Pursue your own career path without fear or procrastination?
   - Start your own business?
   - Become more physically active?
   - Write a book?
   - Find and begin a new hobby?
   - Lose or gain weight?

You can probably think of many more ideas. Write them down. You may want to keep them in your journal.

2. List those obstacles that have kept you from pursuing the activities you wanted. Perhaps it has been a lack of money or education. Maybe your distractions or feelings of being overwhelmed have been too severe. Maybe it was one of your toxic habits, choices, people, or relationships blocking or delaying you from moving forward.

Now write down ways you could work on overcoming those obstacles. As you do this, remind yourself that you are an intelligent person. You have the ability to resolve problems. You can resolve these problems slowly or quickly. You can take small steps or big steps—whatever feels right and is possible for you. But you must do it if you want to take back control of your life.

In the process of taking control of your own life, you must identify and defeat all toxic habits, choices, people, and relationships that exist in your life.

In each moment, you have the opportunity to decide how life will be for you. How do you want it to be? Take control of your thoughts and make them positive. Take control of your actions and make them effective. Take control of your feelings and make them empowering.

Choose to take control right now, and you will add energy to your moments as you transform your burdens into positive opportunities and your opportunities into blessings.

Minimizing the Distractions

> *"Toxic distractions are the challenges of the world forcing your focus to turn or go in a meaningless direction."*
>
> — Ty Howard

If you observed many people today, you would realize, like I have, that a large number of them fail to complete tasks or accomplish their goals due to distractions. People who are easily distracted cannot concentrate on completing tasks or even writing them down.

They are afraid they will miss something. Distracted people use excuses and statements like these:

"I can't work on my personal goals on the weekends because Friday evening, Saturday, and Sunday are my party and fun times."

"I can't get a second job to pay down my debt because I'm going to miss my favorite television shows."

"I can't go back to college to get a degree because that will cut into my Internet, video game, or social time."

"I can't stay focused long enough to complete anything because I'm too busy and there isn't enough time in the day to get anything done."

Concentration is "focused" thinking which enables us to think with precision and get tasks done. The ability to concentrate varies greatly from one person to another; however, with practice, you can improve your level of concentration.

People who are easily distracted cannot concentrate on getting tasks done unless their work environment or life is free of distraction. Distractions can either be external (physical) or internal (psychological) in nature. To achieve greater concentration, you must improve the conditions that promote concentration. You must commit yourself to minimizing your distractions.

Types of Distractions

Internal or psychological distractions

Internal distractions originate within YOU. YOU create these distractions, and only YOU have the power to eliminate or control them. Included in internal distractions are daydreams, personal problems, anxiety, indecision, and unrealistic goals.

External or physical distractions

Anything that stimulates the senses and in the process interrupts concentration can be considered an external distraction. To concentrate effectively, you must reduce sights and sounds, work in an appropriate study environment, and use the proper equipment.

Ways to Reduce Internal Distractions

Keep track of your lapses of concentration. It is suggested that you use a "concentration scorecard" to record your personal interruptions. Indicate on a sheet of paper by a check mark or notation of time (4:35, 4:43, 4:51) the number of occasions when you are aware of your mind wandering while trying to complete a task. When you total these distractions, you realize how intrusive distractions and lapses in time are. The mind can be trained to concentrate for longer periods.

Record stray thoughts on a "worry pad." Write down personal thoughts that intrude on your concentration, and deal with these thoughts when you have completed the task. These distractions can include family problems, financial concerns, work-related matters, and more. Take the time, before or after a task, to analyze why the problem exists and identify possible solutions. Usually you can analyze the cause of the problem and some options for resolution. If it is a serious or sensitive concern, seek professional help.

Ways to Reduce External Distractions

Choose an appropriate work environment.
-   Select a place designed for writing or working on a task such as a separate, quiet room in your house, the community library, or create your own. In the library, choose a corner carrel or a seat facing the wall. If you begin to daydream or nap while writing and thinking, take a break. Do not become conditioned to anything, but think and write when you're in your personal work environment.

Eliminate noise that can be a major obstacle to staying focused.
- Turn off the music when working on your personal tasks and writing.
- Keep the TV off. Television is a distraction to both vision and hearing.
- Choose adequate lighting. Good lighting is essential to staying awake.
- Health problems such as headaches, eyestrain, or tension can develop from poor lighting.
- Minimize visual distractions. Remove from your view items that might interfere with concentration. Examples are photos, gadgets, books, or activity outside the window.

Use a written Personal Life Plan and written Goals Worksheet to keep you focused.
- When you find yourself in a position where your friends and family members are distracting you by competing for your time, review your written Personal Life Plan and Goal Worksheet. This will help you stay focused and committed in completing the task. There will be plenty of time for you to have fun and play later. Remember, sacrificing now will bring your life increased happiness and longer quality fun in your future.

Strategies for Enhancing Concentration

- Maintain a positive attitude. Realize that some tasks, activities, and personal planning processes may be uninteresting. To meet the goal of "untying your knots," however, it is necessary to stay focused and get the job done. Keep the positive mental attitude of "Whatever it takes" and stay the course.
- Prepare to work by setting realistic time goals. Break a large personal task or project into manageable blocks that can be accomplished one at a time. Add the task to your daily "to do" list.
- Stay in good physical shape. Get sufficient sleep. Eat nourishing meals. Exercise regularly. Take a short, 15-30 minute power nap if needed.

- Deal with any life challenges or problems when they arise. Putting challenges and problems off only decreases your ability to concentrate and think effectively.
- Use outside help when needed. If you begin to struggle, find a caring person to support and encourage you to stay focused and committed. Don't procrastinate!
- GET ORGANIZED with an appointment book. Learn to control your time. Use a monthly calendar and schedule to keep and monitor your daily routine. Make weekly and daily "to do" lists.
- Take breaks after a sustained period of focused work, writing, and journaling. Reward yourself with a ten-minute break.

Take control of your life today by deciding to minimize your distractions. Begin to stay focused on the tasks that are most meaningful and beneficial to your life right now, and you will find yourself living a life with less worries, stress, health problems, and trouble.

A distraction-free life with fewer worries, stress, health problems, and troubles is worth holding onto. Isn't it?

Bringing Your "A" Game

"Nothing great was ever achieved without enthusiasm."

— Ralph Waldo Emerson

In his abbreviated debut season of 1996 -- at age 20 -- Tiger Woods won twice. The next year, he became the first African-American to win a major when he dominated the Masters. In 2000, he became only the second golfer -- Ben Hogan was the first in 1953 -- to win three professional majors in a year. He was the youngest -- at 24 -- to complete a career Grand Slam. And it took him just 21 starts in the majors, the fastest ever. That year, he captured 11 titles, nine on Tour, and had record Tour earnings of more than $9 million for his 20 starts.

In an interview about being the first of his race to win at Augusta, Woods said, *"I wasn't the pioneer. Charlie Sifford, Lee Elder, and Ted Rhodes played that role. I said a little prayer and said thanks to those guys. You are the ones who did it for me."*

I would sit and watch Tiger Woods on television in total awe of his dedication, focus, character, and ability.

Still, one of the most powerful statements I ever heard anyone say came from Tiger Woods in an interview at the end of a career Grand Slam at the age of 24. Tiger during the interview explained to the interviewers, *"When I step out onto the golf course to compete, I expect to win. I may not win every game; however, I expect to win. I strive to bring my 'A' Game."*

Once I heard Tiger's response, it inspired me from that day forward to strive to always bring my "A" Game! No, I may not win or achieve every goal exactly the way I planned; however, if I put forth my best effort, what may first seem impossible can become possible. Just like the many impossible to possible accomplishments I watched Tiger Woods create.

Do you bring your "A" Game to every situation in which you have to perform?

You may not win or achieve every goal exactly the way you planned it; nevertheless, you come prepared to perform your best and expect to win.

Or does your performance reflect whatever your mood or mind tells you to put out that day?

You know you have the potential to perform beyond your own expectations; however, you choose to allow your emotions or negative way of thinking to put out whatever level of performance it sees fit for the situation. So, you may come unprepared and deliver your "B," "C," "D," or "F" Game. To you it really doesn't matter because you feel and think, "Hey, at least I showed up."

Woody Allen says, "Eighty percent of success is showing up." The other 20% is showing up prepared, motivated, and expecting to succeed.

If you truly want to create and live the life you desire for yourself, from this point forward you must bring your "A" Game to every task, goal, project, and life situation where you are required to perform. I want you to perform at your best; however, I do not want you to become some crazed toxic competitor with everything that crosses your path. You do not have to become a perfectionist or crazed person who feels you must win the big trophy all the time.

Write this next statement down in your journal, and put an asterisk besides it: "You do not have to come in first to win."

Just show up prepared, motivated, expecting to succeed, and with your "A" Game!

Soon you too will be turning impossible situations into possible celebrations. Bring Your "A" Game!

Stretching Yourself

> *"One can never consent to creep when one feels an impulse to soar."*
>
> — Helen Keller

The successful people in life learn at a certain stage in life that if they are going to be continuously successful, they have to stretch themselves and their goals more and more after each accomplishment.

It's in the actual stretching of yourself and your abilities where true change and growth takes place.

I'm reminded of a story of a little girl being chased through the jungle by a hungry lion. She was terrified and running for her dear life. She could hear and feel the lion getting closer and closer as she continued to run. The little girl came to a cliff, and she was faced with two options: 1) jump off the cliff into the shallow waters below and risk her life; or 2) jump up to reach a protruding branch from a tree right next to her and pull herself to safety. The little girl jumped, and she missed the branch. At this point, the lion was so close that she could hear and feel him breathing on her back. Scared and fearing for her life, the little girl squatted down into a stoop—then she leaped up with all her might. And again...she missed the branch...but this time, she caught it on the way down.

When you decide to commit and follow-through on making the Untie the Knots Process a natural way of life for yourself, you will set new points in your life that will cause you to stretch. Stretch out of your comfort zone, stretch to increase your level of education, and stretch to change and develop your skills and abilities.

When we concentrate and focus on what we are doing or going to do, that's when we're able to do just as the little girl did in the story, exceed our normal potential, and soar to new heights.

Saying "YES!" to Your Future

> *"The greatest revenge is massive success."*
> — Willie Jolley

Life is too short to spend it getting back at someone else and trying to get even.

The best thing to do when it comes to living life at our best is to say, "YES!" to our future.

Your first step in saying, "YES!" to your future is to set your intention.

Setting intentions is the most powerful way to focus your energy and attention in a chosen direction. It is much easier to keep your intentions when you identify the reason why you want to make a change in your life. Why are you setting a particular intention? What motivates you to set this intention?

When he was at the top of his game, Lance Armstrong, the American professional bicyclist, was literally forced off his bike in excruciating pain. He was told that he had cancer. Lance Armstrong said, "YES!" to his future, fought cancer, and won; he then went on to win seven Tour de France victories.

Joe Louis Dudley, Sr., who was labeled mentally retarded early in his childhood, said, "YES!" to his future. He is President and Chief Executive Officer (CEO) of Dudley Products, Inc., one of the world's largest manufacturers and distributors of hair care and beauty products.

Tawana Williams was a victim of brutal medical negligence. Born without arms and with impaired use of her legs, she said, "YES!" to her future. Her compelling life story reveals a will to survive the anguish of physical defect and the shame of abuse and isolation. Unable to fight with human hands, she fought in spirit and lives to stand and share her inspiring motivational story, "Unarmed but Dangerous," as a full-time professional motivational speaker.

Have you said, "YES!" to your future? Have you said, "YES!" to life?

If "YES!" that's GREAT!

If "no," what's holding you back?

It's time to identify and write down your intentions for life from this point forward.

Why do you want to identify and untie your knots?

Why are you setting this bold and challenging goal?

What motivates you to set this intention?

You truthful and heartfelt answers will reveal to you your updated world of passion, hope, and purpose.

So, start right here and now by saying aloud, "YES! YES! YES! To My FUTURE!"

You have just made a confirmed commitment to LIFE!

You can now monitor your confirmed commitment to your future by using the following strategies:

1) Maintain a positive mental attitude.
2) Check every two to three weeks to see if you still are in complete control of your life.
3) Address all problems, challenges, or issues that come into your life's path as soon as possible.
4) Choose to stay on a journey that is constantly green and growing versus ripe and dying.
5) Look for continuous opportunities to learn, stretch, and bring your "A" Game.
6) Make necessary adjustments that will keep you saying, "YES! YES! YES!" to your future.

When you say, "YES!" to your future, you know you are the embodiment of Spirit, that you have come here to evolve your Purpose, and that you are always living at your "Passion of Choice Point."

I connected with my "Passion of Choice Point" when I left Corporate America, and I took what at first seemed impossible to the possible. When I started my motivational speaker business, at first it seemed hopeless and destined to fail. Then I once again said, "YES!" to my future by commanding myself to stretch, move forward, and bring my "A" Game. I began to constantly monitor my mental attitude, self-talk, and focused actions. I minimized my distractions and stayed true to my personal commitment to life.

Within a year's time, what was once hopeless became hopeful, and I have been green and growing ever since.

You too have the same capability and Spirit to turn the impossible into the possible.

Chapter Conclusion

In this chapter, you learned the importance and benefits of *Making "A" Commitment to Life*. You learned strategies about how to take back control of your life and how to minimize the many distractions the world will throw your way. You learned about the power of personal commitment. You learned the value of bringing your "A" Game and not settling for putting out just an "okay" or "mediocre" effort. You learned that even when you've brought your "A" Game and given your best effort, you can still make another effort to S T R E T C H even more. I explained to you how powerful saying, "YES!" to your future can be and how to monitor your life for continuous commitment once you have officially said, "YES!" to your future.

Remember: The power of personal commitment can turn what may at first seem impossible into the possible.

Chapter 14

Step 8: REWARDING, ASSESSING, MANAGING, AND PERSISTING

"Stop worrying about the potholes in the road and celebrate the journey!"

— Barbara Hoffman

Before you plunge yourself into reading this chapter, congratulate yourself on *Making "A" Commitment to Life* by choosing to learn and master the Untie the Knots Process. Making that commitment is challenging, but it will provide you substantial immediate and long-term benefits when you stay the course. You may find it difficult to maintain your progress; however, with the Untie the Knots Process, you do not have to come in first to win. As you have read and learned already, there are several principles and strategies you can use to help you stay on track. Although no one principle or strategy can motivate all people to stay actively committed, the following principles and strategies you will read and learn in this chapter may make it a little easier for you to continue learning, practicing, and staying the course.

Five years ago, I wrote a fable about "The Father and His Daughter." It's a short story that brings to light the importance of self-reward for successfully completing any task: large, medium, or small.

The Father and His Daughter

A Father and his Daughter were working hard in the flowerbeds around the house planting tulip bulbs in the fall in preparation for next spring. The entire time the Father and Daughter worked, the Daughter frowned in disgust because she'd rather be doing anything else than digging in the dirt. Still, the Father continued to work alongside his Daughter, encouraging her to put her best effort into the task at hand. He explained to his Daughter that even the most challenging task could become pleasing if one focused on the reward in the end. The Daughter moaned in dissatisfaction and continued to dig. Three hours and six flowerbeds later, the job was complete. The Father first thanked his Daughter for her help. Then he asked his Daughter, "So, what are you going to do now?" The Daughter replied, "Clean myself up by washing my hands, body and hair...after that, nothing." The Father swiftly responded, "Well, I plan to do the same exact thing as you; however, I will not end at nothing...I will end with a self reward." "A self reward?" inquired the Daughter. "Yes, I will treat myself with a reward of my choice for the time and effort I put into today's yard work." Then the Father helped his Daughter set a new standard for herself by teaching her, "From this point forward, no matter how big or small the goal or task you accomplish, make it your personal purpose to stop and reward yourself. By doing so, any meaningful goal or task you work to accomplish will have an appeal worth completing because you've set a personal self reward for yourself in the end."

Moral of the Story: Any task worth completing deserves a reward.

Rewarding Yourself

"When you know that you are doing your very best within the circumstances of your existence, applaud yourself!"

— Rusty Berkus

Is it me, or have you noticed too, that most people today do not reward themselves for their accomplishments unless they feel the accomplishment of the task or goal warrants it. For the most part, we're talking about high priority tasks and goals like graduations, job promotions, the start of a new business, completion of a long training program, or release of a new book, music cd, or product.

It doesn't matter if the task, project, or goal is large, medium, or small. What does matter is that you do not neglect yourself by recognizing the tasks you have accomplished. There's no need to feel guilty or self-centered; you've earned it. If you've paid your bills on time each month for the past six months, that's an accomplishment. If you forgave someone who has hurt you in your past to bring closure to that segment of your life, that's an accomplishment. If you successfully completed a college or training course, that's an accomplishment. If you finally paid your debt on a credit card and then cut it up, that's an accomplishment. If you encourage your child to do better in school and his or her grades improved tremendously, that's an accomplishment. If you completed writing the manuscript for your book, that's an accomplishment. If you finally bagged all the old clothes you had in the attic that you no longer wear and took them to a homeless shelter for others to use, that's an accomplishment. It doesn't matter how big or how small the goal, task, or project is; you should reward yourself. You are worthy of a reward, and you deserve rewards continuously.

The purpose of a reward is to provide motivation and to reinforce positive behaviors. Rewards can play an important role in helping you stay motivated and committed to a goal, task, or project. The reason rewards work is that your brain automatically links an action taken after a behavior to the behavior. So if you just cleaned out a disorganized and cluttered closet in your house, and immediately afterwards you went out and purchased the CD you've been wanting, your brain links those positive feelings associated with buying your CD to getting the task of organizing your closet completed. This motivates you to repeat the behavior. But be careful because you can reinforce negative behaviors without even knowing it.

For example, let's say you are exercising every other day at 6:00 p.m.; one night you are set to go to the gym and an interesting TV show comes on. You say, "Just this one time, I'll watch the show and skip my workout. It won't hurt; it's only one workout." Chances are you won't be sticking to your workout schedule much longer. Your failure to stay focused was due to a toxic distraction. Had you put a reward in place, you might have increased your chances of staying focused and committed. Never underestimate the power of a reward!

What's the best way to reward yourself? If you are trying to lose weight, it is definitely not going to your favorite restaurant. The best way to reward yourself is by doing something you enjoy doing, but generally don't take the time to do often. It doesn't have to be expensive. It doesn't have to be elaborate. A reward can be as simple as calling a friend you haven't talked to for a while or reading your favorite magazine.

Recently, I informally polled about 25 people what they thought would be a good reward for completing a small task like putting your clearly defined goals in writing with deadlines. Here are some of the rewards they mentioned: buying clothes, watching a movie, visiting an amusement park, eating a bowl of ice cream, writing an encouraging letter to myself in my journal, hanging out with friends or family, going to the theater, attending a spa, going bike riding, purchasing a cd, going to a club, getting a massage, getting a manicure, going for a drive, going to a sporting event, taking a bubble bath, buying something for the car, going to the park to run and play with my dog, and reading a book. You can probably think of a number of rewards that you enjoy doing but have trouble finding time to do. These types of activities make great self-rewards.

Another caution you should take when rewarding yourself is to not allow your personal rewards or celebrations to become your new toxic distractions. If you reward yourself too frequently by eating, spending, or doing anything compulsively, you will only create a new toxic habit. Do not overdo your personal rewards or celebrations; what might start out as motivating and refreshing can quickly become toxic.

How frequently should you set rewards? The answer is as often as you need to. It may take some trial and error to find out what is most effective for you. For some people, a larger reward at the end of the month works best. For others, small daily or weekly rewards seem to keep them motivated. Generally, the sooner after the behavior you reward yourself, the better. So now that you understand why it is important to reward yourself and how to reward yourself, you can begin experimenting today with self-rewards.

Make rewarding yourself a key part of your Untie the Knots journey, and you will find yourself working harder and staying motivated to make it to your next self-reward.

The Importance of Looking Around and Writing Things Down

"You may find your best friend or worst enemy in yourself."

— English Proverb

Once you start identifying and untying the knots in your life by applying the Untie the Knots principles and strategies, it will be your responsibility to look around and write things down, frequently.

Set a timeline for yourself, once a week, every two weeks, or once a month to schedule a personal sit-down session with yourself in a quiet, non-distracting place. Bring your personal journal, writing pads, pens, and personal scheduler with you. Then answer the following ten questions:

1) What have I learned?
2) Where and how have I grown?
3) What areas in my life still have challenges?
4) What distractions, if any, are hindering my progress?
5) At the present time in my life, do I rate my daily efforts as an "A," "B," "C," "D," or "F"?

6) Who can help me grow and improve at this point?
7) In 40 words or less, how do I honestly feel about my life?
8) What are the four most important things or people in my life?
9) What are the top three goals I'm currently striving to accomplish?
10) What two activities am I doing to bring my life balance?

After you have answered all ten questions, move onto this next step that will give you a clearer indication of the current balance of your life. Complete the "How Balanced or Unbalanced is Your Life" assessment tool.

Assessment Tool: <u>How Balanced or Unbalanced Is Your Life</u>?

Balance is the ability to manage the sometimes conflicting demands of work and personal life. A lack of balance leaves many people feeling over-stressed and unfulfilled. Rate the current balance in your life by circling the appropriate numbers below.

Note: This is not a pass or fail evaluation. Go with what your heart tells you, and most importantly, be true to yourself. Only through self-awareness can we make the necessary life changes to move us toward the life we desire.

	I have difficulty taking care of		Fair		I care for myself well in this way
1. Eating healthy	1	2	3	4	5
2. Exercise	1	2	3	4	5
3. Sleep	1	2	3	4	5
4. Time alone	1	2	3	4	5
5. Time with partner	1	2	3	4	5
6. Time with family	1	2	3	4	5

	I have difficulty taking care of		Fair		I care for myself well in this way
7. Play time (recreation, hobbies, sports)	1	2	3	4	5
8. Finances	1	2	3	4	5
9. Spirituality	1	2	3	4	5
10. Setting realistic expectations	1	2	3	4	5
11. Setting limits	1	2	3	4	5
12. Self-comforting	1	2	3	4	5
13. Personal growth or development	1	2	3	4	5

Add your circled numbers = _____

Now look below to view the **"Sliding Scale Responses."**

Sliding Scale Encouragement Responses

If your circled numbers totaled:

13 - 23   It's "time" to pick yourself up, dust yourself off, and move forward. What happened to you isn't the problem; what you feel about what happened to you is the problem. Forgive yourself, forgive the other person(s) involved, accept your mistake, and learn from it. Begin to remove clutter, confusion, and unwanted stress from your life. Remember: **You May Be Delayed, but YOU Are RARELY Denied!**

24 - 35   You are either sliding down or climbing back up the hill of life. I hope it's the latter of the two. There is hope for you! There is a purpose in this lifetime for you! Quit marking time—and move forward. Welcome back!

36 - 47   You have your good and bad days; nonetheless, you still manage to keep hold of the reins. Watch yourself though; you're in the middle and your life can go either way. **Inactivity** will succumb to *mediocrity*. Continuous **Action** will move you forward to brighter *future opportunities* and *success*.

48 - 56   You are only a few steps away from creating the life your desire...keep moving forward. Now that you have identified the other self-nurturing areas in your life that can use some enhancing, begin working on those areas today. **Note:** don't allow your strong areas to slip because you're focusing too much on your weak areas.

57 - 65   You are someone others should model. If everybody were like you there would be world peace. Give yourself a pat on the back.

There are many ways to assess your life. There are numerous assessment tools like the one you completed. These self-evaluation tools can be helpful for assessing where you are in your life. I use many in my programs to help people see and understand as much as possible: where they are with their health and quality of life, mentally, emotionally, physically, and spiritually. One of the best ways though is to write: journal about your feelings, your thoughts, and how you see your life. Is your perception of your life reality? How do you want to see and think about your life? Is that perception realistic? Reflect, spend time alone, write, but above all, be honest!

Things work out.

No matter how hopeless or stressful a situation may appear to be, it does, eventually, change. And when it does, it's almost always for the better. If you graph your life, you'll get peaks and valleys, but the overall trend is upwards.

Don't get discouraged by first drafts when you're looking around and writing notes down. Continuous peaks are on the horizon. Remember, your first draft isn't THE final draft; there's more positive and productive living to come.

Adapting and Adjusting to Whatever the World Throws Your Way

"If there is no wind, row."

— Danish Proverb

Creating a healthier and happier life is a process. Many of us live in a fast-paced society that focuses on getting instant gratification. However, if we live the life we are meant to live, we must be as healthy as possible to have the strength, energy, and stamina to create and achieve the goals we want. This takes a combination of many tools and techniques and information and education, but mostly it takes managing. Effective managing gives us the courage to first go within ourselves, so we can honestly admit where we are in our lives right now; identify where it is we want to be in the future; create a plan that will move us in the direction we want our lives to go; and finally, begin taking action on our plan.

Managing allows us to adapt and adjust to whatever the world throws our way. When we learn to effectively manage our lives, we empower ourselves to "press on" through periods of disappointments, frustrations, failure, struggles, and being overwhelmed.

The one fact we all know is that life happens and for the most part there are events we can and cannot control. From this point forward whenever the world throws you a curve ball, here are a few strategies to help you adapt and adjust to maintain or bring yourself back on your Untie the Knots path:

1. Know what you want.
Self-discipline is impossible without knowing your objective. Knowing what you want is the beginning point of discipline. People with direction have purpose. If you want to run a marathon, you must know how many miles you need to train each day to complete the race. If you want to lose weight, you must know what size you want to be.

2. List the important things.
Grab a sheet of paper, and make a numbered list, 1 through 10. Then, list the items in your life that are most important to you. Once you do so, take some quiet time and ask yourself if the way you currently spend your time matches your list. You'll then have a better idea of what items you need to spend more time on.

3. Determine what you're doing now.
For the next two weeks, write down everything you do and the amount of time you spend doing it. At the end of the two-week period, analyze your log, and determine what areas of your life can be streamlined. Example problem areas are spending the majority of your time at the office or doing four hours worth of chores each day.

4. Learn to say No to lesser things.
Your capacity to say no often determines your capacity to say yes to greater callings. Discipline is a matter of choice. One of the telltale signs of maturity is this ability to say no. An author was told early in his career, "You'll have to decide whether you are going to be a great writer or a great date. You can't be both." To say yes to certain desires, you may have to say No to many others.

5. Perform the hard part first.
The principle of delayed gratification is often expressed as "Save the best for last" or "Do your homework first" or "Pain now, plea-

sure later." Delayed gratification involves routine daily choices: skipping a late-night television program to go to bed early allows one the opportunity to be fresh in the morning; pushing back from the table with a single helping of food enables a person to fit into clothes a size smaller; and attacking home chores and responsibilities immediately after school or work frees up the rest of the evening for special family time.

6. Have a purpose in everything you do.
This is the principle of intention. Here, we need to ask a few questions. Will this activity help me reach my final destination? Does it enhance the priorities I've established as my life's purpose? Can someone else assist me in doing it better?

7. Streamline your work.
Are you always working late at the office? If so, does your job offer work-at-home options? Can you delegate more? Can you use your computer to speed up the time it takes to complete a regular task? Can you speak with your boss about hiring an assistant?

Perhaps you may consider getting your own business off the ground, so you can reduce your hours at your job. Or, if you do really well with your home business, you can then work at home full-time. If you have your own business already, is it possible to outsource some of your work? If you're the "only person that can do the job right," your schedule will always be full.

8. De-clutter and de-stress.
When you begin to de-clutter your home and office, you'll realize how much time it can save you to live and work in an organized environment. When your surroundings are de-cluttered, your mind has a chance to relax and focus.

Weed out old and outdated paperwork. Donate things you no longer use. Give items you do use a permanent home. Get rid of old e-mails. Lighten your wardrobe, your pantry, your basement--you'll be amazed at what you can actually live without and what you WON'T miss. You will spend less time looking for stuff and fretting over feelings of chaos, resulting in lower levels of stress and more enjoyable living.

People who learn how to effectively manage their lives are happier and healthier because they are better able to adapt and adjust to whatever the world throws their way.

Creating an Effective Support System

"Whatever my individual desires were to be free, I was not alone. There were others who felt the same way."

— Rosa Parks

A few years back, I went to a motivational event in Greenbelt, Maryland. On that evening, I listened to world renowned motivational speaker Les Brown explain, "You win in life with people. You cannot and will not achieve the level of success you aspire by yourself."

Mr. Brown is 100% correct!

In 1996, I created what I now call my "Fab Five Support Team." The significant support team members on my "Fab Five Support Team" assist in the following 11 areas of my life:

1) Education
2) Business
3) Mental Health
4) Family
5) Spiritual
6) Relationships
7) Financial and Investment Learning
8) Humanitarianism
9) Real Estate
10) Resource Management
11) Career Management

Imagine, whenever you have an accomplishment, challenge, or crisis in one of the above 11 areas of your life, you could pick up the phone and call a knowledgeable, caring, and supportive person who you can rely on to share honestly with you. To either teach you, point you in the right direction, or let you know truthfully how they think your decision or behavior is impacting a particular situation.

The moment you decide to build your own "Fab Five Support Team," you have to consider finding reliable, quality team members who have the stability, knowledge, professionalism, and confidence in helping you accomplish your goals and live your dreams. Your "Fab Five Support Team" members should be accomplished professionals or role models who are not fighting to be your best friend or looking to sugarcoat the feedback they are giving you.

Consider asking yourself and your potential "Fab Five Support Team" members the following questions when seeking and recruiting reliable, quality members:

- Does this person have a genuine interest in your well-being and future success?
- Will this person relate to your desires, goals, background, and life challenges?
- Is this person skilled and knowledgeable in the areas of your life you wish for them to support and assist you in?
- Will this person motivate, energize, and guide you tactfully towards your personal vision?
- Will this person have time to commit to mentoring and coaching you?
- Is this person trustworthy enough to share anything about your life and livelihood?
- Does this person have a non-judgmental and positive mental attitude?
- Is this person a good and patient listener?
- Does this person know how to give constructive feedback honestly and without tearing you completely down?

- What forms of communication does this person prefer to use when it comes to effective communications (telephone, e-mail, fax, mail, etc.)?
- Is this person a reliable role model, coach, and mentor that will enhance the quality of your "Fab Five Support Team"?

A reliable and quality "Fab Five Support Team" builds relationships that will help you tap into your potential and help you grow. The quality of your life can be enriched by strong "Fab Five Support Team" connections.

Once you have successfully assembled your "Fab Five Support Team," make sure you keep them informed of your life's progress, digressions, accomplishments, obstacles, and crisis. Never take any of your support team members for granted or abuse their support for foolish gains that equate to misuse of their time.

A good "Fab Five Support Team" will be around to share in your good times, your accomplishments, your moments of challenge, and your times of crisis. Today, make one contact to seek and recruit a reliable, quality "Fab Five Support Team" member. You and the enhanced quality of your life will be glad you did.

Staying Committed to Your Actions

"You can't spell SUCCESS without U!"

— Keith Harrell

If you are like most people, you are embarking on a new way of living right about now. Within six weeks, many readers of this book will deviate from their Untie the Knots journey, half will quit within six months, and less than one third of those who begin seeing and experiencing real-life results will still be practicing and mastering the Untie the Knots Process by the end of their first year.

Where will you be on your journey six weeks, six months, and a year from now?

If you plan to be living and enjoying a life of better health, balance, harmony, potential, significance, and prosperity a year from now and beyond, it will take constant persistence. Persistence wears down resistance. Persistence can turn a life of chaos and struggle into unleashed potential and prosperity. Persistence empowers you to successfully identify and untie your toxic knots of delay, decay, and disappointment.

The following nine simple tips can help you stay committed to your actions and goals while making the transition from toxic living to living significantly:

1. Don't try to do too much, too soon; you will end up burnt out and discouraged. It is always better to take baby steps. Spend at least 15-30 minutes each day learning and working on your Untie the Knots journey. Consistency is the key.

2. Schedule your Untie the Knots learning and development sessions on your calendar as if they were any other important appointment. This way, you will be able to balance your Untie the Knots journey with family, work, and social activities. You will be more successful if you fit your Untie the Knots journey into your current lifestyle. A little is always better than NONE.

3. If possible, plan your Untie the Knots learning and development sessions in the morning. You will get it done, feel energized all day, and avoid "life" getting in the way of achieving your goals.

4. Choose a role model. Ask a mentor or person who cares about your future success for suggestions and advice about how you can most effectively reach your goals. There are also a variety of other resources available for achieving your goals and living your life's purpose.

5. Keep an Untie the Knots journal. Chart your progress and accomplishments.

6. Give yourself some leeway – if you miss an Untie the Knots learning and development session or an entire week, get back on track as quickly as possible. Setbacks

and challenges are normal. The quicker you get back on track, the quicker you will reach your goals. Remember, "identifying and untying your knots" is not about being perfect, but about a series of positive choices that you make consistently. It is not an all or nothing process.

7. Evaluate your progress every three to six weeks and increase the intensity of your Untie the Knots practice and mastery to stay challenged and inspired.

8. Feel like skipping an Untie the Knots learning and development session? Get yourself to do something for at least 10–15 minutes. Most likely, once you start you will complete your entire planned session (If not, don't worry, 15 minutes is better than nothing).

9. Bored? Unfocused? Change your routine a bit. Add a mentor–mentee conference call to your planned session. One morning instead of going to the same quiet room where you have your planned sessions, get dressed and walk around your neighborhood thinking, assessing, learning, and practicing. Schedule a telephone conference call with your mentor or a caring support person to discuss your progress and development. Managing, adapting, and adjusting will aid you in staying focused and inspired throughout your Untie the Knots journey.

The tips outlined above could be used in or out of order. There is no sequence; the only consistent theme is that to stay committed to your actions you must keep choosing and using one of the above tips no matter what! You must stay persistent and consistent with positive and productive steps of action.

This week pay attention to your thoughts. Thoughts are like magnets: they go out into the world and attract the substances that match them.

Your emotions energize your thoughts: the stronger your emotions, the quicker you create what you want. Because energy follows thought, it's more important to focus on what you do want instead of what you don't want. Whatever you focus on is what you get!

The moment you catch yourself thinking, "Maybe I need to just forget about this," replace that thought with "I am committed to my goals and dreams." Then persist so you can arrive at each new goal and your updated dream on time.

Chapter Conclusion

In this chapter, you learned the importance of rewarding yourself for each Untie the Knots success you generate, no matter how big or small the accomplishment. You learned the importance of constantly looking around and writing things down by checking to see how balanced or unbalanced your life is at any given time. I encouraged you to seek out and create your own *"Fab Five Support Team"* for additional guidance, honest feedback, and support. I shared with you sound strategies to keep yourself focused on your Untie the Knots path, regardless what the world may throw your way. I explained to you that even with a green and growing attitude, determination, focus, persistence, and action, your life will never become 100% knots free. However, staying committed to your positive actions and personal action plan will elevate you to a new plane in life that is far more promising and rewarding than being on a level where you are so tied up you feel you can't think, produce, move, or breathe.

When you learn and develop an Untie the Knots approach to life, you will become more skilled at celebrating, assessing, managing, and persisting in the face of life's many great tests and challenges.

Chapter 15

Step 9: LEAVING A LASTING LEGACY: CREATING A LIFE OF SIGNIFICANCE

"The energy of the mind is the essence of life."

— Aristotle

In 1998, I met with Mr. Willie Jolley, internationally known motivational speaker, outside the Sheraton Hotel near the Baltimore-Washington International Airport. Willie and I sat in his car discussing my purpose and passion to speak. He asked me questions like "Why do you want to speak? What's your message? What stories about your life are you now sharing? Who are you doing this for? What purpose are you looking to fill? Do you consider being a speaker a form of service or a quick hustle?"

On that day, I learned and grew as a professional speaker, as a businessman, and as a human being. Willie taught me that what I had embarked on should not be about me; it had to be about a higher purpose that would advance someone else, a group of people, or a cause for the better. Willie instructed me to sit and think right there in his car and answer, "What purpose are you looking to serve as it pertains to becoming a successful professional speaker?" My answer was this: "The reason why I want to become a successful professional speaker is to advance my daughter, nephews, and family to a new level of thinking, acting, and being—a new standard in life. I want the depth of my commitment and work to impact and advance generations to come. I've also begun to stand up and make a difference in my community by explaining to and showing teenagers and young adults that there are other positive options they can choose to assist them in creating the life they want."

Willie made me think, grow, and connect to my "Why" like never before. He ended our meeting by stating, "Ty, if your 'Why' and purpose is strong enough and high enough (meaning it extends beyond selfish interests or gains), you will bring great value and passion to the professional speaking industry and your life."

I learned on that day that significance happens and lasting legacies are born when your life's purpose and passions are not focused primarily on you.

Why Leave a Lasting Legacy?

"More important than leaving an inheritance is leaving a legacy."

— Author Unknown

We should strive to create and leave a lasting legacy because it helps to preserve our memories and heritage for generations that follow. A lasting legacy can become the new standard for excellence or the foundation of values for a family, group of friends, community, or business.

There is one fact about life: we all are born and we all die. So, the straightforward question is, "What are you going to do in between?"

Our legacy is a reality, and we all have one. Even the baby that dies in infancy has some effect on the family he or she was born into. Something changes with the existence of each human life, and each day we are building a legacy, whether we are aware of it or not and whether we like it or not. Our personal lives will have an impact on others, even those yet unborn.

As I observe the world today, I find it interesting when I drive by a church and see each side of the street packed with people in line waiting to get inside to pay their last respects to someone who left a significant mark on the world. Someone who left a lasting legacy, a mark that empowered, encouraged, enriched, and inspired family, friends, business colleagues, the community, and the world. Conversely, it's also interesting to see a funeral hearse driving down the road toward a cemetery to lay someone to rest with only one car following behind. Here's a person who lived but did little to enrich his or her family, friends, community, business colleagues, or world in any way. Each time I observe this outcome the experience forces me to reflect, "What was each deceased person's life like? What did each person do or not do to have such an outcome?"

People want to leave a mark on the world. I believe everyone wants to be remembered in some special way. Legacies are special gifts from one generation to another.

What do you think about when you think of a legacy? Dictionary. com defines a legacy as "Something handed down from an ancestor or a predecessor from the past." It may or may not be from an ancestor, but for the purpose of this chapter, it is assumed to be so. We are not talking about the furniture your Aunt Janice had in her dining room, the car your father owned, or the large financial inheritance your grandmother left you, but rather the intangibles that are a part of you that came from your family.

We will all leave a legacy of some sort; the question is, "What will it be?" A legacy is something that remains after we leave this world: something that speaks of our lives. If you were to leave this world peacefully this evening in your sleep, what would your family, friends, co-workers, and community have to say about you?

Why leave a lasting legacy? A true lasting legacy comes from going beyond your own limited interests. The more you take into account the interests and improvement of others, the more significant and prosperous your life becomes.

A lasting legacy comes not from having the right job or having the right contacts or from becoming famous or amassing great financial wealth. A lasting legacy comes from taking genuine steps of action in your life to be of service, not for monetary gains, but for the enhancement of others. When you find and champion a cause that will improve some aspect of your family, a group of people, a community, or the world—that's when you will find yourself on the path to creating a lasting legacy because the focus is no longer on your personal interests.

Think of someone who you believe without a doubt created and left a lasting legacy. I think you would agree with me that the person you thought of found an effective way to be of service. The person you thought of found a cause to champion, and financial gains, rewards, or accolades were not the primary focus. Still, they managed to impact, touch, inspire, and improve the lives of many.

Constant steps of action that serve, help, and empower others create a true lasting legacy.

The more valuable you can make yourself to others, the more value you will see flowing into your own life. That holds true no matter what your circumstances, past experiences, or background may be. If you have a pulse, a body that is able to move and willing to inspire others, a vision and a positive mental attitude, and a cause backed with the humbling passion to serve others, you too can create and leave a lasting legacy. You too can leave a mark on the world that will show and prove you gave and did the best you could with what you knew here on Earth.

Go beyond the mere survival dictated by your own narrow self-interests. Fill your moments with service and your purpose with a cause, and you will create and leave a lasting legacy that will preserve your memories and enrich your family's heritage for generations to come.

Why Live a Life of Significance?

"Great minds have purposes, others have wishes."
— Washington Irving

When you possess a healthy character and the constant willingness to serve and help others, regardless of whether you have a billion dollars or a single penny in your life, this spirit will not allow you to fail. The purpose of everything we decide should be about having significance and leaving a lasting legacy. Having significance and leaving a lasting legacy is far more important than becoming the richest man or woman in the world or the best-looking man or woman in the world.

What is the significance of life? This is an important question. After birth, a human being rapidly ages and then dies. Between the processes of birth, aging, being healthy, being sick, and dying, he or she is busy learning, working, eating, grooming, and growing. What is there to achieve? What is the significance of this? These questions are the puzzle. In childhood, we unconsciously follow social norms and often live without thinking about these questions. This is common. But for those who have a more sensitive perception of their situations, those living in unfavorable environments, those experiencing failure in their career, or those who are debilitated by illnesses, these individuals may lose some or all of their hope. Then the questions arise, "What is the significance of life? What are we busy indulging in?" Although these questions that sometimes come to us linger in our mind, we feel there is no way out. We keep on indulging in learning, working, eating, grooming, and growing.

Life is meaningful. Not only should we discover its worthiness, but we should also realize its ultimate significance. With significance, we evolve our everyday routines, goals, opportunities, successes, dreams, and life to a level of meaning far beyond our pre-conceived expectations or common normality.

You should never quit dreaming and never quit on your dreams no matter how often people may discourage or disagree with you or your dreams. When you quit and give up on your dreams, you have chosen to quit living, to end your opportunity to live a life of significance, and to abandon and leave whatever legacy your life has at that time. And you're much better than that!

Do not yield to people who say, "You can't do this or that." My siblings didn't believe I could start and operate my own successful professional motivational speaking business; I can hear them still saying, "You were the little knucklehead who ran around the neighborhood always getting in trouble. Everyone in our family has always worked for an employer that was safe and reliable. Boy, go back and get your old job." One of my teachers back in high school said, "Mr. Howard, you won't be able to actualize your dreams because you can't even name five past Nobel Peace Prize winners."

When you choose to create and live a life of significance, it is not required to gain the support of other people, especially family, nor is it necessary for you to know five past Nobel Peace Prize winners.

A lasting legacy comes from finding your purpose in life. Once your purpose is found, it becomes your passion, which manifests into your goals, then into your cause, and then into your life of significance. Your driven purpose and life of constant service becomes your ultimate success.

Remember, you can achieve success without significance, but you cannot achieve significance without success.

I encourage you to keep your dream alive. If you gave up on or abandoned your dream some time ago, go back and pick it up again, or look deep within yourself, your heart, and your spirit to find a new dream to begin pursuing today. You are never too young or too old to have and pursue "your" dream. I encourage you to do this because it will bring true meaning and purpose to learning, practicing, and mastering the Untie the Knots Process.

Why live a life of significance? When you allow your passion for significance to drive your purpose, you will find yourself doing things you never thought you could do, no matter how old you are. You will be accomplishing goals in your life that others doubted you could achieve or tried to discourage you from even attempting. You will create and live a life of significance because you decided to help, inspire, care for, and serve someone or a cause other than yourself with a healthy character and a positive mental attitude. Living significantly is always possible.

Significance is as significance does.

Will you create and live a life of significance?

Discovering and Connecting to Your Life's Purpose

"Your work is to discover your work and then with all your heart give yourself to it."

— Buddha

How do you discover your real purpose in life? I'm not talking about your job, your daily responsibilities, or even your long-term goals. I mean the real reason why you're here at all—the very reason you exist.

Perhaps you're a rather pessimistic person who doesn't believe you have purpose and that life has no real meaning. Doesn't matter. Not believing that you have a purpose won't prevent you from discovering it, just as a lack of belief in gravity won't prevent you from tripping. All that a lack of belief will do is make it take longer, so if you're a pessimist, instead of seeing yourself discover and connect with life's purpose today, envision yourself discovering and connecting with your life's purpose tomorrow. If you're really stubborn, it's okay to envision yourself discovering and connecting with your life's purpose next week or next month.

Here's a story about Bruce Lee, actor and martial arts expert, which will set the stage for your "Life Purpose" exercise. A master martial artist asked Bruce to teach him everything he knew about martial arts. Bruce held up two cups, both filled to the brim with liquid. "The first cup," said Bruce, "represents all of your knowledge about martial arts. The second cup represents all of my knowledge about martial arts. If you want to fill your cup with my knowledge, you must first empty your cup of knowledge."

If you want to discover your true purpose in life, you must first empty your mind of all the false purposes you've been taught (including the idea that you may have no purpose at all in life).

So, how do you discover your purpose in life? While there are many ways, and some are fairly involved, here is one of the simplest anyone can do. The more open you are to this process and the more you expect it to work, the faster it will work. Not being open to this process or having doubts about it or thinking it's a meaningless waste of time won't prevent it from working for you—again, it will just take longer for you to discover and connect with your life's purpose.

As you go through this process, some of your answers will be very similar. You may even restate previous answers. Then you might head off on a new tangent and generate more answers about some other theme. That's fine. You can list whatever answers pop into your head as long as you keep writing and answering openly and honestly.

Answer and use the following questions to help you gain insight into your life's purpose.

Write every thought you have. Let the words flow. Keep writing until there is no more response.

What are you good at?

What are your gifts, talents, and abilities?

What do you love to do?

What makes you come alive?

What were you doing when you were the happiest in your life thus far?

What are you most proud of having accomplished at this point in your life?

What characteristics right now are you most proud of?

When you were young, what did you know you would do when you grew up?

When you are on your deathbed, what five activities will you hope you completed in your lifetime?

If you could fix one major problem in the world right now, what would it be?

Who in history do you admire most and why?

If you were financially able to retire one year from today, what would you begin working on to prepare for your retirement?

What would you most like the people at your funeral to specifically say about you?

What do you feel is your purpose or vision in life right now?

What is in the way of you getting ahead in life right now?

List three possible life purposes:

1. _____

_____

2. _____

_____

3. _____

_____

Clarifying Your Purpose

Imagine you are at a dinner party in your honor. Everything has been laid out for you in the most beautiful way. Your family, friends, colleagues, and local news reporters are there. Three people are about to stand to talk about you. They will explain these statements to everyone in the room:

Who you are;
What you have achieved;
How you did it;
Where you failed, yet persevered;
Your value to family and friends; and
Why it's an honor to know and interact with you.

What would you like them to say?

Stop here and write exactly what you would like them to say about you, your life, and your achievements. Let your highest aspirations flow from within without judgment or censorship.

Did you know that 80% of success comes from being clear about who you are and what you want to accomplish?

My own purpose statement is to — "Inspire A Generation: one person at a time, one audience at a time, and one community at a time."

Discovering your life purpose will allow you to reconnect with your soul and enable you to make a significant contribution to the world. Your life purpose will often seem "bigger than life." You may even wonder if you have the right assignment. The truth is your purpose was designed especially for you, and it will fit you like a glove, so no one else needs to understand and believe in it except you.

When you decide to live your life "on purpose," you become more fulfilled. As a result, you can show others how to live to their full potential. When who you are and what you do are in alignment with your authentic self, anything is possible. When you are living your purpose, you feel more passionate about life, more excited about waking up to each new day; and you have a brightness that shines from within. You will have more meaning, a greater sense of self-worth, and a stronger spiritual connection with life around you.

Becoming the Example and Setting the Standard

> *"Example is not the main thing in influencing others. It's the only thing."*
>
> — Albert Schweitzer

Leaving a lasting legacy and living a life of significance have two meanings: 1) you accept the challenge of becoming the example, and 2) you have no problems in setting the standard.

Many people today are not living a significant life or leaving behind a lasting, meaningful legacy because they do not desire anything that will cause them to stand out from the crowd.

World-renowned motivational speaker Les Brown said it best: "If you don't stand up for something, you may fall for anything."

People who know me know that my positive and enthusiastic way about life is not a façade. I really am that way from the inside out. If you were to come across me in public and ask me, "Ty, how are you today?", my response would most likely be, "I'm doing GREAT! Thanks for asking. How are you?" I've had people question me on numerous occasions about every day being a "GREAT Day or an 'A' Day." I choose to be this way so I can be the example and set a new standard. I have learned over the years from reading and listening to other great minds that YOU determine how you will think and respond to the world each and every day. This doesn't mean I am immune to life's great challenges and problems. We all have our challenges, problems, and tests. With a positive and enthusiastic state of mind though, I'm able to see the light at the end of tunnel versus a constant string of dead end streets.

This standard allows me to have big ideas and enough energy to follow through on them. Those who are around me often eventually catch on that this is how I operate. It's a good approach that obviously works. It's contagious in the best sense of the word. One fact everyone knows about me and InspiraGen Institute, Inc. is that we get work done. A big reason for this is because I've set the new standard and choose to lead by example.

If you like to work hard, you will attract people with the same ethic. The people who work with me enjoy the daily challenges and set their own standards to meet those challenges. Their pattern of thinking matches mine: How do we accomplish more? How do we get to where we want to go? It's a combination of vision, courage, determination, purpose, and discipline to realize that the possibilities are always there. But if you're thinking too small, you might miss them.

Ask yourself the following questions: Am I the example for my family, friends, or community to follow? What standard would you like to be known for? Then go about becoming the positive and healthy example and setting that standard for yourself and others. No one else can set it for you. I remember when my mother couldn't understand why I wanted to leave a job where I was making $70,000-80,000 a year to become a motivational speaker. I had my eye on speaking to youth and young adults worldwide since speaking at the school in the Washington, D.C. area back when I was in the U.S. Navy; it was now my passion, my life purpose.

My family was never known for being entrepreneurs. We were mainly blue-collar workers who worked hard and made an honest living. I'm sure we all had goals, aspirations, and dreams; however, no one had ever stepped up and out to pursue them. This was my time and my opportunity—so, I did. I stepped out on faith to become the example and to set a new standard. My stepping up was not about me though. Becoming the example and setting a new standard was and still is mainly meant to show my daughter, my nephews, my siblings, and the generations to follow that it's possible. You can have a dream, a purpose, and create and live a life of significance. It's not only meant for other people who we see on television each and every day; it's meant for us too!

I began speaking to youth audiences, and the feedback I received was encouraging. This fueled my passion, which drove my purpose to continue living significantly and creating my lasting legacy. There are tens of thousands of other speakers throughout the world. I learned that the difference doesn't lie in what I do as a speaker, but in the fact that I constantly strive to do it better than anybody else can. The great speakers that I admire and learn from on a daily basis perform routine tasks but with extraordinary skill.

So the secrets to setting new standards and becoming the example and new standards setter is relatively simple. If you invest the effort to make sure that everything you do exceeds expectations by a healthy margin, you become the example and set new standards. And you move steadily ahead of the pack.

If you stay alert, you will see that every day presents you countless opportunities to become the example and set new standards for others to follow:

- **Show up ahead of time for all appointments.** If someone expects you to arrive at an appointment at noon, make it your purpose to show up at 11:45 a.m. Leave your home or previous commitment well in advance to avoid excuses about traffic or any other challenges. Exceeding expectations is a quick path to setting new standards.
- **Keep every promise you make.** If you tell a friend or family member that you will help them pack and move, don't make them call to remind you. There are no small promises - only small people who don't fulfill them. Here's where you can set the standard for others to follow.

- **Be a better communicator than everyone around you.**
  Listen to people and ask follow-up questions to be sure
  you have understood. Strive to learn and use a new vocabulary word correctly each day. Not many people invest even a few extra minutes in these steps. Yet if you do,
  you will become the example for the way people should
  communicate in your family, community, or workplace.
- **Respect everyone, especially people who are different
  from you.** That's not simplistic advice. Stop and think
  about how rare genuine respect for others can be in our
  world. Practice it and watch your leadership profile grow.
  Practice a new standard long enough and it becomes a
  way of life for others to follow.
- **Admit when you're wrong and then apologize.** If you
  find out that you have made a mistake or were wrong
  about anything, and it has impacted or affected someone's life, admit you were wrong and then apologize. This
  is a new standard that will definitely separate you from
  the rest and win you the admiration of others because
  you've become the example for others to follow.
- **Look and act the part.** If you want others to take you
  and your life purpose seriously, make it your priority to
  look and act the part. Do not think that when you're not
  working directly in your purpose, cause, or career field,
  people aren't watching you, because they are and they do.
  Example-setters often look and act the part because of
  their positive character and mental attitude.
- **Give continuously.** When you give your time, money,
  and material possessions to others who need them more
  than you, you become the example that shows service to
  others is your way of life. Make it your goal each month
  to give your time, money, or material possessions at least
  twice a month. When you give, give unconditionally; do
  not expect anything in return.
- **Participate in your community.** Do not be the neighbor
  who doesn't know the neighbors who live next door. Set
  the new standard for your community; say, "Hello" and
  make friends. Even when community efforts may seem
  corny, participate anyway. Remember, it's not always

about you. It is about you becoming the example and setting new standards. Smile, and become an active participant in your community. Your idea may be the idea that brings more of your community together.

Opportunities to become the example and set new standards are literally right before you every minute of the day. I now look for them and seize them, and my efforts are rewarded with exceptional recognition and the continuous development of a significant life for others to learn from and follow.

You can do the same. Just focus on becoming the example by taking determined and disciplined steps of action. Focus on implementing positive and healthy standards into your way of living and stay with them tenaciously. Do not allow anyone or anything to force you to abandon what you've now decided to stand up and step out for—to become the example and set a new standard for you and others to follow. Do this fearlessly and you will be defining yourself and your future success in the process.

Gathering and Maintaining Your Life's History

"A page of history is worth a pound of logic."

— Oliver Wendell Holmes

Your stories of "way back when," your knowledge of family history, and your perspective on life may be lost forever unless you begin recording them now.

Begin with your best stories first. You know the ones your family, siblings, children, and friends have asked you to tell repeatedly. And then there are those you use to illustrate a point.

But why those? Your siblings and children already know those. They've heard them frequently. So why shouldn't you move on to stories they've never heard?

For one thing, they want to hear those anecdotes again because the stories remind them of their childhood. Like the *Little Engine That Thought He Could* tales, your family stories are a part of its personal folklore.

Ask your relatives what they want to know about. Wouldn't it be terrible if you proudly presented your finished product to a parent, sibling, or child, and they moaned, "Oh, you forgot to tell the story about the time when we broke Mommy's lamp playing football in her living room. We tried to make paste with flower and water to glue the lamp back together. It held temporarily until Mommy turned the light on that evening to read her newspaper." To your brother, that was a major event.

Your nieces and nephews will want to know about their own mother or father's childhood antics. Your cousins will surely want you to include a profile of your grandparents.

Carry a notebook with you everywhere you go. When you have to wait in a doctor's office or in your mechanic's waiting area, never waste time reading a magazine; get busy on your life history project.

Select your medium. Would you feel more comfortable using a notebook and writing by hand? Will the finished product be a journal? A self-made scrapbook? A commercial fill-in-the-blanks book? A typed and photocopied booklet? A self-published book? Audiotapes just for the family? Home DVDs for the family?

A typed and photocopied booklet can be the simplest way to get your life history into many hands quickly and inexpensively. With a soft cover, it is semi-permanent. A hardcover should last as long as the paper does.

A self-published paperback or hardbound book can be expensive, but the more copies printed, the less the cost per copy. This is more likely to be saved for many generations and will be a source of great pride for the author.

Do not look at this project or process as work. Look at it as setting the new standard and example for how you and your family will capture, record, and pass on your family's heritage and history. We live in a world of awesome technology and software; there is no excuse for a family's history to be lost, fragmented, or forgotten. At least do your part.

Purposely Passing on Your Legacy

"The only gift is a portion of thyself."

— Ralph Waldo Emerson

Think about the lasting legacy you want to give. We all have good and bad parts to the legacy we have inherited. The key is to move forward from here. For some, taking a closer look at the legacy they've been given helps them assess the legacy they want to create and pass on. After considering your past, it's now time to look forward to the future of your family and generations to follow.

Decide what you will keep. You probably have things you received that are wonderful and need to be kept and passed on. Other things may need to be thrown out. Or, perhaps, you have a weak legacy that needs strengthening.

In spite of whatever you received, you can now intentionally pass along the good. This isn't always easy. If you saw or experienced a bunch of negativity in your parents' lives, you may be tempted to throw everything out, good with the bad. Don't. That would be like burning down the house to get rid of some bugs.

Always look for the silver lining: look for the good in the bad. Your history and heritage is just that, yours. There is no need to look for the erase or rewind button. When you decide to purposely pass on your lasting legacy, step back, reflect, and share the good with the bad. Let those who will get to know you learn about the mistakes you made, the lessons you encountered, what your family and growing experiences were like, and the periods in your life where you triumphed, persevered, and accomplished your goals, aspirations, and dreams.

Now that you're on your Untie the Knots journey and are striving to create and live a significant life, as you share your life history, it will become more and more inspiring, encouraging, empowering, and enriching for all who get to know you.

Decide on a format. You could use an anecdotal style or a flowing life-story approach. Or you might write vignettes and profiles with "bridges" to take the reader from one story to the next. The same would be true if you used cds or DVDs (audio or video).

Be prepared to change your medium or format. With good notes and a running list of what to include, you can switch from one medium or format to another without great difficulty if you become uncomfortable with your first choice.

Decide who your stories are for. Do you expect your parents, siblings, children, grandchildren, and others in your direct line to be the only ones to care? Or would your extended family want to know more about you and the people who touched your life? Will your friends want a copy? Are you into genealogy? If you include ancestors and currently living relatives in your vignettes, you may want to make your work available to your entire genealogical family and people you may have never met.

Express your feelings. Anyone can record dry history. People (especially your family) years from now will want to know how you felt about major events that occurred during your lifetime.

Expect rewards. Do not be surprised when you find a new sense of purpose. The joy of accomplishing your goal and handing the finished product to your loved ones can be indescribable. During the process, you may be building closer relationships with the ones you love. The more they find out about your past and understand how you feel, the more they will truly know you.

Today, you can begin to take positive steps to capture and prepare a new heritage for yourself and your family to begin purposely passing down for generations to come.

Chapter Conclusion

In this chapter, you learned the importance of creating a lasting legacy by creating and living a significant life. I shared that you can be successful without having a significant life, but you cannot have a significant life without being successful. I explained why you should answer the questions "Why leave a lasting legacy?" and "Why live a significant life?" I shared a simple process about how to discover and connect with your life's purpose so you can add meaning and passion to your life. I shared with you eight secrets to keep yourself alert so you can become a constant example and new standard setter for others to follow. I encouraged you to purposely record, capture, and pass on your life history so the current and future generations of your family can learn and benefit from who you are and maintain your family's heritage. This step, among all the nine Untie the Knots Process steps, will be your greatest challenge to accept and fulfill; however, I think you will agree with me at this point that when you decide to live a significant life and leave a lasting legacy, everyone wins. Learn, practice, and master the principles and learning lessons of this chapter, and you will find yourself and your significant life repeatedly back at step one of the Untie the Knots Process because you're enjoying and managing your new happier and healthier and more harmonious, prosperous, and purpose-driven life.

NEVER QUIT! NEVER STOP! DON'T EVER GIVE UP! Your significant life and lasting legacy are worth standing up for, fighting for, and purposely living for daily. Your future and future generations are depending on you.

Unit Summary

NEVER QUIT! NEVER STOP! DON'T EVER GIVE UP!

To add true value to your life takes commitment, reward, assessment, management, persistence, and significance. When characteristics like these are actively in play within your life, it increases opportunities to leave a lasting legacy. A lasting legacy that will show and prove that you boldly and courageously stood up within to "Never Quit! Never Stop! And Never Ever Give UP!"

Chapters 13, 14, and 15 were written to 1) propel you to Make "A" Commitment to YOUR Life; 2) inspire you to alertly reward and manage your life for continuous learning, development, and accomplishment; and 3) provide you with sound practical reasons and processes to hopefully drive you to having a dream, purpose, passion, and commitment to live a significant life with the discipline to creating a positive and valuable lasting legacy.

Let's recap the three chapters that make up Unit 5, Part 4: NEVER QUIT! NEVER STOP! DON'T EVER GIVE UP!

Chapter 13, Step 7: Making "A" Commitment to Life

Chapter 14, Step 8: Celebrating, Assessing, Managing, and Persisting

Chapter 15, Step 9: Leaving A Lasting Legacy: Creating A Life of Significance

We've encountered the following **Infusers** *(Freedom Break Away Tools)* that were explained in the introduction of this book:

Infuser #1: Reinstate a Positive Attitude
If you are serious about breaking free and away from the knots that tie up your life, you will be required to put into place a positive mental attitude. You will have to be committed to developing and working constantly with a positive attitude, regardless of your past experiences or current situations or circumstances.

Infuser #2: Refocus
How are you going to change the direction of your life if you're not aware of what direction you're currently going in?

Infuser #3: Choose
Decide true freedom and life is what you want and then go where you can produce those results.

Infuser #4: Identify
To successfully break away from anything that has delayed or derailed your life in the past, you must summon the bold confidence to now identify it as a toxic habit, choice, person, or relationship.

Infuser #5: Simplify
Remove clutter, confusion, unwanted stress, and sabotaging distractions from your life daily, and watch new, desired opportunities appear.

Infuser #6: Believe
It takes your strong will and unshakable faith to make the impossible possible.

Infuser #7: Move
Don't just stand there knowing how...do it! Quit procrastinating and making excuses. My ultimate goal is to inspire, teach, and empower you to create an updated personal life plan; boldly face your fears; and move forward daily in executing your new personal life plan.

Infuser #9: Persist
How bad do you want what you now see? No more excuses...no more procrastination...no more string of bad and unproductive days! Stay the course!

Infuser #10: Leave a Mark of Significance
It's one experience to live and simply to have come and gone. It's another experience to have purposely decided to create and live a life of significance. A life that will enable you to leave behind a

lasting legacy that will contribute to your family's heritage and that will also allow many others who come after you to learn and grow from your efforts.

This unit (Chapters 13 through 15) is where your purpose and passion connect you to your planned life of significance, which will later connect you to your lasting legacy. Make sure you read it more than once because the material in this unit is meant to keep you enthusiastic, committed, focused, and disciplined to the Untie the Knots Process.

You too have the ability, creativity, passion, and energy to leave a valuable mark of significance on the world.

NEVER QUIT! NEVER STOP! DON'T EVER GIVE UP!

To gain immediate access to a practical, comprehensive, step-by-step guide that will help you break free of the 50 Most Common Toxic Knots, visit the following link on the Internet, right now:

http://www.tyhoward.com/KnotsFree_SpecialGuide.html

(Or turn to Appendix C for more information about the Knots Free Special Guide.)

Time OUT!

Just to recap some of the major concepts you've read about thus far, find and write in your journal the answers to the following questions:

- What are the two types of distractions?
  Refer to the "Types of Distractions" section in Chapter 13 for the answer.

- How can you begin monitoring your confirmed commitment to your future?
  Refer to the "Saying 'YES' to Your Future" section in Chapter 13 for the answer.

- What is the purpose of rewarding yourself after you have accomplished a task, goal, or project?
  Refer to the "Rewarding Yourself" section in Chapter 14 for the answer.

- What are four strategies that you can use when the world throws you a curve ball or challenge?
  Refer to "Adapting and Adjusting to Whatever the World Throws Your Way" section in Chapter 14 for the answer.

- Why does Ty encourage you to leave a lasting legacy?
  Refer to the "Why Leave a Lasting Legacy?" section in Chapter 15 for the answer.

- Why does Ty encourage you to live a significant life?
  Refer to the "Why Live a Life of Significance?" section in Chapter 15 for the answer.

"You're not obligated to win. You're obligated to keep trying to do the best you can every day."

— Marian Wright Edelman

PART 5

ONCE IS NEVER ENOUGH—LET'S DO IT AGAIN!

"Repetition is the mother of skill."

— *Anthony Robbins*

In Part 5...

You will find out how to put the Untie the Knots Process to work and how to avoid self- and outside-sabotage. I will also show you the importance of applying the T.A.P.P. (Think, Act, Pray, and Prosper) method to empower yourself to move forward whenever you have reached a period of stagnation. You will learn that the Untie the Knots Process was designed to become a permanent part of your life. Learning and applying the process once will never be enough. We will never be 100% free of toxic knots. So, it will be smart and effective for us all to embrace and utilize a "Once Is Never Enough—Let's Do It Again Philosophy!" Let's have fun with life and not allow it to drag us through it.

Let's create and maintain a life with fewer knots so we can live a significant life with improved health, happiness, balance, harmony, potential, and prosperity.

Chapter 16

MAKING THE
UNTIE THE KNOTS
PROCESS A CONTINUOUS CYCLE

*"Efficiency is doing better than what already is
being done."*

— Peter F. Drucker

Putting knowledge and honest self-discovery to work is the objective of the Untie the Knots Cycle. The cycle's model is a 12-phase cycle guided and driven by five components (Initiating, Diagnosing, Establishing, Acting, and Learning).

The cycle was developed to give your Untie the Knots journey true meaning, guidance, and focus. It communicates that to achieve the desired results you truly want from the Untie the Knots Cycle you must continuously develop and practice the process of awareness, discovery, design, development, action, evaluation, revision, refinement, reward, and persistence.

To get the most from this cycle, you should journal, take notes, record times and commitments, and involve your stakeholders (caring supporters) throughout the cycle. Your caring supporters or sponsors (stakeholders) will be there to advise, guide, cheer, mentor, and coach you throughout the entire process. They will assist you in staying focused and committed to the personal vision and plan of action you create.

The 12 phases and five components of the cycle are linked together in a circular pattern as shown in the illustration on the next page.

The Untie the Knots Cycle
A 12-Phase Cycle

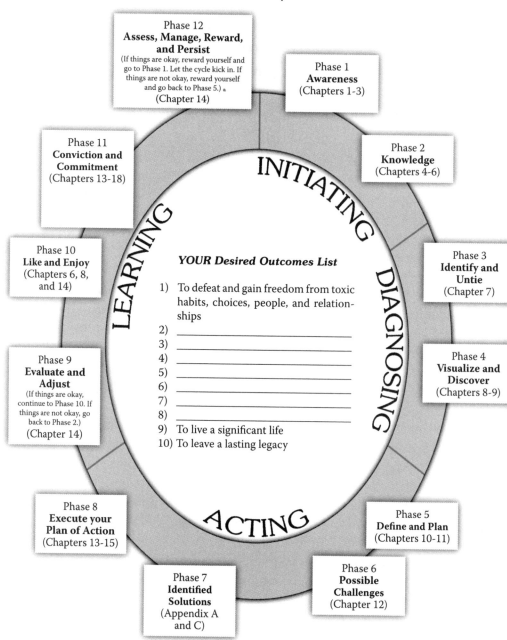

Phase 12
Assess, Manage, Reward, and Persist
(If things are okay, reward yourself and go to Phase 1. Let the cycle kick in. If things are not okay, reward yourself and go back to Phase 5.)
(Chapter 14)

Phase 1
Awareness
(Chapters 1-3)

Phase 11
Conviction and Commitment
(Chapters 13-18)

Phase 2
Knowledge
(Chapters 4-6)

INITIATING

Phase 10
Like and Enjoy
(Chapters 6, 8, and 14)

LEARNING

Phase 3
Identify and Untie
(Chapter 7)

DIAGNOSING

YOUR Desired Outcomes List

1) To defeat and gain freedom from toxic habits, choices, people, and relationships
2) _____
3) _____
4) _____
5) _____
6) _____
7) _____
8) _____
9) To live a significant life
10) To leave a lasting legacy

Phase 9
Evaluate and Adjust
(If things are okay, continue to Phase 10. If things are not okay, go back to Phase 2.)
(Chapter 14)

Phase 4
Visualize and Discover
(Chapters 8-9)

Phase 8
Execute your Plan of Action
(Chapters 13-15)

ACTING

Phase 5
Define and Plan
(Chapters 10-11)

Phase 7
Identified Solutions
(Appendix A and C)

Phase 6
Possible Challenges
(Chapter 12)

To achieve the best results possible with the Untie the Knots Process, you will need to repeat the cycle by accomplishing a second Untie the Knots success. The second should be followed by a third, etc. Each continuous success will move your life toward your ultimate growing expectations and desires.

Stage Components and Phases of the Untie the Knots Process

"No matter how carefully you plan your goals they will never be more than pipe dreams unless you pursue them with gusto."

— W. Clement Stone

Initiating Component

The Initiating Component is where you enter the Untie the Knots Process to increase your awareness and knowledge for improvement. This covers issues such as establishing initial self-awareness, knowledge of the Untie the Knots Process, general goals and plans for self-discovery and self-improvement, and evaluating your personal readiness for the cycle in general. This phase starts when stimulus for improvement is recognized and understood, and the work for establishing the Untie the Knots Process starts, initially as a task of self-discovery through increased self-awareness and knowledge. The phases within the Initiating Component are as follows:

Phase 1   Awareness
Phase 2   Knowledge

The purpose of Phase 1 – the Awareness Phase – is to increase your awareness to a level of clarity and understanding that toxic knots are hazardous and harmful to your life, relationships, health, career, and dreams. In this phase, your attitude and desire to change is primed and set to a position that will eventually help you establish a designed plan of action for implementing the Untie the Knots Process to work for continuous improvement. The Awareness Phase consists of Chapters 1-3.

The purpose of Phase 2 – the Knowledge Phase – is to increase your knowledge to a level of clarity and understanding so that the Untie the Knots Process is just that—a process. In this phase, you are introduced to the 9 Step Untie the Knots Process and are encouraged to 1) boldly stand up within for continuous change and growth and 2) to make the process a lifelong hobby. The Knowledge Phase consists of Chapters 3-6.

The Diagnosing Component

The Diagnosing Component is where you establish a more meaningful understanding of the Untie the Knots Process. It provides you with a table listing the 50 Most Common Toxic Knots tying up many people and organizations today. This is the stage where the reader is charged and challenged to "Get Real" and "Be Honest" because this stage sets the baseline for self-diagnosing and self-improvement. The phase within the Diagnosing Component Stage is as follows:

Phase 3   Identify and Untie

The purpose of Phase 3 – the Identify and Untie Phase – is to bring you face-to-face with yourself and the list of the 50 Most Common Toxic Knots so you can assess and diagnose yourself for toxic knots in the areas of habits, choices, people, and relationships. In this phase, the information revealed, acknowledged, and recorded will later support, focus, and drive your ability to successfully identify and untie your toxic knots when working through Phases 4 through 12. The Identify and Untie Phase is Chapter 7.

The Establishing Component

The Establishing Component is where you establish the necessary groundwork to create improvement actions that will drive and maintain the Untie the Knots Process. It is also largely a repetition of the tasks done in the Initiating and Diagnosing Components, now repeated with a clearer view of what is ahead. This is the stage where you decide to do you, face your fears, set unstoppable goals, and command yourself to move forward continuously. The phases within the Establishing Component are as follows:

Phase 4   Visualize and Discover
Phase 5   Define and Plan

The purpose of Phase 4 – the Visualize and Discover Phase – is to bring you to a courageous point where you decide to do you and acknowledge and face your fears. In this phase, you create and see an updated vision of yourself and your future. You begin to see a person and a personal vision that is capable of taking on and pushing through one fear after another. The Visualize and Discover Phase consists of Chapters 8 and 9.

The purpose of Phase 5 – the Define and Plan Phase – is to bring you to the point in the process where you take the necessary time to sit down, think through, and write down new unstoppable goals that will now guide and direct your life. You will seek out and recruit stakeholders (caring supporters) who will advise, mentor, and coach you along your Untie the Knots journey. You will also create commands for your life that are needed and necessary to command yourself to move forward once again. In this phase, the information you write down becomes the new definition, meaning, and plan for your life and your Untie the Knots journey. The Define and Plan Phase consists of Chapters 10 and 11.

The Acting Component

The Acting Component is where you think through, write down, review, and execute your actual plan for improvements. You will oversee the activities unfolding, support them, and ensure that you stay on course. The activities in the Acting Component unite your personal vision, action plan for success, and desired outcomes for working through the Untie the Knots Process. This is the stage where you take responsibility for the improvement project or action, identify possible challenges, develop the solution, practice it, validate and refine it, develop a plan for rollout, execute your plan of action, and evaluate the solution in use. The phases within the Acting Component are as follows:

Phase 6   Possible Challenges
Phase 7   Identified Solutions
Phase 8   Execute Your Plan of Action

The purpose of Phase 6 – the Possible Challenges Phase – is to bring you to the point of thinking about what could happen to distract, delay, or derail you on your Untie the Knots journey. You must record each possible challenge for further planning and action. In this phase, you are provided with practical strategies that empower you to identify and defeat toxic habits, choices, people, and relationships in your life. The Possible Challenges Phase is Chapter 12.

The purpose of Phase 7 – the Identified Solutions Phase – is to bring you to the point of thinking and practicing the following pattern: for each possible challenge you identify, you must find a practical solution to respond to and push through it. In this phase, you should take your recorded list of the possible challenges you created in Phase 6 and identify two or more practical solutions. The Identified Solutions Phase consists of support and solution resources, and can be found in Appendix A and C.

The purpose of Phase 8 – the Execute Your Plan of Action Phase – is to bring you to the ultimate point of acting—the actual execution of your Untie the Knots Process plan. The main purpose in this phase is to install your new Untie the Knots habits improvement plan. This is the phase where you are to inform and continuously update your stakeholders (supporters of your personal vision and journey) so they can assist you in looking after and maintaining your Untie the Knots Process plan. The Execute Your Plan of Action Phase consists of Chapters 13 through 15.

The Learning Component

The Learning Component is where you evaluate, analyze, record, adjust, refine, reward, and persist based on the improvement activities completed and lessons learned. This is where you assess and measure your true growth and development in the process. It also prepares you for the next step by providing you with information and outcomes that will allow you to develop refined strategies for future actions. This component also duplicates some activities from the Initiating Component through the Acting Component such as visualizing, discovering, planning, reviewing, executing, and evaluating motivation, goals, sponsorship, possible challenges, identified solutions, etc. The phases within the Learning Component are as follows:

Phase 9	Evaluate and Adjust
Phase 10	Like and Enjoy
Phase 11	Conviction and Commitment
Phase 12	Assess, Manage, Reward, and Persist

The purpose of Phase 9 – the Evaluate and Adjust Phase – is where you and your stakeholders (supporters) look at the outcomes and lessons learned after you have installed and executed your plan starting from the beginning. This action is required to help insure that the lessons learned during the past phases in the cycle are working correctly and effectively in the beginning of the Learning Phase. It also gives you an opportunity to check the commitment your stakeholders promised you with their support. This is the phase where you make any adjustments necessary before you continue. If you and your stakeholders say that things are okay, continue to Phase 10. If you or your stakeholders feel that something needs to be adjusted, go back to the Initiating Component and begin again. The Evaluate and Adjust Phase is Chapter 14.

Journal Assignment #1 for the Cycle

After you've reached and completed Phase 9, meaning that both you and your stakeholders have given permission to continue with your plan of action in defeating and removing a particular toxic habit, choice, person, or relationship from your life, answer the following questions in your journal:

1) What did I intend to do?
2) What did I do?

3) What did I learn?
4) How successful was I?
5) What will I do differently next time?

The purpose of Phase 10 – the Like and Enjoy Phase – is where you personally stop to recognize and access the new feeling of living without a particular toxic knot in your life. Stop to answer and write down your answers to questions like these: Do I like this feeling? Is my life more manageable now? Is my life less stressful? Do I honestly now see more opportunities for myself on the horizon? Do I now like myself even more? This is the phase where you begin to like and enjoy the new you. The Like and Enjoy Phase consists of Chapters 8-14.

The purpose of Phase 11 – the Conviction and Commitment Phase – is where you personally announce your conviction (beliefs) and commitment (promise) to living without a particular toxic knot from ever impacting and tying up your life again. This is the phase where your passion and life purpose summon the power to push you closer and closer to your desired Untie the Knots outcomes. The Conviction and Commitment Phase consists of Chapters 13-18.

The purpose of Phase 12 – the Assess, Manage, Reward, and Persist Phase – is where you take responsibility and accountability to assess, manage, reward, and persist based on your new change, development, and growth. This is the phase where you make necessary adjustments and refinements before you continue. If you and your stakeholders say that things are okay, reward yourself, and continue to Phase 1. If you or your stakeholders feel that something needs to be adjusted, reward yourself, and go back to the Establishing Component. The Assess, Manage, Reward, and Persist Phase is Chapter 14.

Journal Assignment #2 for the Cycle

After you've reached and completed Phase 12, meaning that you have successfully defeated and untied a toxic knot in your life, answer the following questions in your journal:

1) Where did I come from (describe how your life was with the toxic knot)?
2) How did I get here (give a brief description of what you did to be at this point)?
3) Who are you today (describe who you feel you are today without this toxic knot in your life)?
4) What do you want to become (describe who you want to become and where you are headed from here)?

***** The Untie the Knots Cycle can only happen when you experience the complete process once.

The Importance of Making the Untie the Knots Process A Continuous Cycle

"Life is either a daring adventure or nothing at all."

— Helen Keller

Making the Untie the Knots Process A Continuous Cycle is important because if you desire to 1) create and live a significant life, 2) create and leave a lasting legacy, and 3) create a life of better health, balance, potential, harmony, happiness, and prosperity—you must continuously identify and defeat toxic habits, choices, people, and relationships in your life. You can no longer ignore, side step, or turn your back on them because you may have already discovered those methods don't work and your toxic knots still exist.

When you initiate the desire and motivation to step forward boldly on faith to improve some aspect of your life, you are at the beginning stage of aligning yourself with significance. However, significance doesn't happen through a one-time shot or one-time effort. Significance happens when a person focuses his or her positive efforts on a continuous basis to reach and accomplish his or her ultimate goals and dreams in life. This continuous effort makes the tasks and goals worthwhile and worth pursuing. It gives life meaning and it makes discovering and living our life purpose important.

When you focus and act on a continuous basis, you summon the courage to take on whatever pains, struggles, fears, or challenges come your way. You put yourself in a positive position to achieve and win in life because you are continuously moving, planning, executing, evaluating, refining, rewarding, and persisting. This puts you on the path toward creating and living a significant life—a life that will also create and leave a lasting legacy for all generations to learn and benefit from.

By continuously executing and successfully completing the Untie the Knots Cycle, you will be able to

- Boldly Stand Up Within to Continuously Change and Grow
- Make the Untie the Knots Process Your Hobby
- Identify, Untie, and Control Your Toxic Knots
- Decide to Do YOU
- Acknowledge and Push Through Your Fears
- Set Unstoppable Goals
- Quit Marking Time—and Move Forward
- Defeat Toxic Habits, Choices, People, and Relationships
- Make "A" Commitment to Life
- Reward, Assess, Manage, and Persist on Your Untie the Knots Journey
- Live A Significant Life, and Leave A Lasting Legacy

More importantly, you will be able to create the relationships, family, career, happiness, health, prosperity, and life you truly want.

Remember, we become what we repeatedly do. Start by Making the Untie the Knots Process a Continuous Cycle!

What Are YOUR Desired Outcomes for the Untie the Knots Cycle?

> *"The will to win, the desire to succeed, the urge to reach your full potential...these are the keys that will unlock the door to personal excellence."*

— Eddie Robinson

To make your Untie the Knots journey a worthwhile journey, you must identify and write down a clear and confirmed list of "Desired Outcomes." Your Desired Outcomes create a meaningful and purposeful reason for why you are learning, practicing, and continuously executing the Untie the Knots Process.

List your Desired Outcomes below:

1) To defeat and gain freedom from toxic habits, choices, people, and relationships

2) _____

_____

3) _____

_____

4) _____

_____

5) _____

_____

6) _____

_____

7) _____

_____

8) _____

_____

9) To create and live a significant life

10) To create and leave a lasting legacy

Now, ponder the words from a few significant people and then move forward with the Untie the Knots Cycle:

"I learned this, at least, by my experiment: that if one advances confidently in the direction of his dreams, and endeavors to live the life which he had imagined, he will meet with a success unexpected in common hours." — Henry David Thoreau

"Give yourself an even greater challenge than the one you are trying to master and you will develop the powers necessary to overcome the original difficulty."— William J. Bennett

"You control your future, your destiny. What you think about comes about. By recording your dreams and goals on paper, you set in motion the process of becoming the person you most want to be." — Mark Victor Hansen

"How do you go from where you are to where you want to be? I think you have to have an enthusiasm for life. You have to have a dream, a goal, and you have to be willing to work for it."— Jim Valvano

"It's not so much how busy you are, but why you are busy. The bee is praised. The mosquito is swatted." — Mary O'Connor

"When a goal matters enough to a person, that person will find a way to accomplish what at first seemed impossible."— Nido Qubein

"You must have an aim, a vision, a goal. For the person sailing through life with no destination or 'port-of- call,' every wind is the wrong wind." — Tracy Brinkmann

Chapter Conclusion

In this chapter, you learned the specific design and purpose for each phase and component of the Untie the Knots Cycle. You learned the importance of making the Untie the Knots Process a continuous cycle. Not only did I share with you the workings of the 12-Phase Untie the Knots Cycle, but I also explained to you the workings of the five components that guide, drive, and give clear meaning to each phase in the cycle. The Untie the Knots Process is only worthwhile if the insight and results lead you to continuously practice and live a life with better health, balance, harmony, potential, significance, and prosperity. This chapter is a brief reminder of the Untie the Knots Cycle in which each phase of development requires self-awareness, determination, focus, action, and evaluation; the whole process is a continuous process of design, development, action, evaluation, revision, reward, and persistence.

When your goal is worthy and filled with meaning, the courage to reach it will be there. When your sense of purpose is strong and clear, your courage to drive your purpose will be there. The Untie the Knots Process and the Untie the Knots Cycle empowers you to continuously establish worthy and meaningful goals and to make your sense of purpose strong and clear throughout your journey.

Remember, courage is what happens when your desire to make continuous positive progress greater than your fear of a negative setback or defeat. It was Winston Churchill who once said, "Success is never final. Failure is never fatal. It is courage that counts."

Chapter 17

AVOIDING SELF- AND OUTSIDE-SABOTAGE

"Knowing is not enough; we must apply. Willing is not enough; we must do."

— Johann von Goethe

Keep You and Others Out of the Way

Where could you take yourself if you put as much energy and creativity into manifesting your goals and dreams as you do procrastinating and avoiding them?

Imagine having control of your time, money, weight, and career. Imagine knowing what to do with a sabotaging friend or spouse. Imagine human behavior making sense. Imagine being able to influence yourself to finish every task you begin.

Tell me if this has ever happened to you: You want to improve an area of your life so you can become healthier, happier, and more successful. You read books, gather information, listen to tapes and cds, map out your new goals, connect with your purpose, maintain a journal, create a new life plan, and embark on the journey toward a healthier, happier, and more successful you. But the minute you begin your journey—procrastination, negative emotions, and self-doubt set in. You put off the time you planned to spend working on the new you, you find excuses to become easily distracted by meaningless activities, and all the almost new materials and supplies for your journey are now sitting in the corner collecting dust. You're now back to once again skipping, cheating, and robbing yourself of the goals, dreams, and life you truly want to live. What's even more upsetting is that you know what you should be doing, but no matter how hard you try, you can't get yourself to do it. Here's another task or goal started but never finished. It's as if some unseen force is sabotaging you and controlling your behavior like you were a puppet on a string.

Has this ever happened to you?

If this scenario sounds familiar, then the answer to your frustrations might lie deep within you—within your beliefs and emotions. Unfortunately, the average person, at the mere mention of self-esteem, self-worth, self-confidence, or self-image usually cries out, "Oh no, not another one of these cheesy self-help concepts!"

The point I'm making is not about reading self-help books or crying out because of negative beliefs regarding self-help concepts; my point is this: if there is anything you really want to do or have, but are unable to bring it into your life, and there is no logical, rational, or otherwise "real" reason why you can't do or have it, you are experiencing self-sabotaging or outside-sabotaging behavior.

For you or anyone else to succeed and achieve the results you desire from your Untie the Knots journey, you first must get the self-sabotaging or outside-sabotaging behavior under control, defeated, and out of the way. Yes, you have to move YOU and your toxic beliefs and emotions out of the way.

The principles and strategies shared in this chapter can put your life in a position where you confidently avoid, control, and defeat the following sabotaging behaviors from this point forward:

- Beliefs and emotions sabotage
- Starting and finishing tasks sabotage
- Time management sabotage
- Self-esteem and self-image sabotage
- Innovation and creativity sabotage
- Positive change and growth sabotage
- Goals and dreams sabotage
- Family sabotage
- Relationship sabotage

- Health and fitness sabotage
- Career sabotage
- Financial sabotage
- Spiritual sabotage
- Significance and prosperity sabotage

You can be one of the most successful people in the world because of your gifts, talents, skills, or accomplishments but suffer from self-sabotaging and outside-sabotaging behavior in other areas of your life, which cause you to fall short of living the life you want. To onlookers, you appear like the duck in the lake: on top of the surface everything appears cool, calm, and collected; however, underneath the water, you're paddling for dear life trying to keep up because your negative beliefs and toxic emotions are sabotaging your goals, happiness, success, and dreams.

It's not a lack of desire, skills, knowledge, or effort that holds people back. There is something inside them that's stronger than their desire, and it sabotages their efforts to do the tasks they truly want and have the life they truly want to live.

To overcome self-sabotaging and outside-sabotaging behavior, we first must use conscious awareness to explore our emotions and beliefs and understand how they influence our actions.

Let's explore and become more aware of a few realities as they pertain to self-sabotage and outside-sabotage.

What Is Self-sabotage?

> *"The passion for destruction is also a creative passion."*
>
> — Mikhail Bakunin

Self-sabotaging behavior is when you say you want something and your actions work in the opposite way ensuring it doesn't happen.

How Will You Know If You're Self-Sabotaging Your Life?

"My mind is my biggest asset."

— Tiger Woods

Self-sabotaging behavior is most recognizable by the experience of an internal "tug-of-war" between having a desire to do something and feeling like you can't or shouldn't do it.

For example, you might believe you are unworthy of a life that is significant and prosperous, yet on a deeper level, you know that everybody is worthy of a significant and prosperous life.

You may realize your inability to feel your heart's full range of emotions (joy, anger, sadness, grief, fear, peace, compassion, motivation, sympathy, empathy, desire, determination, etc.). For example, you want to work through and make your Untie the Knots journey your new way of life; however, your inability to feel motivated causes you to procrastinate and lose interest.

Or you feel that you can't fully choose what comes in or out of your life. For example, you might have a boundary problem around relationships, feeling that you are not able to attract and build quality healthy relationships, or you compulsively strive to be friends with everyone regardless of whether they add positive or negative energy to your life.

What Are the Patterns of Self-sabotage?

"The injuries we do and the injuries we suffer are seldom weighed on the same scales."

— Aesop

Let's take a look at a few key patterns that hinder and stop most saboteurs today:

Negative Self-Talk

- There's not enough time in a day—I will never finish it.
- What if I fail - how will I face everyone?
- Who am I to even try something like this?
- What if I succeed - then what will I do?
- Everyone in my family has the same body type and bone structure. Why work out?
- It's foolish of me to even think I could do that.
- Don't do it! Do it! Don't Do it! Do it! Wait and see.

Do you hear and feel the toxic emotions and self-sabotaging behavior in the above patterns? When we listen to and adhere to our negative self-talk, it stifles our progress and opportunities for growth.

Here are three practical strategies to control, defeat, and prevent the self-sabotaging behavior of "negative self-talk":

1) Focus on solutions. Assume most problems have solutions, and ask, "How can I successfully get past this situation?" Focus on what YOU can do to promote a solution to the problem.
2) Stop beating yourself up. Be realistic in your assessment and stop scaring yourself. Yes, bad things do happen, and many bad things are often inconveniences, mistakes, and foul-ups—not necessarily traumas, tragedies, or disasters.
3) Use empowering affirmations. Remind yourself that "I am a human being with unique personalities" or "I may encounter shortcomings; however, they help to create new opportunities."

Avoidance and Procrastination Behaviors

- Not doing what you feel you should be doing.
- Not managing or prioritizing your time.

Procrastination is a toxic habit that results from the toxic choice of poor time management.

Here are three practical strategies to control, defeat, and prevent the self-sabotaging behavior of "avoidance and procrastination":

1) Look at the effects of procrastination versus not procrastinating. What rewards lie ahead if you get the task done? What are the effects if you continue to delay it? Which situation has better effects? Chances are you will benefit more in the long term from facing the task head on.
2) Set reasonable goals. Plan your goals carefully, allowing enough time to complete them.
3) Break the task into smaller parts. How can you approach it step-by-step? If you can concentrate on achieving one goal at a time, the task may become less burdensome.

Inability to Focus on and Filter out Distractions

- You're distracted by internal negative self-statements, fears, emotions, and beliefs.
- You have friends, family, a job, a spouse, and children, and all want your attention, but you haven't found a way to structure distraction-free conditions.
- You're not doing something you're truly passionate about.

Focusing your attention like a laser beam on a target is the key to Untie the Knots success. Scattering your attention across various tasks, projects, and chaotic situations is a road to self-sabotage.

Here are three practical strategies to control, defeat, and prevent the self-sabotaging behavior of being "unable to focus on and filter out distractions":

1) Align your daily work with your goals. The most important task you can do to increase your focus is to have goals. If your goals are clear, which includes having them

written down, it is much easier to re-focus your efforts towards them. Goals provide a compass for your efforts. Make sure your list for the day includes items specifically related to your goals.

2) Inform your family and friends. Sometimes it can be very advantageous to inform a caring family member or friend about a personal task or goal you're working on. This support person will help you to stay focused by reminding you of what you should be working on when you become distracted.

3) Prioritize the list. If you have the long list syndrome, identify the five items that are most important to be completed that day. Make sure that at least one of those things is in service of your most important goals, not just in putting out the urgent fires you are facing.

Decreased Self-motivation

- You have not learned how to motivate yourself.
- You are in the habit of relying on outside motivation factors.
- Your fears, self-doubts, and concerns zap your motivation.
- You are using the wrong factors to try to motivate yourself.

Self-motivation is taught to us at a young age. The ways in which we were raised and the feedback we receive from our environment help us to learn how to become self-motivated. When we receive little positive feedback about our accomplishments, we are conditioned to believe that our achievements are not important.

Here are three practical strategies to control, defeat, and prevent "decreased self-motivation":

1) Make a change in your life. Sometimes, the routine of daily life can lead to decreased self-motivation. If you feel your daily routine is becoming boring, sign up for a class at your local community college, volunteer at your town's animal shelter, or call up a friend to play tennis.

2) Surround yourself with supportive people. When laziness begins to set in, one of the worst reactions you can have is to surround yourself with other lazy people. Instead, actively seek out people—in both professional and personal settings—who will support your ideas, encourage your success, and embrace you as a person.

3) Do something that motivates you. All too often, laziness stems from boredom or a complete disinterest in your daily tasks. If you don't feel your work is rewarding, consider changing careers. Likewise, if your child isn't inherently motivated to do schoolwork, set up a reward system that gives them something to work toward. Also, if a particular task seems overwhelming to you or your child, and therefore causes you not to do it, take small steps to make the task more manageable.

Poor Conflict Resolution Skills

- You tend to act aggressively with people when simple assertiveness will work better.
- You passively let others walk all over you because you don't know how to say "no".

Conflicts with others are generally a part of life, but how we handle them can actually strengthen relationships or can cause additional mental stress for all involved and create bigger conflicts that take on a life of their own. Interestingly, many people who act aggressively are not fully aware that they're doing harm to their relationships and are not familiar with a better way of handling things.

Here are six practical strategies to control, defeat, and prevent "poor conflict resolution":

1) Remain calm. Try not to overreact to difficult situations. By remaining calm, others are more likely to consider your viewpoint. Express feelings in words not actions. Telling someone directly and honestly how you feel can

be a powerful form of communication. If you start to feel so angry or upset that you feel you may lose control, take a "time out" and do something to steady yourself: take a walk, do some deep breathing, pet the cat, play with the dog, do the dishes - whatever works for you.

2) Be specific about what is bothering you. Vague complaints are hard to work on.

3) Listen and ask questions. Ask fact-based questions (who? what? where? when? how?) to make sure you understand the situation.

4) Deal with only one issue at a time. Don't introduce other topics until each is fully discussed. This avoids the "kitchen sink" effect where people throw in all their complaints while not allowing anything to be resolved.

5) Agree to the best way to resolve the conflict and to a timetable for implementing it. Who will do what by when?

6) If the discussion breaks down, reschedule another time to meet. Consider bringing in a neutral, skilled third party to mediate the conflict to an agreed upon solution.

Pessimism

- You see events as worse than they really are.
- You pass up opportunities to improve your situation.
- You overlook solutions to problems.
- You cause yourself mental stress in many other ways as well.

Pessimism is more than just seeing the glass as half-empty; it's a specific worldview that undermines your belief in yourself, brings poorer health outcomes, fewer positive life events, and other negative consequences. Because the traits of optimists and pessimists are specific and slightly elusive to someone who doesn't know what to look for, many people with pessimistic tendencies are completely unaware of it and view themselves as optimists.

Here are three practical strategies to control, defeat, and prevent "pessimism":

1) Admit that your pessimism and negativity are not productive behaviors.
2) Identify the feelings that precede your negative attitude and then the feelings you have after the negativity; recognize that your emotional life suffers by negative behavior.
3) Watch for the reactions your negativity and pessimism bring out in others; if it's not a positive reaction, begin working on yourself to soon change the reaction you're currently receiving to a positive and healthy one.

Taking on Too Much

- You constantly over-schedule and over-stress.
- You take on too much and put yourself under undue pressure because of it.

You mainly take on too much because you're not sure how to say "NO" to others' demands on your time. This often puts you in a state of chronic stress because you've once again taken on more than you can handle.

Here are three practical strategies to control, defeat, and prevent "taking on too much":

1) Learn to say "No." After you've said, "No," do not give an explanation. Any type of explanation after you've said, "No" only makes you feel guilty and feel you're letting the other person down.
2) Pre-plan and confirm your schedule each morning. This way your day is confirmed before you start. When someone asks you to take on another task, if it's not your direct responsibility or a family emergency, respond by saying, "I can't do it because I already have scheduled commitments and projects that I need to get done today." Again,

you do not have to explain what your commitments or projects are.

3) Schedule personal time for yourself each day, each week. When you schedule personal time, write it in your schedule and do not allow anyone or anything to replace it. The only reality that can replace it is a "real family emergency" or a job or assignment that must get done; outside of that, it's your time, even if you choose to sit in a quiet place to read *Untie the Knots That Tie Up Your Life*.

Imagine how much happier and more successful your life would be if you were able to finally defeat and prevent the internal tug-of-war your self-sabotaging behaviors have caused; they have hindered and kept you from your optimal performance. You, your goals, your success, your dreams, and your significant life would be unstoppable.

There's no reason why every human being shouldn't do the internal exploration necessary for change. Such a change requires will and hard work, but it's the only way to remove self-sabotaging behavior once and for all.

Learn, practice, and master the practical strategies above, and you will soon find yourself doing and having the life you really want because self-sabotage will no longer be blocking your way.

What Is Outside-sabotage?

"Tricks and treachery are the practice of fools who don't have brains enough to be honest."

— Benjamin Franklin

Outside-sabotage behavior is when a friend, co-worker, stranger, spouse, or relative contributes to the reason why you can't perform the tasks you want to achieve or why you can't have the life you want to have.

How Will You Know If Outside-sabotage Is Happening to You?

"Keep your friends close, and your enemies closer."

— Sun Tzu

The truth of the matter is there are times in life when another person makes it open and blatantly obvious that they are trying to sabotage our opportunities, goals, dreams, and life. How? They either tell you or show you through their actions.

Then there are other people, the silent snipers, who could be a close friend, co-worker, stranger, spouse, or relative. They slowly and silently feed and condition your belief system to whatever they want you to believe. They do it so much that after a while, you begin to take ownership of the thoughts and emotions they have projected on you, and their outside-sabotaging behavior becomes your internal self-sabotaging behavior.

Let's take a look at a few outside-sabotaging examples:

A successful entrepreneur: "I always thought of my friends as supportive until I started making some pretty good money. It was an eye-opener for me to discover that if I were really, really rich, some of my friends would be really, really gone."

A hard-working husband: "She wanted the weight on me because she thought I'd be less attractive to other women. I didn't realize this until she started doing the same thing with our teenage daughter. Sexuality of any kind really frightened my wife, and she fought it by feeding us. She thought she was protecting us."

A girlfriend: "My boyfriend and I always talked about going onto college together after high school. I took the SATs, filled out the college applications, and did what I had to do to get myself into college on time right after high school. He talked about it but did nothing to get himself in college. Even though I went to college locally and was still in the neighborhood, my boyfriend began psychologically and verbally attacking me. Every now and then he'd make sly remarks like 'I guess you think you're smarter than me now, huh. My wife will be at work and then at home taking care of the kids and not wasting her time in some useless college program. You think I'm dumb because I am not in college; stop talking down to me.'"

A son: "I thought I would make my mother proud by becoming a positive, responsible, and self-sufficient man until I purchased my first home. It blew me away when I learned that my own mother was talking negatively about my accomplishment behind my back to other family members."

A co-worker: "Our little workplace click went out to lunch everyday. I must admit sometimes we returned to the office maybe 10-15 minutes late about once or twice a week. I was surprised to find out on the day my employer decided to terminate me for repeatedly returning late from lunch that the leader of our little lunch group had provided the Human Resources Manager with a list of days and times spanning a three month period for each day I returned late from lunch."

An employee: "When I started working at company A, the people were helpful, cordial, and all team players. It was almost too good to be true. My boss would often work right along side us. One day for some unknown reason I became very ill and had to miss several days from work. I felt guilty because there was a pressing project my team was working on. The project was completed in my absence; however, when I returned, my boss began to interact with me in a totally different way. Based on his direct feedback he said that my tasks were never done correctly and the deadlines that I thought we confirmed were never the deadlines he had. My life where I spent most of my time had become a living hell. I became so stressed that it caused me to become ill again and this time I had to be hospitalized."

When you choose to *"identify and untie the knots that tie up your life,"* don't be surprised when you learn that a few of your friends, who are still tied up, think that you now believe you're better than them. It takes an aggressive person to do that; however, it happens every day. If for instance your partner is very "understanding" about you not being able to go back to school to get the required education needed for advancement at work, perhaps they're too accommodating. If you spend more money shopping with your impulse buying friends than you do shopping alone, take a look at your behavior.

Ask yourself:
   • What do they gain by sabotaging my efforts?
   • Am I easy to control and sabotage?
   • Do I make them "right"?
   • Do I cut myself off from activities because of this sabotage?
   • Am I less active?
   • Am I less accessible to other people?
   • Am I more dependent on the saboteur because of this sabotage?
   • Am I less powerful?

If you don't feel you're in control of your health, your weight, your finances, your choices, your career, your self-esteem, your self-confidence, or your life, perhaps there are people around you who subconsciously want you to feel that way.

NOW what?

If you suspect that someone else is contributing to your sabotage, what do you do about it?

"When there is no enemy within, the enemies outside can't hurt you."

— African Proverb

You have many options; here are three:

a) Negotiate a change in the person's behavior.
b) Change yourself.
c) Change the situation.

Let's see how these three options work and how you can use them in your own situation.

A. Negotiate a change in the person's behavior.

When you feel and discover that someone has been contributing to your sabotage from the outside, this is not the time for you to cry "Wo Is Me!" It can be very beneficial and advantageous for you to negotiate a change in his or her behavior.

Here are two options about how you can change another person's behavior.

1) Cordially confront and openly tell the person about his or her behavior.

Request a meeting with your saboteur to sit down and discuss what is causing or forcing this person to project that behavior into your life. Stay calm, listen, and hear the person out. After you learn what has been happening and why, offer a few positive, healthy, and practical suggestions about how the person can change his or her behavior to strengthen your relationship.

2) Figure out how you want to be supported and ask the person to support you in the positive way you create for them.

If you honestly think and are certain that your saboteur really cares for you and your future success, you can create a written plan of goals to discuss at your meeting. This plan can be designed to ask the person to support your Untie the Knots journey. Sometimes, when you seek the support of others, especially family and friends, they feel honored and thankful that you asked them.

The two above options are civil, cordial, and respectful. Nowhere did I mention arguing, fighting, or contributing more to the already existing sabotaging behavior.

People can only treat you the way you allow them to treat you.

B. Change yourself.

If someone has control over your goals, health, career, self-image, or self-confidence, you can take back that control by changing yourself.

Here are two options about how you can change yourself.

1) Decide to do you. Decide that you will no longer allow this saboteur to continue his or her sabotaging behavior in your life.

If you're trying to lose weight and your partner decides to order twice as much junk food than in the past to entice you to abandon your "eating right and eating healthy" plan, when they walk in the house with buffalo wings, sodas, subs, and pizza, change your normal reaction to their actions. Instead of running to the kitchen to chow down, go and take a nice hot bath while listening to soothing music and relax.

2) Create and write your own potential saboteurs list and have an action plan.

My Saboteur's Name	His or Her Method of Attack	My Civil and Cordial Response	My Self-Reward

The two above options are civil, cordial, and respectful. Nowhere did I mention arguing, fighting, or contributing more to the already existing sabotaging behavior.

You can have anything you want if you give up the belief that you can't have it!

C. Change the situation.

If you've negotiated with your saboteur and have changed yourself, yet you discover that your saboteur is still hard at work trying to sabotage your life, you must now change the situation with more extreme methods.

Here are two options you can use to change the situation.

1) Change the situation.

If your saboteur only attacks you when you're alone, try your best not to allow him or her the opportunity to catch you by yourself. If your saboteur attacks you through e-mail, cell phone, text messaging, instant messaging, or your home phone, either block the person or change your contact accounts and telephone numbers.

What you must do is assess the situations in which your saboteur is able to launch an attack on your life, and change it to best protect you and keep him or her out.

2) Change your position.

There are situations and times in your life when you must "cut-all-ties" and terminate an unhealthy relationship or interaction with a person. This is definitely tough when it comes to a close friend, spouse, relative, or even a job where you have worked for a long period. But it's necessary! To allow sabotaging behavior to continue to destroy and bring down your life is like agreeing to allow yourself to be continuously injected with small doses of poison daily. That's not healthy! That's not living! And you cannot convince me on your best day that sabotaging injections are what you truly want.

When any situation or relationship that involves toxic outside-sabotaging behavior reaches this point, cut it loose and move on! It will hurt, but you're a much better and deserving person who shouldn't allow such malice to continue in your life.

The two above options are civil, cordial, and respectful. Nowhere did I mention arguing, fighting, or contributing more to the already existing sabotaging behavior.

Once you break free from the sabotaging behaviors surrounding your goals and life, your internal guidance system will easily and effortlessly move you toward success.

Will I Ever Be Completely Free of Self- and Outside-sabotage?

"Our bodies are our gardens...our wills are our gardeners."

— William Shakespeare

No, we will never be 100% self- and outside-sabotage free.

However, it is definitely time to stop destroying your goals and dreams by allowing self- and outside-sabotage to be unmanageable obstacles in your life. Right here and right now is where YOU will get out of your own way so you can finally create and live the way you want to live!

Chapter Conclusion

In this chapter, you learned that self- and outside-sabotaging behavior can destroy your motivation to complete the tasks you
really want to complete by creating an *internal tug-of-war*. You
learned how to recognize when you have self- and outside-sabotage taking place in your life and what you can do to defeat and
prevent it from tying up and delaying your future success, significance, prosperity, and happiness. I shared with you that you will
never be completely self- or outside-sabotage free; however, you
can still gain control over your beliefs and emotions to empower
you so that you are able to have the life you really want. When
you develop clarity and insight about the outcomes you want to
create and the awareness for potential setbacks, you can stop
self- and outside-sabotage right in its tracks. You can also focus
your energies on working toward new goals that will fully enrich
your life in every way. You will then look back one day and see
that instead of being our own worst saboteur, you have become
your best friend and supporter. When you look in the mirror,
you will see someone who took the necessary steps of action
to learn how to prevent and defeat the hindrance of sabotaging
behavior in your life, once and for all.

Chapter 18

WHEN ALL ELSE SEEMS TO NOT WORK, T.A.P.P. — THINK, ACT, PRAY, AND PROSPER

"This time, like all times, is a very good one, if we but know what to do with it."

— Ralph Waldo Emerson

YOU and I started this journey together with me confessing and sharing with you the toxic knots that tied me up beginning from early childhood. I told you that for over 19 years I was being suffocated and strangled by the toxic knots of anger, fear, excuse making, self-doubt, regret, self-sabotage, and low self-esteem. As we continued the journey, you learned and hopefully changed and grew as I shared with you principles and strategies about how I "untied the knots that tied up my life." In my efforts to educate and help you "untie the toxic knots" in your life, I made clear one simple and practical point by stating, "We will never become 100% toxic knots free; however, a life with fewer toxic knots can become a significant life with greater potential."

Yes, there will always be challenges, problems, disappointments, frustrations, obstacles, loss, tragedy, and setbacks. It's called life. There will be events and obstacles we can control and others that we cannot.

As you learn, practice, manage, and strive to master the Untie the Knots Process, expect life to still happen. You will still struggle, become exhausted, contemplate quitting, and even put yourself in park mode from time-to-time.

Why?

We have all experienced situations and challenges in our lives where we felt that everything we tried and the people we called on did not seem to slow, control, or fix our problems. When this happens, we become worried, exhausted, stressed, and overwhelmed. Some people climb in bed and try to sleep their worries and problems away. Some people go on an eating frenzy because if they are chewing continuously they don't have time to think or hear about their worries and problems. Some people go on a shopping spree or stay super busy to avoid dealing with their worries or problems. They've tried self-help and professional help, and neither worked, so now they're on the run from their worries, challenges, and problems.

Have you been at this point in your life before?

I have!

And the truth of the matter is—more likely than not, we will all go through similar experiences time-and-time again due to Murphy's Law (a universally accepted principle or rule), which states if anything can possibly go wrong, it can and will.

I once heard a professional speaker explain to an audience, "When it comes to dealing with life, Murphy's Law will always come into play." He then stated, "Learn to accept that trouble is either now in your life, leaving your life, or on its way to your life. You can learn right now how to effectively prepare and respond to it or be bulldozed by your troubles or challenges time-and-time again each time Murphy's Law shows up in your life."

The speaker was correct; we can learn how to effectively prepare and respond to challenges and troubles that will come our way. However, what should you do when you have exhausted your efforts and resources on trying to slow, control, or fix your troubles or problems?

When all else seems to not work, T.A.P.P. Don't Quit! Don't Stop! And Never Give Up! Think, Act, Pray, and Prosper.

If you still have a pulse, an able body, and a focused and positive mind, your spirits and hopes can be strengthened to pick you up and move you forward in life once again.

When all else seems to not work, T.A.P.P.—Think, Act, Pray, and Prosper!

Think

> *"Thinking is the soul talking with itself."*
>
> — Plato

When I was tied up and being suffocated by toxic knots early in my life, the one behavior I could not do or failed to do effectively was THINK.

When your mind is filled with chaos, anger, confusion, frustration, fear, and worry, thinking effectively becomes almost impossible. Life becomes one long string of chaotic reactions versus positive responses.

From this point forward, I want you to learn, practice, and realize the benefits and rewards of developing and teaching yourself to "think" positively and effectively. When you think positively, you increase the opportunities to create and generate positive results in all areas of your life. When you can think effectively, you increase awareness and the ability to acknowledge, withstand, and work through the many challenges and toxic behaviors that enter your life. With constant positive and effective thinking, your life will become healthier, happier, empowered, and rewarding.

When all else doesn't work, here is what you can do to bring yourself back to positive and effective thinking.

1) **Identify and untie the toxic knots that are blocking or suffocating your ability to think**. Before you can do anything, you must clear away any and all toxic confusion and behavior.

2) **Reinstate a positive mental attitude.** Once you have cleared and controlled all toxic confusion and behavior, reinstate a positive mental attitude. If you want positive results, you have to make sure you have on the correct hat for the job.

3) **Find a quiet place.** If you're not dealing with a situation that is urgent or immediate, find a quiet place that will allow you to think clearly about the situation or challenge at hand.

4) **Calm yourself and clear your mind.** If you're in a quiet place or being confronted by a more immediate situation, calm yourself. Use positive affirmations like "I am in control of my thoughts, my actions, and this situation" or "I will not allow this person or this situation to upset my spirit."

5) **Think twice before you speak.** If you're being confronted by a more immediate situation and you're unable to step away into a quiet place, think twice before you speak. Our natural emotions often drive us to blurt out the first thought that comes into our mind. However, frequently in a heated situation, our first thought is a negative thought. So, think twice...calm yourself...restrain yourself...think again...then respond...don't react in a toxic way like the other person or persons involved. Remember, "I am in control of my thoughts, my actions, and this situation."

6) **Ink what you think.** If you're in a quiet place, open your journal or organizer and write down what you're thinking. When you put your thoughts in writing, it gives you an opportunity to logically review and assess them for the most effective outcomes possible.

7) **End with a positive thought of encouragement.** Give yourself something meaningful to make of your positive time alone. You guessed it; this is your self-reward.

Transforming your thinking into positive and effective thinking can indeed change your world. So choose the best thoughts that you can possibly imagine, and the rewards and benefits will be enormous.

Act

"Moving water makes stagnant water move."

— African Proverb

In ancient Greece, Socrates was reputed to hold knowledge in high esteem. One day a fellow met the great philosopher and said, "Do you know what I just heard about your friend?" "Hold on a minute," Socrates replied. "Before telling me anything, I would like you to pass a little test. It's called the Triple Filter Test." "The Triple Filter?" the fellow replied. "That's right, The Triple Filter Test," Socrates continued. "Before you talk to me about my friend, it might be a good idea to take a moment and filter what you're going to say. That's why I call it the triple filter test. The first filter is Truth. Have you made absolutely sure that what you are about to tell me is true?" "No," the man said, "actually I just heard about it and wanted to tell you." "All right," said Socrates. "So you don't know if it's true or not. Now let's try the second filter, the filter of Goodness. Is what you are about to tell me about my friend something good?" "No, on the contrary it's somewhat negative." "So, it's not something good," Socrates continued, "you want to tell me something bad about him, but you're not certain if it's true. You may still pass the test though, because there's one filter left: the filter of Usefulness. Is what you want to tell me about my friend going to be useful to me?" "No, not really," replied the man. "Well, let's review," concluded Socrates, "if what you want to tell me is neither true nor good nor even useful, why tell it to me at all?"

This is why Socrates was a great philosopher and held in such high esteem. Use the Triple Filter Test each time you hear loose talk about anyone. Use it mainly to control and guide your actions.

Our thoughts become our actions, our actions become our habits, and our habits become our future. What we must learn and work cautiously and consistently on doing daily is practicing effective strategies that will put us in a position to respond to the world versus react to the world. When we are reacting to the world, we are not in control of the situation nor ourselves. When we are responding to the world, we are in control of the situation and ourselves. We're about to positively and effectively think and act, which can lead us to a positive and desirable outcome.

Get in the habit of seeing that every situation and every possible challenge provides fuel for positive action. Use that positive fuel to move you forward, and before long, you will be back on the path to enjoying your Untie the Knots journey once again.

Pray

> *"The less I pray, the harder it gets; the more I pray, the better it goes."*
>
> — Dr. Martin Luther King, Jr.

Because of the many and varied problems, crises, tragedies, and human needs that we or qualified professionals cannot control or solve, prayer calls upon our determined Higher Power for answers, directions, and guidance.

Even if you are not a religious person by nature or training—even if you are an atheist—prayer can help you much more than you believe, for it is a practical practice. What do you mean by practical? I mean that prayer fulfills three basic psychological needs which all people share, whether they believe in God or not:

1) Prayer allows us the opportunity to put our thoughts into words.
2) Prayer provides us an opportunity to openly share our burdens and regrets.
3) Prayer puts into force the active principle of doing, which is normally the first step to taking action.

My now deceased grandfather, Senior Pastor James C. Howard, taught his grandchildren how to pray and why to pray. Pop-Pop was a Senior Pastor in Baltimore, Maryland for over 30 years before God brought him home. It was not unusual to hear Pastor Howard preach to his congregation to pray in good and bad times. He taught us that prayer increases your relationship and connection with THE Higher Power. Whether your prayers are for yourself, for a family member or friend, focused on a group of individuals, or a general request for world peace, it is your intention that stirs healing into action. Prayer really does offer a powerful effect on our well-being.

The intention of closed eyes during prayer is to quiet the mind whereas the intention of two hands placed together during prayer is to quiet the physical body's activities. When the mind and hands are silenced, the spirit is allowed a more focused communication with a place of knowing and THE Higher Power.

It was Abraham Lincoln who confessed by saying, *"I have been driven many times to my knees by the overwhelming conviction that I had nowhere else to go."* Prayer isn't only meant for those who are on their sick beds, in poverty, or experiencing tragedy. Prayer is for and can help everyone—even the most powerful leaders and most successful people in the world.

That's why when all else seems to not work, most people Pray!

I'm sure you may have heard at least one person say, "We've done all we can. The only thing we can do now is pray." Prayer really should be our first resort rather than our last resort. It's powerful and meaningful.

Much prayer = OVERFLOWING POWER
Little prayer = Little Power
No prayer = Absolutely no power

When you choose to live daily in the strength and spirit of a Higher Power, you increase your ability to cope, withstand, and work through the many challenges of the world—especially when it appears that all else seems to not be working. Our children need to see and learn from us the purpose, practice, and power of prayer. Not only when our life is in turmoil, but when our life is being continuously blessed as well. It has been said, "A family that prays together, stays together." Prayer increases hope, inspires life, and has brought families, communities, and nations back together during tragedy and crisis. I encourage you to connect the dots in your life through prayer.

Prosper

"The best way out is always through."
— Robert Frost

A rich man asked a Zen master to write something that could encourage the prosperity of his family for years to come. It would be something that the family could cherish for generations. On a large piece of paper, the master wrote, "Father dies, son dies, grandson dies."

The rich man became angry when he saw the master's work. "I asked you to write something down that could bring happiness and prosperity to my family. Why do you give me something depressing like this?"

"If your son should die before you," the master answered, "this would bring unbearable grief to your family. If your grandson should die before your son, this also would bring great sorrow. If your family, generation after generation, disappears in the order I have described, it will be the natural course of life. This is true happiness and prosperity."

True prosperity is:

- Caring for, loving, and participating in the life of your family.
- Nurturing and maintaining healthy relationships.
- Working for all you get.
- Giving away the first 10%.
- Paying yourself the next 10%.

- Putting into a savings account the next 10%.
- Living on less than you earn.
- Avoiding debt.
- Building long-term security.
- Building reliable resources and networks to empower your family, friends, community, and you.
- Participating in your community.
- Identifying and championing a cause meaningful to you.

Strive not to become the richest person (solely driven for financial gains) in the world, but the wealthiest person (a person rich in wealth because of the healthy relationships, character, and a lasting legacy he or she is building over time) in the world due to constant acts of service to family, friends, community, or a cause.

Prosperity is a matter of choice. Decide for yourself which of your beliefs promote prosperity in your life and which promote scarcity and poverty. Decide for yourself which beliefs to encourage and which to actively and aggressively transform. When you learn to attentively and successfully transform your negative beliefs into positive and healthy ones, you put yourself on the path to lifelong prosperity.

Become the humbled, prosperous person who is determined to contribute to and leave this world in a much better condition than when he or she came into it. Now THAT'S living prosperously!

Chapter Conclusion

In this chapter, I shared with you a healthy and positive mind, body, and spirit-focused process that has the power to liberate you should you find yourself idle or wanting to quit your Untie the Knots journey. The T.A.P.P. (Think, Act, Pray, and Prosper) process is especially designed for periods when you encounter Murphy's Law and when your challenges and troubles overwhelm you to the point where you no longer desire to apply the principles or strategies taught to you throughout the Untie the Knots Process. I explained to you the individual reward and benefit in committing yourself *unreservedly* to Think, Act, Pray, and Prosper through challenging and traumatic periods in your life.

When you learn to continuously and effectively raise your hopes and spirits during turbulent times, you too will be able to pick up, dust off, and put your life back on the path to healthier, significant, rewarding, and prosperous living sooner than later. You too will be able to stay connected to your life's purpose, dreams, significance, and the continued creation of your lasting legacy.

Unit Summary

ONCE IS NEVER ENOUGH—LET'S DO IT AGAIN!

The Untie the Knots Process is a philosophy designed to free and improve one's life. This book is not a "reading book" in the ordinary sense; it was written as a "guidebook" for a new way of life.

Chapters 16, 17, and 18 were written 1) to explain how to effectively put the Untie the Knots Process to work; 2) to avoid both self- and outside-sabotage so you can stay green and growing; and 3) to provide you with a practical process that will get you through more challenging and turbulent times. This unit was the funneling process for the principles, strategies, tools, and activities you encountered throughout your Untie the Knots journey. It is designed to spell out and explain to you exactly what to do with all the information and practical strategies you received while reading, participating, changing, and growing on your journey.

Let's recap the three chapters that make up Unit 6, Part 5: ONCE IS NEVER ENOUGH—LET'S DO IT AGAIN!

Chapter 16: Putting the Untie the Knots Process to Work

Chapter 17: Avoiding Self- and Outside-sabotage

Chapter 18: When All Else Seems Not To Work, T.A.P.P. — Think, Act, Pray, and Prosper

This being the final Unit Summary of this book, let's review all of the *Untie the Knots* **Infusers** *(Freedom Break Away Tools)* you first encountered in the introduction of the book once again:

Infuser #1: Reinstate a Positive Attitude
If you are serious about breaking free and away from the knots that tie up your life, you will be required to put into place a positive mental attitude. You will have to be committed to developing and working constantly with a positive attitude, regardless of your past experiences or current situations or circumstances.

Infuser #2: Refocus
How are you going to change the direction of your life if you're not aware of what direction you're currently going in?

Infuser #3: Choose
Decide true freedom and life is what you want and then go where you can produce those results.

Infuser #4: Identify
To successfully break away from anything that has delayed or derailed your life in the past, you must summon the bold confidence to now identify it as a toxic habit, choice, person, or relationship.

Infuser #5: Simplify
Remove clutter, confusion, unwanted stress, and sabotaging distractions from your life daily, and watch new, desired opportunities appear.

Infuser #6: Believe
It takes your strong will and unshakable faith to make the impossible possible.

Infuser #7: Move
Don't just stand there knowing how...do it! Quit procrastinating and making excuses. My ultimate goal is to inspire, teach, and empower you to create an updated personal life plan; boldly face your fears; and move forward daily in executing your new personal life plan.

Infuser #9: Persist
How bad do you want what you now see? No more excuses...no more procrastination...no more string of bad and unproductive days! Stay the course!

Infuser #10: Leave a Mark of Significance
It's one experience to live and simply to have come and gone. It's another experience to have purposely decided to create and live a life of significance. A life that will enable you to leave behind a

lasting legacy that will contribute to your family's heritage and that will also allow many others who come after you to learn and grow from your efforts.

This unit (Chapters 16 through 18) was designed to explain and provide you with a clear and simple next step plan. I kept you, the reader, in mind, along with life's many challenges, when providing you with practical sabotage-preventing strategies to help ensure you continuous success. Make sure you read this unit more than once. The material in this unit is meant to keep you committed and connected to your Untie the Knots journey and your desired outcomes for taking the journey.

Remember, we may never be completely toxic knots free; however, a life with fewer toxic knots becomes a significant life with greater potential.

No matter what has happened to you in the past, this moment is filled with positive possibilities. Now is where your whole life has come. Now is the time. You are more than worthy. You can create something that has never existed before. Add energy and enthusiasm to your positive steps of action as you continue to transform your toxic knots into significant and prosperous blessings.

Stay the course. Continue to enjoy your journey on route to creating and leaving a lasting legacy filled with T.A.P.P.ing significance!

> *To gain immediate access to a practical, comprehensive, step-by-step guide that will help you break free of the 50 Most Common Toxic Knots, visit the following link on the Internet, right now:*
>
> *http://www.tyhoward.com/KnotsFree_SpecialGuide.html*
>
> *(Or turn to Appendix C for more information about the Knots Free Special Guide.)*

Time *OUT!*

Just to recap some of the major concepts you've read about thus far, find and write in your journal the answers to the following questions:

• How many phases are in the Untie the Knots Cycle?
Refer to the first page of Chapter 16 for the answer.

• What are the five Components of the Untie the Knots Cycle?
Refer to the "Components and Phases of the Untie the Knots Cycle" section in Chapter 16 for the answer.

• What are the patterns of self-sabotage?
Refer to the "What Are the Patterns of Self-Sabotage?" section in Chapter 17 for the answer.

• What are the three options Ty recommends for you to use if you suspect outside-sabotage?
Refer to "If you suspect that someone else is contributing to your sabotage, what do you do about it?" section in Chapter 17 for the answer.

• What do the letters of the word "T.A.P.P." stand for?
Refer to the first page of Chapter 18 for the answer.

• What is true prosperity?
Refer to the "Prosper" section in Chapter 18 for the answer.

"Success doesn't come to you, you go to it."

— Marva Collins

Epilogue

"We should not only master questions, but
also act upon them, and act definitely."

— *Woodrow Wilson*

I have shared with you throughout **Untie The Knots That Tie
Up Your Life** many practical and useful strategies, principles,
assessment tools, and concepts. My purpose in doing so was to
hopefully make your reading journey easy, inspiring, doable, empowering, rewarding, and fun. By providing you with purposeful, valuable, and timely information, I believe from the deepest
level of my heart that you can move yourself from where you are
now to where you want to be in the near future.

If you continue to learn, apply, practice, and master the "untie
the knots" process, you will find yourself defeating and untying
one toxic knot after another for the rest of your life. It will be
necessary, fun, and liberating.

Untie The Knots That Tie Up Your Life is far more than a motivational speech or an inspiring program; it's a process, cycle,
and positive way of life. It has substance, a practical teaching
style, grounded principles, and is applicable to people and professionals on all levels of life. It's a tested and proven philosophy
that will put you and your life on a path to confidently answer
three simple questions at the end of each day:

1) Where have I been?
2) Where am I now?
3) Where am I going?

As I look into the mirror of my life today, I share with you my
answers to the above three questions:

1) Where have I been?

> I have been tied up and bound down by toxic habits, choices, people, and relationships. These toxic habits at one time pushed my life further and further away from my dreams. Toxic choices made my life very difficult, painful, overwhelming, unhealthy, and non-productive. Toxic people would inject negative emotions and situations into my life to immediately frustrate and anger me. And toxic relationships continuously sabotaged and zapped happiness, significance, and prosperity from my life time-and-time again.

> This is where I've been.

2) Where am I now?

> Right now, I'm at a point in my life where the "untie the knots" process is a hobby that has become a continuous cycle and a faithful way of living. I start each day by stating the following three affirmations: 1) A life with fewer knots becomes a significant life with greater potential; 2) I'm green and growing—and bringing my "A" Game!; and 3) Today is the BEST day for me to continue living a significant life and to add to my lasting legacy.

> This is where I am now.

3) Where am I going?

My heart...my vision...my spirit...my life purpose...and my faith communicates to me each day that I'm headed onward and upward. I know now I am here to humbly serve others by sharing the wisdom and principles of the "untie the knots" process with everyone I'm privileged to encounter.

I see myself on big stages, television shows, radio programs, movie screens, and in the mass media throughout the world encouraging and empowering people of all ages and backgrounds to become masters at freeing themselves from toxic habits, choices, people, and relationships.

This is where I am going.

It was Mahatma Gandhi who said, *"You must be the change you wish to see in the world."*

I believe in helping people become more aware of and driven toward creating a life with fewer toxic knots. With an unwavering conviction, I also believe the "untie the knots" process will encourage and empower countless people to be the change they wish to see in the world.

I conclude **Untie the Knots That Tie Up Your Life** by affectionately saying that I hope and pray that one day soon you will courageously welcome and make the "untie the knots" process a continuous cycle in your life. Your future depends on you. Your life of better health, happiness, significance, and prosperity anticipates your arrival. You are more than worthy! And you deserve to live a quality life of fulfilled dreams!

Thank you for your support and your commitment to the "untie the knots" process.

Make Today & Every Day—An "A" Day!

Best Wishes,
Ty Howard
Mr. Untie the Knots
December 2006

Appendix A

You, a friend, or loved one may be in a situation and feel hopeless or confused about what to do. There are many organizations and people available who want to help. You don't have to cope or resolve challenges alone. Please call or visit the Websites below. The numbers listed are all toll free—you can dial the numbers from anywhere within the United States and it won't cost you a cent. These organizations provide support, information, and referrals, and in some cases, crisis counseling. Remember: There are always organizations or people who can help you move from hopeless to hopeful!

Special Note: The many resources listed below do not constitute an endorsement by Ty Howard, Knots Free Publishing, or InspiraGen Institute, Inc., nor are these resources exhaustive (there are many additional organizations throughout the nation that can help). Nothing is implied by an organization not being referenced.

Substance Abuse

If you suspect that you may be drinking too much and you don't know what to do, call the National Council on Alcoholism and Drug Dependency Hopeline:
1-800-NCA-CALL (622-2255)

If you are worried about a family member or friend who drinks too much and are not sure how to help, call Al-Anon / Alanteen Family Group Hotline:
1-800-356-9996

If you or a friend are using illegal drugs or abusing any drug and you don't know who to talk to, call
1-800-662-4357

For information about drugs, alcohol, and tobacco, call:

The American Council for Drug Education
1-800-488-DRUG (3784)

The American Lung Association
1-800-LUNG-USA (5864-872)

Cocaine Anonymous National Referral Line
1-800-347-8998

You may also want to visit these Websites for more information:

Marijuana Anonymous
http://www.marijuana-anonymous.org

Cocaine Anonymous World Services
http://www.ca.org

Narcotics Anonymous
http://www.wsoinc.com

Comprehensive Addiction Programs, Inc.
http://www.helpfinders.com

Partnership for a Drug-Free America
http://www.drugfreeamerica.org

Eating Disorders

If you or one of your friends may have anorexia, bulimia, or an overeating disorder and you want help, call the National Eating Disorders Association (for referral not counseling):
1-800-931-2237

You man want to visit these Websites for more information:

Eating Disorder Recovery Online
http://www.edrecovery.com

Anorexia Nervosa and Related Eating Disorders, Inc
http://www.anred.com

Physical and Mental Health

If you or a friend are considering suicide, PLEASE call the American Foundation for Suicide Prevention:
1-888-333-2377

National Institute of Mental Health
1-800-64-PANIC (72642)

If you are attempting or contemplating suicide right now, call:
911

You may ant to visit these Websites for more information:

Depression FAQs
http://www.mentalhealthscreening.org/infofaq/depression.aspx

Depression and Bipolar Support Alliance
http://www.dbsalliance.org

If you or your friends are concerned about having a venereal disease or contracting AIDS or Sexually Transmitted Diseases, call:
1-800-227-8922

National AIDS Hotline
1-800-342-2437

If you are pregnant or worried about becoming pregnant and need more information about your situation and possible choices, call the Pregnancy Crisis Hotlines:
1-800-550-4900
1-800-228-0332
1-800-826-9662

Abuse

If you or a friend (female or male) are a victim of rape, incest, or any form of sexual abuse, call the National Sexual Abuse Hotline:
1-800-656-HOPE (4673)

If you are in a dating relationship with a person who is abusive, call the Dating Violence Information Line:
1-800-897-LINK (5465)

If you or a friend or another family member is being physically abused at home, call the National Domestic Violence Hotline:
1-800-799-7233

National Abuse Hotline
1-800-422-4453

National Child Abuse Hotline
1-800-4-A-CHILD (224453)

You may want to visit this Website for more information:

Sexual Assault Information Page
http://www.rainn.org

Gambling

If you suspect that you or a friend my have a gambling problem, call the National Council on Problem Gambling:
1-800-522-4700

You may want to visit these Websites for more information:

The National Council on Problem Gambling
http://www.ncpgambling.org

Gamblers Anonymous
http://www.gamblersanonymous.org

Council on Compulsive Gambling
http://www.800gambler.org/Councils.aspx

Financial Debt and Problems Resources

If you suspect that you or a friend may have debt or financial problems, call the National Foundation for Credit Counseling:
1-800-388-2227

You may want to visit these Websites for more information:

Family Economics & Financial Education
http://www.familyfinance.montana.edu

Credit Counseling Centers of America
http://www.cccamerica.org

Marriage, Family, and Relationship Resources

If you suspect that you or a friend may have family problems, call the National Marriage Centers:
1-866-392-4141

National Divorce Care
1-800-489-7778

You may want to visit these Websites for more information:

National Clearinghouse on Family and Youth
http://www.ncfy.com

National Premarital Institute
http://www.premarriage.com/index.htm

Education

If you are considering college or a vocational school and have questions about funding your education, call:
1-800-USA-LEARN (872-53276)
1-800-4-FEDAID (33-3243)

If you are interested in information about training programs in your state for such jobs as carpenter, receptionist, computer programmer, call Job Corps:
1-800-733-JOBS (5627)

National Hotline Reference List (At-A-Glance)

800 ALCOHOL	**800-ALCOHOL**
Abused Registry (Elderly, Disabled, and Child)	**800-962-2873**
ADRDA (Alzheimer's Disease)	**800-272-3900**
AIDS Hotline	**800-342-AIDS**
AIDS and STD Info Clearinghouse (through CDC)	**800-458-5231**
Al-Anon/Alateen	**800-356-9996**
American Red Cross	**800-234-5ARC**
Alzheimer's Education and Referral Center	**800-438-4380**
Attorney Referral Network	**800-624-8846**
Brain Injury Association	**800-444-6443**
Cancer Information Service	**800-4-CANCER**
CDC National STD and AIDS Hotline	**800-342-2437**
Center for Substance Abuse Treatment	**800-662-HELP**
CHADD (Attention Deficit Disorder)	**800-233-4050**
Child Abuse Hotline	**800-422-4453**
Child Find of America, Inc.	**800-426-5678**
Compulsive Gambling Hotline	**800-LOSTBET**
Credit Counseling Center of America	**800-761-0061**

Down's Syndrome Hotline	**800-221-4602**
Drug Abuse Hotline (Focus On Recovery)	**800-888-9383**
Dyslexia International	**800-222-3123**
Hotline for Services for Child Support	**800-537-7072**
Hospice, Inc.	**800-767-4965**
Lawyers United for Debt Relief	**877-833-5227**
National Addictions Hotline	**800-252-6465**
National Adoption Center	**800-TO-ADOPT**
National Child Abuse Hotline	**800-422-4453**
National Clearinghouse on Child Abuse and Neglect	**800-394-3366**
National Coalition Against Domestic Violence	**800-799-SAFE**
National Depressive and Manic Depressive Association	**800-826-3632**
National Health Information Center	**800-336-4797**
National Institute of Mental Health	**800-421-4211**
National Alliance for Mental Illness	**800-950-6264**
National Information for U.S. Vets	**800-452-8906**
National Mental Health Association	**800-969-6642**
National Runaway Switchboard	**800-621-4000**
National Youth Crisis Hotline	**800-448-4663**
Pet Loss Support Hotline	**888-478-7574**
Sexual Assault/Domestic Violence Hotline	**800-825-1295**
Suicide Prevention Hotline	**888-784-2433**
Teen Help, Inc.	**800-637-0701**
Y-ME National Breast Cancer Hotline	**800-221-2141**

Appendix B

Here is a list of books suggested by the author for continual learning and development.

Attitude is Everything
by Keith Harrell

A Setback Is a Setup for a Come Back
by Willie Jolley

Cashflow Quadrant: Rich Dad's Guide to Financial Freedom
by Robert T. Kiyosaki and Sharon L. Lechter

Speaking to Excel
by James Amps

The Nuts and Bolts of Public Speaking
by Craig Valentine

If You Can't Say Something Nice, What Do You Say?
by Sarita Maybin

Kick Your Own Butt
by Pegine Echevarria

The 7 Habits of Highly Effective People
by Stephen R. Covey

Over the Top
by Zig Ziglar

Major in Success: Make College Easier, Fire Up Your Dreams, and Get a Very Cool Job
by Patrick Combs and Jack Canfield

The Journey from Success to Significance
by John C. Maxwell

Success Is a Choice
by Rick Pitino

Eliminate Chaos: The 10-Step Process to Organize Your Home and Life
by Laura Leist and Adam Weintraub

Focal Point: A Proven System to Simplify Your Life, Double Your Productivity, and Achieve All Your Goals
by Brian Tracy

How to Talk to Anyone: 92 Little Tricks for Big Success in Relationships
by Leil Lowndes

Being In Balance: 9 Principles for Creating Habits to Match Your Desires
by Wayne W. Dyer

Get Out of Your Mind & Into Your Life (Workbook)
by Dr. Steven C. Hayes and Spencer Smith

How to Be Your Own Therapist: A Step-by-Step Guide to Taking Back Your Life
by Patricia Farrell, Ph.D.

The Measure of Success
by Marian Wright Edelman

Real Gorgeous: The Truth About Body and Beauty
by Kaz Cooke

Anthony Burns: The Defeat and Triumph of a Fugitive Slave
by Virginia Hamilton

The Artist's Way: A Spiritual Path to Higher Creativity
by Julia Cameron

Letters to a Young Poet
by Rainer Maria Rilke

The Power of Focus
by Jack Canfield, Mark Victor Hansen, and Les Hewitt

Rich Dad Poor Dad
by Robert T. Kiyosaki and Sharon L. Lechter

A Child Called "It":
One Child's Courage to Survive
by Dave Pelzer

The Procrastinator's Handbook:
Mastering the Art of Doing It Now
by Rita Emmett

How to Win Friends & Influence People
by Dale Carnegie

"Learning is a treasure that will follow its owner everywhere."

— Chinese Proverb

Appendix C

WHAT TO DO NEXT?

Gain Immediate Access to a Practical, Comprehensive, Step-by-Step "Special Guide" That Will Help You Break Free of the 50 Most Common Toxic Knots

The Knots Free Special Guide: 50 Most Common Toxic Knots Defined is a must-have "special guide" and companion to this book. It's relevant, time-saving, and invaluable. Ty Howard provides you with terms and definitions, causes and effects, and easy-to-apply strategies for each of the 50 Most Common Toxic Knots listed in the table found in Chapter 7 of his book, *Untie the Knots That Tie Up Your Life*.

This guide will save you from investing countless hours of your own personal time in research. Ty Howard has researched and tested all the strategies on either him or the many other people he's coached in the past 11 years.

With your "Knots Free Special Guide" at your fingertips, you will have sound additional insights that focus individually on each of the 50 Most Common Toxic Knots. This step-by-step guide will equip you with additional, in-depth tools and strategies that will allow and empower you to assemble a personal action plan that will have no gaps. This is an absolute gold mine of information that will offer you a clear understanding on why your toxic knots exist and how to defeat and break free from them. If you're serious about experiencing continuous "untie the knots" success, then your next step will be to gain access to this 68-page Special Guide.

ISBN: 978-0-9724040-1-3

Visit the following Website:
http://www.tyhoward.com/KnotsFree_SpecialGuide.html
or
Call InspiraGen Institute, Inc.
Phone: (410) 737-6839 • Toll Free: 1-800-385-3177 Ext. 3

"Some people drink deeply from the fountain of knowledge. Others just gargle."
— *Grant M. Bright*

Share Your Personal *"Untie the Knots"* Story with the Author

Dear Friend:

Here is your opportunity to share your personal Untie the Knots story or experience with the author of this book, Ty Howard.

Your personal story should be 750 words or less and as detailed as possible. Your story should have a clear premise, setting, problem or challenge, and solution that will benefit readers. Please proofread and edit your story before you e-mail or mail it to Ty.

Your knot (obstacle or challenge) should reveal to Ty a toxic habit, choice, person, or relationship that you decided to break free from to improve and empower your life. It is also helpful if you refer to your knot as one of the 50 Most Common Toxic Knots listed in the Appendix of this book.

Please change all names of any additional characters and organizations to protect their identity. This opportunity is meant for you to share your personal story with the author, not to slander or make known the names of organizations or people who have hurt you.

Indicate in a separate paragraph at the end of your story if Ty Howard has your full-permission to share your story in a future keynote speech or presentation or use it in a future book or article to help readers improve and grow like you. Also, write a second, separate sentence or paragraph at the end of your personal Untie the Knots story clearly stating that your personal story is 100% your personal story and is 100% true.

No compensation is provided for your story. This is solely an opportunity for you to share your past or present Untie the Knots story with the author of the book, and potentially, others.

We are eager and look forward to hearing your personal Untie the Knots story soon.

As Ty often says, "Make Today & Every Day—An 'A' Day!"

Sincerely,
Knots Free Publishing

<u>Special Note</u>: All submissions must be in Microsoft Word or PDF electronic file format only.

Mail or email your personal story to:
Mr. Ty Howard, Author
c/o Knots Free Publishing
6400 Baltimore National Pike, Suite 134
Baltimore, Maryland 21228

Email: mypersonalstory@tyhoward.com

ABOUT InspiraGen Institute, Inc.

Ty Howard is the founder, Chairman, and CEO of Inspira-Gen Institute, Inc.

InspiraGen Institute, Inc. (IGI) is a professional, personal, and management development firm in Baltimore County, Maryland, dedicated to assisting organizations in effectively enhancing the lives of their professionals and the people they serve. Through our knowledge-based actionable strategies, you get:
- Long-term measurable business results;
- A workplace or person of better health and harmony; and
- An outcomes-focused guarantee that produces tangible results.

InspiraGen Institute, Inc. will deliver increased Performance, Productivity, and Perseverance to organizations and people facing challenges in a demanding, growing, and competitive society.

What Differentiates IGI?
There are other professional and personal development companies out there, so why choose IGI? Our qualities set us apart from other vendors. They include *Integrity, Accountability, Focus, Dignity, and Follow-up*. IGI provides first-rate value added programs to help clients generate the maximum Performance, Productivity, and Perseverance within their organization.

InspiraGen Institute, Inc. is a professional and personal development firm with several key advantages:

- **Proactive:** We are constantly researching and creating new ways to improve client potential and are committed to relieving executives, managers, and organizations of headaches, lost talent, corporate apathy, and less than desirable results.

- **Transparent:** We work closely with our clients to become a transparent extension of their organization. Everyone at IGI is familiar with on-going programs, there is never any transition to new account teams, and our service is seamless.
- **Flexible:** As client scenarios change, IGI adapts quickly to provide new programs that assure client organizations a calm and more productive transition.

Working closely with top professional organizations, universities, associations, national conferences, and youth, IGI offers several competitive advantages. IGI program design management is able to leverage experience and knowledge in critical areas, and our staff members are knowledgeable in key terms, applications, and industries.

The IGI approach to professional and personal development is a philosophy of unification. All our clients and projects are managed by a single, scalable program management system that is customized to fit each client scenario. IGI is accountable for long-term measurable results, not just process improvement. This approach creates incomparable benefits for our clients; their employees feel rewarded, company costs and turnover are reduced, and executives and managers are able to lead and manage more effectively.

For more information on InspiraGen Institute, Inc's products, services, and programs, call or write:
InspiraGen Institute, Inc.
6400 Baltimore National Pike, Suite 134
Baltimore, Maryland 21228
Toll Free: 1 (800) 385-3177 Ext. 0
International Callers: 1-(410) 737-6839
Internet:
http://www.tyhoward.com
http://www.tyhowardseminars.com
http://www.baltimorespeakersbureau.com

Ty Howard's products and programs provide a range of sources for individuals, families, businesses, government resources, non-profit organizations, and education organizations, including the following:

Programs: (Available in Keynote, Training, and Intervention Formats)

- ✳ Untie the Knots ™ That Tie Up Your Life or Organization
- ✳ Service Excellence through Personal Excellence
- ✳ Leading With Confidence, Integrity, and by Example
- ✳ Moving from Thinking Teams to Working As Successful Productive Teams
- ✳ Stop Saving YOUR BEST for Last! ™
- ✳ Working Positively Through Workplace Negativity ™
- ✳ STRETCHING and Focusing for Continuous Success ™
- ✳ Tying Into A Better YOU ™
- ✳ You Make A Difference!
- ✳ Networking 101: The Fundamental "How To's" for Successful Networking
- ✳ Conflict Coaching Training

Additional Programs Available On:
Personal or Professional Development, Support Staff Development, Employee Recognition, Respect, Diversity, Youth Development, College and University Programs, and Black History Programs

Products:
Untie the Knots that Tie Up Your Life (workbook)
Untie the Knots poster series
How to Get and Stay Motivated (audio cds)
Presentation and Public Speaking Skills (audio cds)
Sales: Live It! Love It! Profit! (audio cd pack)
31 Daily Inspirational Boosters (12-book series, one for each month)
How to Build Ongoing Healthy, Rewarding Relationships (audio cds)

Ty Howard's College Scholarship Program

The **Ty Howard College Scholarship Program** was established to elevate and continue the humanitarian efforts of InspiraGen Institute, Inc.'s founder, Chairman, and CEO, Mr. Ty Howard. Those who know Ty well witness his passion and commitment for helping youth and young adults excel in life through the enrichment of a good education. He works diligently every day to encourage, motivate, teach, inspire, and support the hopes and dreams of tomorrow's community and business leaders.

In this spirit and in his legacy, InspiraGen Institute, Inc. molded the **Ty Howard College Scholarship Program** to continue providing assistance in perpetuity. Scholarships are provided annually to energetic first-generation or disadvantaged college-bound students graduating from high school and moving into a two-year or four-year college or university program within the United States.

Average scholarship award amount = $1,000 to $2,000 per student

Average number of awards per year = 5 students

For an application or to learn more about Ty's scholarship program, write, call, or visit:
InspiraGen Institute, Inc.
c/o Ty Howard's College Scholarship Program
6400 Baltimore National Pike, Suite 134
Baltimore, Maryland 21228
Toll Free: (800) 385-3177 Ext. 0
Phone: (410) 737-6839
Internet:
http://www.tyhoward.com
http://www.dynamicyouthspeaker.com
http://www.dynamiccollegespeaker.com

"From what we get, we can make a living; what we give, however, makes a life."

— Arthur Ashe

Order Form for the Untie the Knots Book

To order your copy of *Untie the Knots That Tie Up Your Life: A Practical Guide to Freeing Yourself From Toxic Habits, Choices, People, and Relationships* please submit your request with payment to the address or fax number listed below:

Knots Free Publishing
6400 Baltimore National Pike, Suite 134
Baltimore, Maryland 21228
Toll Free Phone: 1 (800) 385-3177 Ext. 0 / Fax: (410) 510-1578

(Print in ALL CAPS)

Name: _____

Address: _____

City: _____State: _____ Zip: _____

Telephone: _____ E-mail: _____

Payment (Check One): ❑ Visa ❑ MasterCard

Card Number: _____

Name on Card: _____

Exp. Date: _____ (mm/yy) Three Digit Code on Back: _____

Address on card (if different from above):

_____

_____

City: _____ State: _____ Zip: _____

My order for *Untie the Knots That Tie Up Your Life* is as follows:

_____ Copies @ $19.95 per copy: _____

5 % Maryland State Tax ($1.00 ea.):   _____

Shipping & Handling ($3.99 ea.):   _____

Total: _____

(Please make copies of this form)

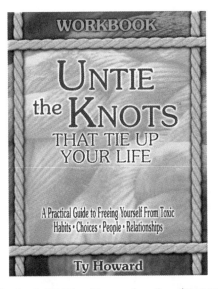

Code # 2251 ◆ Paperback ◆ $15.95
Release Date: September 2007

Now, just in time after the recent release of *Untie the Knots That Tie Up Your Life* comes the *Untie the Knots That Tie Up Your Life Workbook* with easy-to-do exercises, tools, self-tests, and questions that readers can use to develop inspired personal and professional success. With this workbook, readers can make significant changes throughout their lives. Straightforward and concise, Ty Howard's advice is made crystal clear in this workbook, which is certain to be the perfect companion to one of North America's most popular self-help guides.

To order direct, call toll free: 1 (800) 385-3177 Ext. 0
www.tyhoward.com
Price does not include shipping and handling.
Your response code is KFP.

About The Author

Ty Howard, a.k.a. Mr. Untie the Knots, is an internationally respected authority on self-development and business-development. He is a habits intervention specialist, relationship expert, teacher, professional development consultant, and author who has dedicated his life to teaching knots-free living and relationship-building to organizations, individuals, and families around the world. His business acumen and easy-to-follow-and-apply strategies have propelled top organizations to frequently seek his counsel and advice. His admirable communication skills have helped him become one of America's most popular professional speakers on the circuit today. Ty's solid research and practical strategies background have made him a trusted source for professional and personal development guidance on five continents.

When Ty was an active part of the U.S. Navy and then Corporate America, he consistently excelled in highly visible positions including Human Resources Generalist, Executive Office Manager, Corporate Training & Development Manager, Intervention and Behavior Specialist Manager, Outside Sales Account Manager, and Sales Trainer. He managed, trained, evaluated, and led employee teams of four to 300 full-time and part-time personnel working in demanding and fast-paced environments.

Ty Howard is the founder and Chairman and CEO of InspiraGen Institute, Inc., a successful, diverse professional and personal development firm based in Baltimore County, Maryland.

InspiraGen Institute, Inc. is a conglomerate of four internationally recognized businesses: TyHoward.com, Ty Howard Seminars, Knots Free Publishing, and the Baltimore Worldwide Speakers Bureau. They share Ty's vision, discipline, and passion to inspire, lift, and provide tools for change and growth for individuals and organizations throughout the world. He lives in Baltimore County, Maryland with his family.

My "Untie the Knots" Journey Notes

(Write and keep your notes below.)

My "Untie the Knots" Journey Notes

(Write and keep your notes below.)

My "Untie the Knots" Journey Notes

(Write and keep your notes below.)

My "Untie the Knots" Journey Notes

(Write and keep your notes below.)

_____

_____

_____

_____

_____

_____

_____

_____

_____

_____

_____

_____

_____

_____

_____

_____

_____

_____

_____

My "Untie the Knots" Journey Notes

(Write and keep your notes below.)

_____

_____

_____

_____

_____

_____

_____

_____

_____

_____

_____

_____

_____

_____

_____

_____

_____

_____

_____

My "Untie the Knots" Journey Notes

(Write and keep your notes below.)

My "Untie the Knots" Journey Notes

(Write and keep your notes below.)

My "Untie the Knots" Journey Notes

(Write and keep your notes below.)